INTERNATIONAL MARINE

Sailing INTO Retirement

7 Ways to Retire on a Boat at 50
with 10 Steps that Will Keep
You There Until 80

INTERNATIONAL MARINE

Sailing INTO Retirement

7 Ways to Retire on a Boat at 50
with 10 Steps that Will Keep
You There Until 80

JIM TREFETHEN

Mc
Graw
Hill
Education

New York | Chicago | San Francisco | Athens | London | Madrid |
Mexico City | Milan | New Delhi | Singapore | Sydney | Toronto

1 2 3 4 5 6 7 8 9 DOC 21 20 19 18 17 16

ISBN 978-0-07-182315-9
MHID 0-07-182315-8

e-ISBN 978-0-07-182451-4
e-MHID 0-07-182451-0

Photos by the author unless otherwise stated

McGraw-Hill Education books are available at special quantity discounts to use as premiums and sales promotions, or for use in corporate training programs. To contact a representative, please visit the Contact Us page at http://www.mhprofessional.com/.

CONTENTS

INTRODUCTION

*Life is but a temporary inconvenience, and if we fail to
appreciate it for the wonderful opportunities it presents to
live it to the fullest, it is diminished in proportion.*

In 1999, International Marine published a book I had written called *The Cruising Life*, wherein I attempted to chronicle my experiences moving out of a 14-room post-Colonial house in Marblehead, Massachusetts, onto a 40-foot wooden ketch and taking my family on a three-year sailboat cruise halfway around the world to Nelson, New Zealand. This small volume has done rather well over time, but after 15 years it had become sadly out of date. Thus, it has been recently updated into a second edition to better reflect today's cruising environment with its ever-increasing forest of electronic gadgetry and doodads that is making the cruising life easier and more accessible to enthusiasts from all walks of life. Among the most important of the walks of life that is becoming increasingly interested in living and traveling on a boat is the vast army of retirees emerging like katydids from the baby boom of the forties.

Perhaps you are among the many recent retirees or soon-to-be retirees who sincerely believe that you want to live at least a part of your retirement aboard a boat. Maybe you dream of cruising the world in a grand sailing vessel, exploring the waterways of Europe aboard a funky canal boat, or visiting all the islands in the Bahamas in a traditional trawler.

According to the AARP (American Association of Retired Persons), more than 8,000 people are reaching the traditional retirement age of 65 every day, and that's only in the United States. When we add Canadians, Europeans, and a major increase in retirees from other affluent countries, the number of bodies entering the ranks of the retired becomes a vast grey tsunami of elderly humanity.

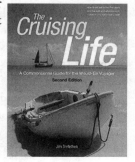

Sailing Into Retirement is a continuation of The Cruising Life, *first published in 1999 and updated 2015. The author has tried to avoid duplicating information wherever possible. Therefore, while not at all necessary, a prior reading of* The Cruising Life, *Second Edition, will help the reader understand some of the concepts in* Sailing Into Retirement.

This worldwide growth in the number of older folks is fueling social change on an unprecedented scale. Everything from rethinking the statutory retirement age to revising the idea of a traditional retirement as enjoyed by mom and dad in years gone by is under close scrutiny by market forces and bureaucrats everywhere. While marketers and sales forces worldwide are investigating how best to capitalize on this free-spending elderly juggernaut, bureaucrats in charge of social services and retirement funds are desperately trying to figure out how to pay for it.

But we aren't concerned with any of that. We will leave the speculation on the social, political, and economic ramifications of the *great grey tide*, as it has been called, to others who are both more qualified to comment on it and more inclined to think their comments are important. Meanwhile, we will focus our resources on the small segment of these multitudes that thinks that they might want to spend their retirement years aboard a cruising boat.

With this lofty goal in mind, I have tried to make this book, *Sailing Into Retirement*, an extension of and sequel to *The Cruising Life*, Second Edition, and as such it would be a benefit to the reader to have read the previous work before starting this one. And no, this isn't a trick to sell more books. In writing *Sailing Into Retirement* I have tried not to duplicate material found in *The Cruising Life*, Second Edition, but to build upon it, especially where specific subjects pertaining to elderly sailors are involved.

Basic Basicism

One pertinent theme of *The Cruising Life,* Second Edition, that I will continue to emphasize is the concept of *basicism* that is central to my philosophy of life. No matter what your dream, be it cruising in a boat, traveling to distant lands by more conventional means, or a cozy retirement home in a warm place, the realization of that dream will be infinitely easier if you learn now to divest yourself of things that aren't necessary for the realization of that dream and to keep only those things that are.

Living a basic life means getting rid of most of your treasured possessions and all of your non-treasured ones. If you can simplify your life to the extent that you are burdened with only the essentials and no extras, both emotionally and physically, nearly anything you want to do and anyone you want to become in your retirement becomes possible. Throughout this book, we will explore ways you can do that, and we will discover that the tyranny of materialistic ownership of objects is among the most restrictive constraints to freedom that life in the consumer society imposes upon us.

This is true in spades for boat ownership; a large expensive yacht can be one of the most tyrannical of all possessions on which we can waste our meager resources. Later, we will explore ways to resist the temptations of large boats. For now, just know that only by breaking away from the oppression that the ownership of useless

One of the worst investments an aspiring retirement cruiser can make is to buy a big, expensive boat. Here are two lovely and powerful motor yachts, well set-up for cruising and living aboard in comfort bordering on luxury. But the big twin turbo-diesels of even the smaller one will go through 100 gallons of expensive fuel an hour at speed. If you plan to go anywhere in your boat, this would be a poor choice, no matter how much money you have to spend.

stuff imposes on us will we ever realize the joy of the true freedom that comes with retiring on a boat.

Divestiture of nonessential possessions is a lot harder than it sounds, so hard, in fact, that many of us who endorse the concept aren't able to face the reality. When it comes time to send great-grandma's grandfather clock to your sister in Poughkeepsie, donate most of your wardrobe to the church bazaar, or take that collection of 137 bowling trophies to the recycling center, we often just can't bring ourselves to do it. Likewise, many of us can't face up to canceling our monthly data contract for our smart phone, or advising our 800 Facebook "friends" that we won't be visiting with them for hours every day because we have better things to do with our time (but we might drop in once a week or so to see how everyone is getting on).

Basicism means dropping all our club memberships, canceling all but one of our credit cards, and completely eliminating any form of debt we might have accumulated during our non-basic years. It means getting by with the smallest and least expensive items (physical things) that will do the job instead of trying to impress our friends (and ourselves) with the hottest new car or the grandest house in the flashiest neighborhood in town. If we must have a TV, we want the smallest one that we can see without eyestrain. We want the smallest refrigerator that will keep our beer cold and our leftover tacos from getting moldy, and the cheapest prepaid cell phone that we can find. If we need a car, we don't need a monster SUV and will seek out the smallest and cheapest used car that will get us reliably to our destinations. And finally, we want to live aboard the smallest boat that will serve our needs without becoming a burden on our mechanical abilities, a strain on our monetary resources, or an infringement on our well-earned creature comforts.

Freedom

Retirement should be all about freedom. Our kids have been raised, our debts have been paid, our sentences have been served, our accomplishments have been acknowledged, our courage has been tested, our rewards have been spent, our mistakes have been regretted, and our crimes have been punished. Our karma is well established and our place among the stars assured, so there is nothing left for us to do but to enjoy the remaining time we have on this wonderful earth. And one really cool way to do that is aboard a boat.

Retirement cruising is one of the last of the true means of achieving freedom left to us in our nanny society. It can take many forms and will mean different things to different people. Lifelong sailors will gravitate toward more high-tech boats, and might find abilities that have deteriorated with age make shifting to a simpler, more basic craft a way to extend cruising years. Rank beginners will find life aboard a basic trawler or small motor yacht to be an easier transition between a boring shoreside existence and the excitement of the cruising life. Some will seek the thrills of long offshore passages, and cover hundreds of miles in a single trip, while others will be perfectly happy to plug along, covering 20 or 50 miles a day, hopping from one lovely anchorage to another.

Some retired cruisers will want to live aboard their boats full-time, and the boat will become their only home. Others will find full-time cruising to be too restrictive and will live aboard for only part of the year. Others, with more resources than most of us, will have their boats delivered by professional crews to interesting spots, so they can enjoy the best destinations without the nuisance of having to get the boat there themselves.

In the coming chapters, we will visit all of these options, and we will try to offer the advice of long experience on how to avoid the alligators and quicksand that lurk in the swamp of boat buying. Since you have divested yourself of useless personal possessions, your physical needs will be small enough to fit comfortably into a small and inexpensive boat. Trading the stress of owning a large home ashore for the often-more-stressful ownership of a big boat, as many misguided dreamers do, is one huge mistake we will help you to avoid. There are lots of other dangers lurking in that swamp, and we will deal with them as we come upon them.

Liveaboards Versus Cruisers

There are among us those who plan to live on a boat tied to a dock at a marina or swinging at anchor with no plans to ever go anywhere else. These are *liveaboards,* and you will find them in many marinas in places where there are low taxes, no restrictions against the practice, and a warm climate.

Understandably, Florida is the liveaboard capital of the world, with thousands of snowbirds living out their retirement years in yachts tied permanently to shore. Many liveaboards choose this option because it is much cheaper than living in a house or condo ashore. Others just love boats but don't necessarily want to go anywhere in them. Many liveaboard boats have permanently installed plumbing, cable, air-conditioning, and electrical hookups. They are more like floating apartments than boats, with tenants who have no interest or need for any nautical knowledge or skill.

If you are among the many who aspire to the liveaboard life as opposed to the cruising life, good for you. Living aboard a permanently moored yacht is an economical and satisfying retirement for many, but it is not what this book is about.

Sailing Into Retirement is written for those of us who live on a boat, full- or part-time, because we want to go places and see things. We are looking to fill the remaining years of our lives with action and adventure; we want to travel to places with strange-sounding names, bizarre creatures, and interesting people. We want to learn things we don't know and to confirm things we do. We yearn for a trip across the wide Atlantic or a leisurely float through the Tombigbee Watershed; the canals of Europe beckon from afar, and the crystalline waters of the San Blas Islands are wishing we were there.

IT AIN'T WHAT YA DO BUT HOW YA DOES IT

This isn't a *Bucket-List* sort of thing, is it. We must guard against rushing about the world in search of brief encounters with a long list of have-to-do-it-before-we-die adventures, as depicted in the movie starring Morgan Freeman and Jack Nicholson. The plot of *The Bucket List* has two terminal cancer patients on a whirlwind tour, cramming all the things they ever wanted to do into their remaining time on this earth. It is a fun and poignant story, and since we are all dying of the terminal condition called life, a comparison here might seem to be appropriate. But it isn't.

Frantically rushing from place to place to jump out of an airplane, climb a mountain, float off into the sunrise in a hot air balloon, or sail nonstop around the world while standing on your head makes for an interesting movie plot, but it isn't a recommended way to achieve tranquility in our retirement years. The frenzy of trying to jam too many or overly challenging activities into a short time is little different than the frenzy of traffic jams, snarly bosses, and unreasonable deadlines that we are supposed to be retiring from. Besides, most of the people who pursue this sort of action adventure are looking to prove themselves and, yes, to show off a little bit (or even a lot).

Pursuing exciting activities just to accumulate the bragging rights is a uniquely human endeavor that drives us to attempt to break records and set new limits of endurance and persistence, but we have already done that. By the time we retire, we should have nothing left to prove to anyone, even ourselves. The tranquility that comes from no longer having to compete in the jungle of life for mates and jobs and ego-boosting accolades is what makes retirement worth striving for.

It isn't that we don't care what others think of us or our chosen lifestyle; we do. It's just that we have come to realize that trying to change ourselves to fit the expectations of others, or to mold ourselves into any of the social stereotypes that have attached themselves to the art of becoming old, is futile at best. At worst, it is dangerous and a sure ticket to a cot in a rest home with tubes up our nose.

Buying Your Boat

Selecting the craft most suited to your type of retirement plans can be one of the most daunting steps on the path to retirement afloat, especially to those among us with little or limited boating experience. More experienced sailors may have a boat picked out, and more than a few of us will already own the vessel of our dreams. The type of craft that you end up living on will be dictated by the type of cruising you want to do, the money you have in the kitty, and where you want to go. There are many options in both the types of boats that are suitable and in how they may be used for a successful aquatic retirement. We can't visit them all but we will call on the best and spend considerable time with the most important.

Once we have you safely aboard your retirement craft, we will offer some of the ways that you can make life afloat easier and more pleasurable than you ever dreamed possible, and we will do it by making your boat into a home, rather than trying to make it into a copy of the house you left ashore.

Old Age Gets Bad Press

As a first step in *Sailing Into Retirement,* we will change our attitudes about aging. Contrary to all you have read and heard, there is nothing wrong with growing old. Our consumer society has a built-in bias against elderliness simply because growing old presents so few opportunities for profit. Except for the lucrative businesses of warehousing older folks in rest homes, selling us overpriced and often unnecessary medications and mobility aids, and exclusive housing, there are few profit centers in the old-age market. In fact, the elderly market when compared to the youth market is miniscule. We can buy many thousands of products that promise to help us think we are younger, healthier, and more attractive than we are or ever will be, and one of the biggest segments of the youth industry, the cosmetic surgery business, adds more than ten billion dollars to the U.S. economy every year, as older folks spend the big bucks altering their bodies in a futile attempt to retain their illusions of looking younger than the are.

But there are very few products to help us realistically enjoy our dotage. Sure, we can buy hearing aids, walkers, and little pills to make us think we are better lovers, but honest products to increase the enjoyment of retirement are scarce. The real joy of growing old comes from vitality and clear thinking, both of which are largely genetic and a matter of luck rather than choice. We can greatly increase the advantages of this genetic good fortune: both are easily achieved with a brisk walk along the beach at sunset and a good meal of natural food that is not laden with chemicals, fat, and sugar. Eating well and getting lots of exercise are available to everyone for free. So where's the profit in that?

In fact, aging is a natural process that all of us lucky enough to make it this far will face, whether we like it or not. And since we consider it to be inevitable, we might as well get to like it.

But old age isn't inevitable, is it. A close friend of mine from high school was killed in a motorcycle crash at 19, a favorite cousin drowned when she was barely 25, and my father died of cancer when he was 59. At 73, I have been to many funerals of friends and acquaintances who were much younger than I when they died, and I know many others who are incapacitated or in rest homes and hospices patiently waiting for that train to the pearly gates to depart the station. And depart it will for a one-way, non-return trip; once we are aboard we can only look back with regret at the life we didn't lead and the things we didn't do.

So aging isn't inevitable at all; in fact it is a privilege that we should embrace with joy and respect while giving thanks to the Supreme Navigator that she has selected us for the honor. Old age is an option that we can pick up with enthusiasm, accept with reluctant detachment, or just leave on the table and die. Life is a temporary inconvenience at best, and if we fail to appreciate it for the wonderful opportunities it presents to live it to the fullest, it is diminished in proportion. The more we fail to appreciate life at any stage along the way, the less we will value the trip. If you aren't happy with your growing age, don't fret about it; it will be over soon enough.

Obviously, you have made the decision to embrace your retirement and eventual elderliness with enthusiasm and resolution or you wouldn't retire. So enough of the philosophical folderol about the agony and hardships of growing old that permeates the consumer society. The only hard ships we want to hear about are the ones with decks to walk on and solid keels to keep us upright and on track toward our ultimate destiny. Okay then, let's get on with it. Life is short and eternity lasts forever. It is time to cast off the lines that tie us to the shoreside life so we can further explore this backwater idea of living on a boat as we enjoy the very act of getting old.

The alert reader has noted the omission of the traditional dedication and acknowledgement pages from this book. These are disposable vanities, and the trees that would have died to provide them are better used to record more useful information to the reader than to curry favor and assuage egos. But Susan, my dear wife and companion, and two of my three children have had books dedicated to them, so it is with great sincerity that I dedicate this one to my youngest son, Phillip, who, though little interested in boats, is a true cruiser in the best sense of the word. That this isn't announced on a separate page matters not at all.

As for acknowledgements, a proper and fair list of the people who helped me bring this project to fruition would take many pages. The danger of omitting those who deserve mention the most or of including some who prefer to remain anonymous is too scary to contemplate. I will, however, risk a special thanks to my friend and former editor, Molly Mulhern, whose early vision and guidance resulted in the product you hold before you.

1 A LITTLE HISTORY

Nelson, on the northern tip of the South Island of New Zealand,
is a fairy tale village in a magical land and a wonderful place to live.

In the autumn of 2012, my wife, Susan, and I celebrated my advancement into dotage by buying and moving aboard a boat. We had been actively looking at various boats for over a year and finally settled on a 37-foot heavy-displacement cruising sailboat made by Northshore Yachts of Great Britain under the Fisher label. When we bought *Vicarious,* Susan was a young and chipper 65, while I, at 70, was just beginning to bask in the glow of genuine antiquity.

Vicarious wasn't our first boat, far from it. Susan and I had first sailed together some 40 years earlier when we were young and stupid and didn't realize how much trouble and expense boat ownership, even very small boat ownership, entailed. Our first boat was a 21-foot "trailer sailer" with a portable toilet, two-burner alcohol stove, and a newfangled pop-top contraption on the hatchway that allowed the builder to maintain a straight face while advertising "standing headroom below decks." *Aquarius* wasn't much of a boat, but we didn't know that at the time, and she was fun to sail. Over the three years we owned her, we spent many nights happily anchored in various coves and harbors up and down the coast of New England from Nantucket to Boothbay Harbor.

Aquarius taught us how to sail, and we sailed a lot. She wasn't an offshore boat by any means but she took us offshore anyway. Our first excursion over the horizon and out of sight of land was aboard *Aquarius,* as were our first overnight passage, our first encounter with thick fog, our first grounding, our first storm at sea, our first lost halyard up the mast, and our first realization that we rather enjoyed this boaty stuff in spite of the expense and the trouble and the all-too-frequent encounters with stark terror that sailing a small boat on a big ocean entailed.

Susan and I learned to sail together 40 years ago on our little
trailer sailer, Aquarius. *She wasn't much of a boat, but she was a*
good teacher. After a few lessons, she had us sailing like pros. More
important, she instilled the germ of the idea that was to become a
lifelong love of boats and cruising.

We were as green as seasick frogs when we first started sailing, but early on we discovered that if you listen to what they say, boats can be brilliant teachers. *Aquarius* gradually taught us to do nautical things in a proper nautical manner by demonstrating what happened when we didn't. We learned that a boat without bottom paint was quickly immobilized by moss and barnacles; we learned that allowing a weather helm to round us into the wind would incite an angry boom into attempted homicide; we learned how to sail backward toward the rocks in the middle of an inky-black and stormy night as our inadequate anchor skittered playfully along the seafloor; we learned new salty-sounding words and terms like "unintentional jibe," "broaching," "hard aground," "fogbound," "dragging anchor," and my personal favorite: "knock-down." We learned that spending half a day watching seagulls as we waited for the tide to float us off yet another clam flat or sandbar wasn't a great way to spend our limited vacation time; and we learned that screaming at each other in anger when things weren't going just right did little to stabilize a wobbly situation, no matter how desperate or trivial it might be.

We learned a thousand lessons from *Aquarius*, and gradually she taught us to be sailors, but not just sailors. Sailors are people who love boats and sail for the joy of sailing, but as much as we enjoyed the challenge of trimming the jenny just so, or getting *Aquarius* to point half a degree higher than the boat trying to overtake us to windward, we needed more. We soon discovered that sailing around the harbor on a sunny Saturday didn't do it for us. The sailing that we came to enjoy most always involved a destination. We needed to be going somewhere. Just where we were going didn't matter that much as long as it was somewhere. Some tiny gunkhole behind an uninhabited island would do fine, as would a crowded anchorage adjacent to some popular tourist spot, or a river we could motor up until the rocks threatened our prop or a low bridge blocked our path.

The desolate Isles of Shoals off the New Hampshire coast became a popular destination, as did historic Plymouth Harbor and quirky Provincetown in Massachusetts. Often we would set out for one distant anchorage and through the fickle vagaries of tide and weather end up in another nowhere near the one we started for. Just as often, a changed mind meant a changed course and off we would go to somewhere else.

Thus, just as we had gradually become sailors, we became cruisers, and becoming cruisers was to change our lives in ways that we could hardly have imagined when we first bought our silly little trailer sailer.

Fifteen years later, sometime in the early 1990s, having raised two children to an age where they were ready for responsibility, we found ourselves yearning for more than our familiar New England and Eastern Canadian cruising grounds. We quit our jobs, stored our stuff, and set sail in *Sultana*, our fifth cruising boat, for a three-year voyage of discovery and adventure around the world. But as often happens in the cruising life, circumstances conspired to defeat our schedule and our goal. Everywhere we sailed we discovered distractions that needed to be investigated,

After a three-year voyage that took us to New Zealand, we were to spend another three years doing a refit. When Sultana *was finally ready to go again, we weren't.*

cultural events that demanded our attendance, and off-course places that required visiting. All this unscheduled activity meant delays, and at the end of three years we were nowhere near our destination. In fact we were barely halfway there. Then a nasty storm between Tonga and New Zealand, an area famous for nasty storms, destroyed our mainsail, snapped our bobstay, and vested mischief and damage on the rest of our sturdy boat. The ensuing repairs in New Zealand turned into a major refit that took the best part of another three years to complete.

When *Sultana* was finally ready to resume her journey, we weren't. One pivotal crew member, our daughter Sarah, had gone off to college in California and to her own life of adventure and romance. Our 16-year-old son, Phillip, was also starting to slip his lines and would soon be off on his voyage through life. Thus, in the southern spring of 1999, the three of us, Susan, Phillip, and I, set sail on one last major cruise in the refurbished *Sultana*, a magical year-long trip that took us to the islands of Fiji and New Caledonia and through Australia's Great Barrier Reef. We welcomed the new millennium in Queensland's Mooloolaba Harbor, which has to be the best place on the planet to change centuries.

After Phillip flew back to New Zealand from Australia to continue his studies, Susan and I were left with what seemed like an empty boat. It had been seven years since we sailed away from our home in Marblehead. We had lived and travelled on *Sultana* as a family for three years and for another three we had worked on *Sultana's* refit. Then we sailed for a year with abbreviated crew through the South Pacific only to be left crewless on the lonely coast of Queensland. Susan and I had an exciting and memorable sail back to New Zealand, as all trips across the Tasman Sea tend to be, but it wasn't the same. Without our crew, cruising seemed pointless somehow, so we tied *Sultana* to a dock and moved ashore.

Nelson, on the northern tip of the South Island of New Zealand, is a fairy tale village in a magical land and a wonderful place to live. Its sunny, tree-lined streets feature sidewalk cafés, bookshops, art stores, a killer Saturday market, lovely weather, and an easy-going atmosphere that makes people approaching elderliness want to stay there. So stay we did. We bought a tiny cottage within walking distance of the markets and shops of downtown and within a longer stroll to the harbor, where *Sultana* lay moored in a slip awaiting the return of her hopelessly dispersed crew.

It wasn't that we ignored our old boat, we didn't, but perhaps she wasn't getting the attention that she had come to expect and fully deserved. We visited often, every month or so, and ran her new engine and cycled her expensive new electronics and rinsed the dust off her shiny new fiberglass decks. We even took her out to the islands of Marlborough Sound on occasion, where we relaxed in some quiet and lonely harbor while we fished for snapper and cod. But *Sultana* wasn't a happy boat. She spent most of her time tied to her slip with her new bowsprit pointing toward Farewell Spit and the open sea. Here, many years before, Captain Cook had departed New Zealand waters in *Endeavor,* bound for even more adventures and discovery. When we visited her, *Sultana* would tug playfully at her dock lines while the waves lapping her boot top quietly gurgled, "Let's go. What are we waiting for? What's wrong with you guys? There's an ocean right out there."

The sunny, tree-lined streets of Nelson, on the north end of the South Island of New Zealand, boast sidewalk cafés, bookstores, buskers, and market stalls. Life here was idyllic for me and Susan, and it was hard to leave, even temporarily. But leave we did, sailing we went, and back we did not look.

But Susan and I had grown too old to go cruising anymore. We had started a business with employees and responsibilities. We had a mortgage and credit cards and obligations. We lived in a wonderful town with wonderful friends, and we were happy with that, weren't we? Who wouldn't be? We were living a life most of humanity could only dream of. How could we leave that? Anyway, we were too old for cruising, right? Eventually we grew weary of *Sultana's* pathetic whimpering, so we sold her.

Now boatless for the first time in more than 40 years, we found ourselves with the leisure and resources to do just about anything we wanted to do. We weren't rich by any stretch, but cruising had taught us to keep our needs small, and our possessions minimal. Thus, we had enough to get by plus a little, and the options were many. We certainly didn't want to go cruising anymore. We had gotten that urge out of our system, and the fetters and expense of boat ownership were far behind us. But Susan and I were both born with a wanderlust that refused to be ignored.

Susan bought a tiny Japanese sports car, and we drove that over the entire South Island enjoying the world-famous vistas and views. But views of what? It seems that everywhere you go in New Zealand you have a calendar-photo view of the sea. There is the mighty Tasman to the west and the endless Pacific to the east, and the waves were constantly whispering, "What are you waiting for?" "What's wrong with you guys?" "There's an ocean out here."

It didn't take long for exploring by car to become repetitious, as New Zealand is a small country with lots of mountains and few roads. We thought of a tour of

Selling Sultana *left us with an empty feeling, much like when the kids left home. Susan bought a small sports car and a smaller dog, and together we traveled the entire South Island of New Zealand trying to fill the void. It didn't work: everywhere we went, the sea beckoned in a voice that would not be ignored.*

Europe, but then decided that since we had seen a lot of coastal North America but not much of the interior, we would start there. In Salt Lake City, Utah, we bought another sports car, just like the one in New Zealand only in a different color and with the steering wheel on the other side, and set out on a three-year tour of Canada and the United States. We travelled the North American highways for three or four months each summer before returning to our business in New Zealand when the weather in North America started to get cold.

We crisscrossed the North American continent seven times in those three summers, driving the back roads through small forgotten towns and living out of a backpack we carried on a rack on the car. We avoided the interstate highways, and except for the interesting ones, like Montreal and New York, we shunned the big cities and population centers. We slept in a tent at night when we could or stayed in modest hotels when we couldn't, and we cooked our food in a pan on a fire. We ate good, slept well, and loved every minute of it.

We had a wonderful time on those trips, and often at night, while listening to the sounds that the deep woods make after dark, we would comment that what we were doing was just like cruising, wasn't it. Well, actually, no it wasn't. Try as we might, we had to admit that driving all over the place in a sports car, as much fun as it was, and camping out in lovely spots that we always wanted to visit, was decidedly not the same as cruising in a sailboat. Something was missing, but defining just what that missing element was proved to be difficult. We even discussed getting a travel trailer or camper thinking that would help, but then decided that wouldn't do it either.

True, there are some compelling similarities between camping in a travel trailer and cruising in a sailboat. You meet wonderful people doing either one, and you get to visit amazing places. But travel campers have to camp where all the other travel campers camp, and they can only go where the others go, since the roads dictate destinations.

And we missed the solitude you can easily find while cruising but which can be elusive while camping. Of course you can find solitude in the backcountry or in any camping area that requires a bit of walking to reach. And the lovely solitude found on a remote mountaintop is familiar to anyone who has ever experienced it. When on a small boat at sea, however, solitude is absolute. There is no one there but you and your crew and the Supreme Navigator, and that extreme of aloneness can be as addictive to a cruiser as heroin to a junkie or paparazzi to a starlet.

Most of the elderly people I know readily admit that as we age we come to value our solitude more and more. It isn't that we are antisocial, not for a moment, but elderly folks who have lived well have a lot of memories, and in blessed solitude it is possible to enjoy the good ones to the fullest. The irony is that as you come to value being alone in a pleasant and relaxing place with the one most important other person in your life, it is becoming increasingly difficult to do it.

In fairness, we did enjoy the odd respite into solitude on our road trips. We had practically an entire campground in Denali National Park all to ourselves,

While we crisscrossed the country looking for a boat, we pitched our little tent by the sea whenever we could. At lonely and desolate Padre Island, in Texas, we found only a few fellow travelers. That it was a lot like cruising made us that much more anxious to get back on board.

and that was rewarding for sure. And there were only one or two other tents in evidence when we visited Padre Island National Seashore on the Gulf of Mexico, but generally we camped with other campers. Some of them had tents like ours and others were in small trailer campers, but a lot of them were in the huge wheeled condominiums that you see lumbering down the highways and clogging the bays in gas stations all across the land.

Nature's night sounds in these popular campgrounds were often drowned out by the muffled noise of TV sets and generators running air-conditioning. We weren't complaining by any means. The other folks in these places were all enjoying themselves. Kids played ball in the narrow lanes between campsites and families gathered around the portable barbecue while dad burned the burgers and charred the dogs. It was great fun, but it wasn't cruising, and solitude remained elusive.

People who know a lot about cruising in boats are going to say that anyone who anchors in a crowded and popular harbor will find the same thing: blaring stereos, Jet Skis zooming about, and generators droning constantly. And they are right. But, while cruising in a boat, noise and crowds are usually optional. Cruisers, no matter where they are, almost always have the option of pulling the hook and moving on to the next anchorage or finding a secluded spot to stay for a while. Even on the super-crowded East Coast of the United States, where the popular anchorages overflow with weekend sailors and day-trippers, we can usually find a small cove or some other remote spot in which to tarry for a day or so. If all else fails, a cruising sailboat can move a hundred miles or so off shore and heave-to for a few days, or simply drift along towing a fishing line in the hope of scoring a piscatorial lunch. You certainly can't do that in a camper.

Susan and I still argue about who first mentioned the possibility of buying another boat, but we do agree that the subject first came up on the shores of Lake Tuscaloosa, part of the giant Tombigbee Watershed in Alabama, where we had stopped to eat our lunch. A traditional trawler, probably a Grand Banks 32, was steaming past a few hundred yards off shore.

"Wouldn't it be fun to have a boat like that," said Susan. (I swear it was Susan who started the conversation. She is equally adamant that I was the one to first mention buying a trawler, but hey, I'm the one writing the book.)

"Yeah, I always thought that cruising these rivers would be worth the effort. Just think, no worries about shortening sail when a storm is coming, and you can stop just about anywhere and not be concerned about the holding ground or shelter. You could just tie the anchor line to a tree if you wanted to," I answered. "And we could catch catfish. I love fried catfish."

"Could you take a boat like that offshore?" Susan asked, moving the conversation back to boats.

"Not really," I answered. "Construction of a lot of the production trawlers can be pretty flimsy, and the semi-displacement hulls aren't designed for big waves. You remember how uncomfortable *Duchess* was at sea." I was referring to the antique 40-foot powerboat we had restored and used for extended cruising on the Maine coast. "We could go out for short offshore hops by watching the weather and could get to places in the Bahamas if we were careful, but any extended offshore trip would be foolish. The best bet for an offshore powerboat in our price range would be a redesigned fishing boat with a true displacement hull and a small-but-strong diesel engine."

"But that boat is so lovely," said Susan referring to the passing trawler, "and *Duchess* was a very comfortable boat in calm water."

Thus went the conversation for the rest of our trip north, and we soon found ourselves looking for excuses to divert to any nearby boatyard or marina that showed on our map. When we reached Elkton, Maryland, for a visit with my sister, Ann, and her husband, Bill, we were ready to take a closer look at these trawler things.

"We aren't really going to buy another boat," I explained to Ann. "We just thought it would be fun to look at a few, just to see what is available. Besides, it will be a good excuse to go to Buddy's for lunch. Do you think that they are still doing the buffet?" I continued, referring to Buddy's Crabs and Ribs Restaurant in Annapolis, one of my all-time favorite eateries, and the site of my personal best in Olympic-class gluttony. Here in the course of a single afternoon I downed six dozen raw oysters nonstop and washed them down with many tankards of ice-cold Blue Moon ale.

So we rang a few brokers in Annapolis, piled into Bill's SUV, and headed west across the stately span of the Chesapeake Bay Bridge for a day of serious yacht crawling. The first boat we investigated was an old Grand Banks, bigger than the one we first saw in Alabama, and roomier than anything of its size you would ever find in a sailboat. Susan liked it right away, but just to starboard of the venerable Grand Banks sat a pristine Lord Nelson Victory Tug, an aggressively cutesy replica of a traditional New York Harbor tugboat, complete with pudding on the bow and a fake smokestack. A big "For Sale" sign was taped to the deckhouse.

"How about that one?" asked Susan.

"Way out of your price range," answered the broker, dismissing Susan's inquiry in a manner that indicated that it wasn't his listing and he wasn't going to offer any information on it no matter what the price.

After we finished our road trip for the year and returned to New Zealand, we continued our fantasy search for the perfect boat on the Internet. As we pored over listing after listing, we would periodically remind each other that we really weren't interested in buying a boat, but it was fun to look. We focused our inquiries on trawler-style yachts, under 40 feet, single diesel with a maximum of 120 horsepower, and in sail-away . . . err, I mean, motor-away condition. We were looking for the perfect liveaboard cruising boat for an elderly couple in reasonable health and with modest means.

On investigation, it turned out that the Lord Nelson Tugs were not out of our price range after all. There were 15 of them listed on the YachtWorld website, http://www.yachtworld.com/. We were still in the depths of recession and some few of them had been on the market for several years with obviously desperate sellers. The Lord Nelsons were interesting boats in spite of their Tubby-the-Tugboat appearance. They were well constructed in Asia by a conscientious builder, and they were marginally sturdy enough to meet Susan's insistence on offshore capability. With a few modifications, I felt they could become reasonable sea boats.

"What if we decided to take it back to New Zealand?" Susan would ask of every boat I suggested she look at. "Could we do it in that boat? Would it be safe to cross the Pacific in it?"

Susan's insistence on a boat that we could safely take across oceans gradually eliminated all of the trawlers that were in our price range. And we eventually dropped the Lord Nelson from consideration as well. There were several available that were in good condition, and they were affordable, but that fake-tugboat look was just too damned cute. I am a form-follows-function sort of guy and the phony smokestack finally did it for me. I informed Susan that if we bought a Lord Nelson, I was going to grow a beard, don a yachting cap, learn to say "Aaaargh" a lot, and find a parrot for my shoulder. I might even consider a false peg leg to round out the package. She didn't mind the cap or the fake leg, but drew the line at the parrot, so we switched our search to a converted fishing boat.

"Now we're talking," I said with enthusiasm after my first search of the YachtWorld database for retired fishing boats. Anyone who loves old boats has to be enamored with these venerable veterans of the fishing fleet. Most of the good ones listed were in the Pacific Northwest, an area where we always wanted to cruise; most were heavily constructed of wood by master boatbuilders in British Columbia, Washington, or Alaska; and there were a fair few listed in our price range. We immediately fell in love with a 40-foot double-ender listed for a reasonable price by a seller in Seattle. We liked it so much that we made an impulsive sight-unseen offer to buy her. Fortunately for us another enamored suitor had also fallen for our prize and got a better offer in ahead of us.

I say "fortunately" because at some point, without our noticing, our fantasy search had become a serious quest. Looking at boats was no longer a joke. We had become determined to get back on the water full time, while we were still young enough to do it. We made that initial offer before our plans had fully gelled and were still subject to change. And change they did.

We spent that entire lazy New Zealand summer looking at boats and discussing our plans and the vessel we would need to realize them. We early on dropped the idea of staying within the comfortable confines of the southeastern rivers; the open sea beckoned to both of us and could not be ignored. At some point we decided that, yes, we would buy a bluewater-capable boat with the vague objective of sailing her back to New Zealand. I say vague because we have always sailed with emphasis on the trip while keeping the actual destination somewhat flexible.

Of the dozens of old fishing boats on the market there were several that caught our attention, but then we started to zero in on the shortcomings of long-distance cruising in a powerboat. Foremost was the obvious problem with fuel economy. Some of the old salmon trollers we found for sale were fitted with small, low-horsepower, high-torque diesel engines that promised seaworthy fuel economy, for a boat. But boats are inherently very inefficient means of transportation, and the best of them would burn a gallon or so of expensive diesel every hour to go an average of about five nautical miles. At a projected five dollars a gallon, that meant we could count on spending about a dollar a mile to get anywhere. With approximately 7,000 miles separating Seattle from Auckland in a straight line, that would be a pretty expensive trip, and we had no intention of traveling in a straight line.

Having spent five glorious summers cruising coastal Maine in an antique powerboat named Duchess, *we know all about the advantages of a big powerboat (comfortable and commodious accommodations) and the disadvantages (fuel burn and an uncomfortable rolling motion at sea).*

A second problem with cruising on a powerboat was the uncomfortable rolling motion that most powerboats exhibit at sea. We had spent five summers cruising the coasts of Maine and Maritime Canada in a 40-foot converted Coast Guard cruiser, so we were all too familiar with this violent side-to-side rocking motion. Any boat without the stabilizing benefit of a deep keel and offsetting windage is going to roll in any sea condition that is much more turbulent than flat calm. True, this rolling can be mitigated to some extent by sensible hull design, but even the best of the old fishing boat designs still roll a lot any time they encounter even the smallest beam sea.

Fishermen deal with sea motion in several ways. The simplest (and least effective) is with a small steady sail rigged fore and aft so that any breeze from the beam will help offset the natural rolling motion of a round hull. These steady sails are used by a lot of the lobster and crab boats on the eastern coast of the United States and Canada, both to stabilize the boat and to keep the bow into the wind while the fisherman is pulling pots with the helm unattended. Steady sails can be very effective roll stabilizers when the wind is strong enough and from the right direction, which in our experience is almost never.

Another popular way powerboats deal with motion at sea is with large steel or iron stabilizers, called flopper stoppers (or any number of other names depending on where you are and who you are talking to). Flopper stoppers are deployed on long booms that look like outriggers and extend athwartship. The effectiveness of flopper stoppers is determined by the length of the boom and the surface area of the bird, the heavy bit that dangles in the water from the boom. The good ones weigh several hundred pounds each and extend up to a boat length from the centerline. Naturally, we are talking about the serious flopper stoppers that are used while under way at sea. There are lightweight ones on the market designed for use at anchor, but that's not what we are talking about here.

Flopper stoppers can work very well indeed, and several of the old fishing boats we ended up looking at were fitted with them. But they are a lot of work, and they take a lot of skill to deploy properly. In a heavy sea, they can even be dangerous if not used with discretion. After thinking about it for a while, we decided that flopper stoppers were not the sort of thing that the elderly-friendly cruising boat we were after would have aboard.

That left the third and most effective of all sea-motion stabilizers: a proper sailing rig. Nothing stabilizes a boat at sea like a billowing mainsail and a full jib; a well-trimmed sailboat can be comfortable in nearly any weather as long as there is enough sail area to offset the roll-producing forces of the waves and swells and enough wind to fill it. Common knowledge will have you believe that you can't have a sailing rig on a powerboat and still have a powerboat, but it just ain't so.

One of the most effective cruising powerboat concepts that came to our attention during our search was the Diesel Duck designed by George Buehler. This utilitarian craft features a sturdily built true-displacement trawler hull fitted with a sail. The

The Diesel Duck design by George Buehler is my idea of the perfect combination of a sensible cruising powerboat and a limited but functional sailing rig. Alas, the Diesel Duck, with all its appeal, was far out of our price range. We should all have our dream boats, and this is mine. You will develop your own idea of the perfect boat for you, and the only guarantee is that it will not be anything like anyone else's. (GEORGE BUEHLER PHOTO)

sail is much larger and more effective than any steady sail, but still not a true sailing rig. However, it is large enough so that it will not only stabilize the boat at sea in most conditions, but will also provide enough sail power to get the boat into port should the engine fail.

Susan and I both fell in love with the Diesel Duck, but alas, not that many of these rugged trawlers have been built, and there were none available in our price range. Just a few years ago I would have jumped at the chance to build one, but this was out of the question if we were going to have any time and budget left to enjoy cruising.

We needed to find our ideal craft in the used-boat market. Thus, as we continued our quest, we shifted our search to eliminate any boats that could not be rigged with a substantial enough sail to provide a get-home alternative to the diesel engine.

So far, our year-long search for the ideal liveaboard voyaging yacht for two elderly cruisers had evolved from a not-too-serious perusal of sedate production trawlers from the seventies and eighties to a determined search for a bluewater capable macho-man of a sail-rigged retired fishing boat. But we weren't done yet. Our quest was to take one last and important turn.

The requirement for the sailing rig narrowed our selection of available fishing boats down to one: a classic old off-shore salmon troller named *Honker*. She was a bit larger than we felt we needed, and she didn't have an effective sail, but she carried a high tower that would have supported quite a large foresail if rigged properly.

Otherwise, she was ideal, so we decided to buy her. And we would have, too, but on his initial inspection the surveyor discovered a significant quantity of soft wood under the fiberglass exterior of the deckhouse and in the forward bulwarks. Nothing too serious, but there was enough superficial deterioration to require a lot of expensive and time-consuming work to fix.

Two of our previous boats—*Duchess*, the old Coast Guard cruiser, and *Sultana*, the ketch we sailed to New Zealand—had wooden hulls, so I was well acquainted with the problem of rot. And I felt entirely qualified and capable of repairing the old boat, but again, time and money dictated otherwise.

While traveling through British Columbia, we came across a grand old retired trawler (similar to this beauty photographed in Nelson Harbour, New Zealand). We decided to buy her, then had to back off when a survey turned up rot in the bulwarks and pilothouse. The rot was minor but more than we, as elderly folks, wanted to deal with, so we had to keep looking.

By now, with our extended list of requirements, we had exhausted all the possible candidates for our ideal elderly-friendly cruising boat. There were two problems getting in the way of our successful purchase of a suitable craft. The first was economic: we simply didn't have enough cash to buy a boat that measured up to all our expectations. There wasn't much we could do about our financial position, so we just had to get used to it. However, the second problem was more manageable. When we first started looking for a boat, we had no real concept of our exact requirements. If we ever wanted to find a boat, we would have to zero in on exactly what we wanted, and this led to the following list:

1. Available for $100,000 or less in sail-away condition (or near)
2. Economical to operate for long-distance voyaging
3. Capable of bluewater voyaging without compromise
4. Heavily built to high standards of construction in wood or fiberglass
5. No longer than 40 feet on deck

6. Fitted with a strong diesel engine capable of moving the boat at five knots or more with a one-gallon-per-hour maximum cruising fuel burn
7. Fitted with a sailing rig, preferably a ketch, capable of moving the boat at a reasonable speed on long ocean passages
8. Designed to be easy to sail. Wouldn't challenge the capabilities of two elderly cruisers
9. Comfortable for two old people in reasonably good health to live aboard

(Reasonable people will argue that if we had come up with this list when we first started our search, we would have saved a considerable amount of time and aggravation, not to mention some scarce cash. And they would be right, of course, but neither Susan nor I are list-makers, and an early list might have snaffled the selection process that eventually led to our purchase of *Vicarious*.)

Once we had compiled our list and were going over it for about the hundredth time, Susan suddenly exclaimed, "Wait a minute, this ideal boat of ours looks just like *Sultana*!" And she was right. In our year-long search for the perfect cruising boat, we had started with the easiest, a traditional production trawler capable of extended in-shore and limited coastal cruising. But as our plans gelled our criteria gradually evolved into the boat we both really wanted. In the end we realized that we had come full circle and ended up with a slightly smaller version of the boat we had sold just three years before.

As I said earlier, old age gets a lot of bad press, and indecision is one of the endearing qualities that popular knowledge attributes to us elderly folks. This is the way it is and probably as it should be, but the foregoing narrative is not the exercise in irresolution that it may appear at first. Susan and I initially gave up cruising because we were facing old age and all the limitations that condition imposes. We were very much aware of the additional aches and pains, the diminished hearing and vision, the deteriorating balance and endurance, and all the other minor ailments that every person, starting from about the age of 25, experiences while getting older. In retrospect, we stopped cruising because we were expected to stop cruising. At 60 we had grown too old for ocean voyages. We needed to go ashore to plan for our sunset years, to establish a beachhead of comfort and convenience, look at moving into a retirement village perhaps, or take up golf and gardening as many of our more well-adjusted and responsible friends were doing.

And we did it, too. Our tiny cottage in Nelson, New Zealand, is the stereotypical retirement home, perfect in every way, and we were happy there. Could anyone with intact senses trade all we had for dragging anchors and midnight watches in stormy seas?

We decided that, yes, we could, so we did.

THE BASIC LIFE

We must free our souls from the prison of obsessive consumption so we can go Sailing Into Retirement with a light heart and a heavy kitty.

First We Need a New "Ism"

Just what is an "ism" anyway?

> *Ism: used as a productive suffix in the formation of nouns denoting action or practice, state or condition, principles, doctrines, a usage or characteristic, devotion or adherence, etc.*
> —WIKIPEDIA

A lot of fuss has been made lately about minimalism as it applies to lifestyle (not to the abstract art movement with the same name) and as exemplified by our hero, Henry David Thoreau. As you undoubtedly learned in high school, H. D. lived for two years in a self-built cabin on the forested shores of Walden Pond in Massachusetts, where he famously proclaimed:

> *I went to the woods because I wished to live deliberately, to front only the essential facts of life, and see if I could not learn what it had to teach, and not, when I came to die, discover that I had not lived.*

This much-over-quoted statement has become the worldwide mantra of the minimalist movement. But minimalism seems to have evolved into a doctrine that focuses on the ". . . essential facts of life . . ." phrase in this quote and has become a lifestyle bereft of all but those few things necessary for survival. Perhaps nourishment, shelter, a few items of clothing, a reliable supply of oxygen, and the affection of someone who is important would comprise the entire list of the needs of a dedicated minimalist.

As I see it, by following a severe doctrine that borders on a religious cult shot through with overtones of Zen, Buddhism, and Essenism, minimalism has become too much of an austere way to live for our purposes. After all, a boat might not be construed by some misinformed souls as necessary for survival. And while there is much to admire in Zen and Buddhism—they aren't quite the same thing really, but we can argue that another time—some of the concepts can get a bit complicated (and you don't even want to think about Essenism). As we sail into retirement, complicated is what we want to avoid, so we need to find another, more adaptable "ism" to apply to our style of living on the cheap while seeing the world from the decks of a cruising yacht.

BASICISM AS AN ALTERNATIVE

Minimalism in its most strict form might lead to an overly austere lifestyle that would miss many of the joys that we adopt the cruising life to seek. So, except for the last few words (" . . . when I came to die, discover that I had not lived."), which we can keep as the ultimate condition to avoid, we can leave Thoreau's most famous quote to the minimalists and move on, seeking a more appropriate slogan for our guidance.

Fortunately, there is another quote by our paragon of parsimonious perplexity, Henry David Thoreau, which will better serve us in our quest to retire to a basic life afloat:

> *Most of the luxuries and many of the so-called comforts of life are*
> *not only not indispensable, but positive hindrances to the elevation*
> *of mankind.*

This remarkable statement, with its artfully constructed double negative, is more focused than the first; plus it is more timely and better serves our newly discovered desire to enjoy the rest of our lives (or the major part) cruising on a boat. We can restate this profundity in language that might be more accessible to modern ears:

The more stuff you've got, the more trouble it will be.

Or:

Stuff you have lying around that you don't need causes more aggravation than it is worth.

Therefore, as we sally forth onto the world's oceans, lakes, rivers, and seas, we will strive to exclude from our lives ". . . most of the luxuries and many of the so-called comforts . . . " that mean nothing to us. But we will retain all of the things that lead ". . . to the elevation of mankind," where "mankind" conveniently refers to you and me.

It is a fascinating study to observe how many of us are quick to quote our hero, Henry David Thoreau, but how few of us ever pay any attention to what he actually had to say. (NATIONAL PORTRAIT GALLERY)

For convention's sake, we will call our newly formed discipline "basicism" and define it (pretentiously perhaps) as a harmonious and spiritually rewarding existence that strives for contentment and comfort by adopting everything that is important for a tranquil life and shunning everything that isn't.

Basicism, as I see it, isn't about deprivation and self-denial; it's about making sensible choices in our material possessions, our individual habits, and in our attitudes that can further our quest for an economical, environmentally kind, healthy, and enlightened life on a cruising boat. We will retain or acquire everything we need and nothing we don't. The difficult part will be to discover the difference between the two.

MINIMALISM VERSUS BASICISM

For an example of minimalism versus basicism, let's examine Susan's linguini and clam sauce, a delectable dish that helps make life worth living. The extreme minimalist diet is likely to consist of only what one needs to sustain life: wheat germ and yogurt perhaps, with a bit of boiled tofu and a handful of nuts when you feel the need to pig out. This may be enough to keep us alive, but unfortunately it leaves no room for my favorite dish, which, of course, makes it unacceptable.

The basicist diet, in contrast, can include anything at all within a broad range of reasonable and easily broken parameters. As long as we try to keep the food we eat as free from processing as possible, as inexpensive as practical, as healthy as palatable, and as tasty as permissible we are doing fine. Healthy eating becomes a beneficial byproduct of our adoptive lifestyle, not a goal that we must strive to reach.

For another example of our desire to embrace basicism instead of minimalism, take the case of a friend we will call Bob (because that's his name) who is inordinately fond of Rolex watches. Bob has drawers and display cases full of the things in a myriad of styles and models. Together they are worth many thousands of dollars. The minimalists would say that Rolex watches are in no way necessary for survival and advise Bob to get rid of the lot. Basicists, on the other hand, would recognize that Bob derives a great deal of pleasure from his Rolex collection, but perhaps more than a little of that pleasure comes from the erroneous belief that he is impressing other collectors with the magnitude of his accumulated hoard. Basicist philosophy would counsel Bob to get over his desire to impress his friends, then to select, wear, and enjoy the most prized and practical example from his collection. He can sell the rest and put the money directly into his cruising kitty.

Bob would be miles ahead if he would treasure the single best example of his watches and divest himself of all the others. Not only would this simple act generate a bunch of cash for the kitty (even though, in truth, more cash in the kitty is the last thing Bob needs), it would also eliminate the expense of maintaining, insuring, and storing the things while reducing the anxiety of a robbery, a worldwide crash in the price of Rolex watches, or (as actually happened) the discovery that several of the most expensive watches in his collection were clever forgeries.

EVILS OF CONSUMERISM

We live in a society where our actions are largely dictated by the needs of our government and of large corporations. The education we receive, the number of children we produce, and our expectations of life are predetermined by the needs of society, and in a consumerist society like ours, this means the corporations that produce the goods we are expected to consume.

A good example of this is the shift in lifestyles that occurred in the fifties and sixties. I was ten years old in 1952 and lived with my family in a ramshackle old farmhouse in the country outside of Washington, D.C. I had three sisters and one brother, making up a household of seven, which was only slightly above the average family size for that time in our history. My dad worked for an environmental lobby group (one of the first) in downtown Washington, and every morning he would trudge the mile or so to the top of the hill that defined our little valley and catch a bus into work. My mother stayed at home where she kept an eye on the kids, tended our small-but-productive vegetable garden, fed the chickens, and did all the other things that the moms of all my friends did.

By the time I was 20, in 1962, my family had moved to a row house in the suburbs, my dad was driving to work in one of our two cars, my mother had a job as a file clerk in a mail-order business (to which she commuted in the other car) while the kids watched themselves. Chickens and vegetables came canned or frozen from the Super Shopper grocery store at the new mall just down the street. I was in the military, stationed in Japan to support what was the beginning of a long and nasty war to make the world safe for big business and the military–industrial complex. (Oops, sorry. Make that truth, justice, and the American way.)

The point here is not to make a political statement or a moral one but to illustrate the profound shift in lifestyles that occurred in the quarter century after World War II. Sometime in the fifties, just before we moved out of the old farmhouse and into the new row house, we acquired our first television set, a monstrous affair with a 20-inch screen in a solid-oak cabinet, and I viewed the first of many millions of TV commercials; the first I can remember featured Howdy Doody explaining to Buffalo Bob what wonderful stuff Wonder Bread was ("Builds Strong Bodies Eight Ways"). Before we got the TV, the only advertisements I could remember were the Maidenform bra ads (hey, I was 13 for Pete's sakes) in the pages of the *Saturday Evening Post* and the Burma-Shave signs that were great fun and populated every roadside on the continent ("Every Tube . . . is like . . . Louise . . . You Get . . . A Thrill . . . With Every . . . Squeeze.").

Television was the juggernaut that led the free world from the pursuit of a complacent and prosperous lifestyle to the consumerist one, and the world has never been the same. Our prosperity is now judged by the amount of stuff we buy, and our personal worth to society is judged largely by our income and the value of our possessions. It seems that the more we quote mid-nineteenth-century existentialists, such as Thoreau, the less we observe their teachings. And in spite of Henry David's shining example, we have become a nation of consumers driven to acquire as many things as our credit cards will allow, and we have been unremittingly successful at it.

I will return here to the comparison of my life as a ten-year-old with that of my youngest sibling, who was ten years younger than me, as a case in point. My ten-year-old life in 1952 was lived with woods and fields to roam, with a mother who was there to kiss my boo-boos and yell at me for climbing too high in the old pear tree. My young sister, on the other hand, lived her ten-year-old life in 1962 in a new house on an eighth-acre lot in a massive suburban housing development. Mom had to work, so sis had to deal with her own boo-boos, and there was no pear tree in which to climb too high. In fact, except for two saplings my dad planted in our tiny front lawn, there were no trees on our property at all.

The Trefethen family gained a lot when we relocated from the country into the suburbs. We moved from a drafty old house into a brand-new one, and we now had a garage to house one of our two not-so-old cars. Or at least it would have if it hadn't been full of new bikes and camping equipment and the new barbecue with the lift-up lid and lawn-care equipment and the new washer and dryer and the new oversized stand-up freezer and lots of other new stuff that we didn't even remember we had.

To say we came a long way in that eventful decade would be an understatement. We progressed from a poor family who needed to raise their own food to make ends meet to a middle-class success story with all the trappings of luxury and prosperity that a young family could want. Of course my mom had to get a job and work to pay for all this stuff, but that was the normal thing to do in the sixties. Everyone accepted the fact that in order "to make ends meet" a family needed two incomes. And besides, women had just as much right to work their lives away at dull, meaningless jobs as men did.

THE FREE MARKET

The success of consumerism and the free-market system has driven one of the greatest social changes since the Industrial Revolution. It has seen a quantum leap in what we call our "standard of living," lifted hundreds of millions of people from the quagmire of endemic poverty, helped to stabilize shaky governments and overthrow corrupt ones, and created international wealth on a stupendous scale.

Unrestrained consumerism is great for big business, the Walmart store just down the road, and the new MegaMall across from it (not to mention the guy who rents you your self-storage bin where you keep all your extra stuff), but it may not be that great for you and me. Measuring the esteem of a person by net worth or by the value of possessions is an effective way to drive the obsessive acquisition of property, but at the personal level the connection between wealth and quality of life is illusory at best. At worst, it is dehumanizing and degrading.

It seems to me that the free-market system isn't free at all, especially when we consider the freedoms and personal liberty that we have to surrender to achieve it.

There is no point here in going into all the negative effects that excessive consumerism has on our environment and on our personal lives. It is a fascinating subject perhaps, but it isn't what this book is about. There is already plenty of reading material in publications and on the Internet on the unprecedented increases in suicide, chronic depression, environmental degradation, climate change, clinical obesity, personal debt, pollution, divorce (and other relationship problems), stress, corporate greed, and (ironically) unemployment levels.

Our list of negative effects of consumerism could go on forever, but, of course, there are also some positive effects. No rational person will argue that the advances in racial and sexual equality, medicine, and information technology haven't had a positive effect on the way we live. Unfortunately most of the positive advances in the past half-century are social, political, technological, and economic rather than personal. We can argue that, while our standard of living has increased remarkably, our quality of life has not. In fact, you can mount a valid argument to the contrary: that as we focus more on ". . . the luxuries and many of the so-called comforts . . ." and ignore the ". . . elevation of mankind . . ." our quality of life has decreased in proportion to the increase in our standard of living.

There is actually a name for this phenomenon. It is called the Esterlin Paradox, after the guy who discovered it, and it states (very basically) that personal satisfaction does indeed increase with a person's net worth, but only up to a point. We need a certain level of income to be comfortable and if we don't have that, it makes us unhappy. The interesting part is that once we reach our comfortable level of income, adding to it doesn't increase our level of contentment at all, and can actually reduce it.

A content consumer is a non-consuming one, and non-consumption is a threat to the very fabric of our society. If we ever stop borrowing money and buying stuff on a massive scale, our economy would collapse, individual net worth would evaporate, unemployment would skyrocket, and governments would be overthrown. This almost happened in 2008, of course, when the *Great Recession*, fueled by a crash in artificially inflated housing prices, caused consumer spending on nonessential goods and services to plummet.

You could easily argue that, because our society depends entirely on consumption for its very existence, it is our civic duty to buy as much stuff as we possibly can. But we have already spent most of our lives doing that. We have done our part, and it is now time to retire and leave the excessive consumption, with all its stress and depression and dissatisfaction, to our descendants whom we can count on to carry on the tradition, max out their credit cards, and dutifully prevent the collapse of society.

CONSUMERISM IS FUTILE ANYWAY

Okay then, our first step in preparing for sailing into retirement is to stop being a consumer and start being a basicist. We must free our souls from the prison of obsessive consumption so we can go sailing into retirement with a light heart and a heavy kitty.

Transcending the allure of owning stuff may sound easy, but it will probably be one of the hardest things you have ever done. We have been saturated since birth with a continuous stream of expensive propaganda admonishing us to buy more of this and lots of that.

Psychologists who work for big companies know that many of our actions are strongly and subconsciously motivated by the way we perceive that others (our friends, family, neighbors, kids, partners, and even the family dog and complete strangers) think of us for taking those actions. We know for sure that buying a new car is going to impress the smart ass across the street and that having a daughter in medical school is going to make us look and feel like good parents or that a membership in the country club will let everyone know that we are people of importance and substance.

Playing to our desire to impress others has been the cornerstone of the advertising industry for generations. Advertisers gear their pitches to emphasize our perception of the envy and admiration that owning their product will generate in the ones who see us owning it, and it works with everything from Froot Loops™ to mega-yachts.

I am sure that this intrepid fisher-person, snapped unaware in a Georgia bayou, does not consider himself a victim of consumerism and the voracious international advertising industry, but why else would a sane person buy a $60,000 boat with a 200-horsepower outboard to use fishing in a swamp for six-inch crappie (a small freshwater fish popular with big-spending sportsmen from the South)? Not shown is the elderly couple sitting comfortably in five-dollar folding chairs while fishing from the opposite bank. They appeared to be catching just as many fish and having a lot more fun than our big spender in the speedboat.

But the psychologists who don't work for big corporations know something else that is even more important to us as cruisers, and it is even more profound. Many studies have proven that what we perceive to be the impression that we are giving to others by our actions is uniformly wrong. The envy we see in the eyes of a neighbor looking at our new $60,000 LunkerBuster Bass Boat is more likely perplexity at why we would want such a thing in Las Vegas or even pity that we would be so stupid to buy a LunkerBuster when everyone knows that Zoomercraft MK-IV with the supercharger option is the one all the really cool guys are driving this year.

The point is that our subconscious motivation to impress others by buying stuff we don't need or even want is largely in vain. Others don't really give a stuff about our stuff because they are too busy accumulating their own stuff so that they can impress us. I suppose that's why they call it a rat race.

FROM CONSUMERISM TO BASICISM

The first thing we must do to make the transition from consumerism to basicism is to stop worrying about what others think about us. We need to stop looking at ourselves through the eyes of others and start judging ourselves on our own personal standards based on our goal to retire on a boat.

We must learn to evaluate everything we do to determine if it furthers or hinders us in our quest; if it is a hindrance, we won't do it, and if it isn't, we will. What anyone else thinks of our actions simply doesn't matter, provided, of course, that the action is legal and within reasonable moral boundaries.

This change in attitude isn't as easy as it seems. Compulsive consumption is so much a part of living in our society that we may not even recognize it is happening.

THE 10-STEP AUSTERITY PROGRAM

Starting right now, we need to focus on basic behavioral adjustments that will get us to stop buying stuff we don't need. The following is a ten-step program that, if followed assiduously, will convert us from the herd-following consumerist sheep we were trained to be from birth to the frugal tightwads we need to become if we are to realize our sailing-into-retirement dreams. Any similarity of these ten steps to the proven effective *Twelve Steps Program* of Alcoholics Anonymous is entirely intentional, as excessive consumption is every bit as addictive as strong drink.

This program is designed around those of us who have limited resources and earning power, such as your elderly-but-humble author, and who want to retire on a boat within five years. But many aspiring retirement cruisers reading this book aren't poor and will have already accumulated substantial resources that can be used to fatten the kitty. Perhaps you are among these lucky individuals who have enough cash in the bank to enjoy a comparatively luxurious retirement cruise, enough to buy just about any boat you want and to go anywhere you want. If so, I would admonish you to follow this program anyway, because doing so will enrich your life in ways that you can only imagine until you try it. In fact, the higher the value of the useless stuff you have accumulated, the more it has become the chain of unquestioned conformity that has kept you shackled to the wall. It isn't an exaggeration to say that the sense of freedom derived from systematically divesting yourself of useless possessions is as intense as that felt by a released prisoner after a long time in jail.

We have all heard that "living within our means" is a great way to go through life, and a few of us are probably actually doing that. But all this means is that you are spending no more than you are earning, whatever the source of our income. This is good news, but it isn't good enough for those of us aspiring to retire on a boat within five years. We must start now to live *below* our means; the more below our means we can manage, the faster we can fatten the kitty and get gone on our retirement cruise.

Here is the step-by-step program for doing it, so let's get started. Forget about boats and cruising destinations for now; first we must get our affairs in order if we are to have any chance of success. Psychologists tell us that changing our habits is far from easy and that behavioral adjustments take at least 21 consecutive days of exposure to become permanent—ex-smokers will easily remember the first three weeks of agony when they finally kicked the butts—so give each step a month before moving on to the next.

Step One: Share the Passion
The very first thing to do before you start: if you are planning to sail into retirement with another person or with several other persons, make sure that everyone involved (spouses, partners, kids, dogs, cats, etc.) shares the passion of your goals. Any cruising plan becomes infinitely easier if everyone is staring wistfully at the same horizon.

Step Two: Clean Up Your Diet
Depending on your habits up to now, learning to eat well might be one of the hardest steps on this list. Eating well is one of the best ways there is to improve your retired life, no matter where or how you spend it, but if you have a lifetime of eating junk behind you, as many of us do, cleaning up your diet can be agony. Forget about any fad diets that may be sweeping the country at the moment, and concentrate on eating good stuff and not eating bad stuff. It really is as simple as that, but it still isn't easy.

To start, except for special occasions or when you want to give yourself an *earned* reward, stop eating in restaurants and prepare all your food at home. If you don't know how to cook, jump forward to Step Six and make learning your way around the kitchen (soon to become a galley) a priority. Shun the fast-food places like a kid shuns cabbage, and gradually change your diet to eliminate as much prepared or packaged food as you can. Learn to eat apple slices or celery sticks for snacks instead of chips and cheese balls, and if you enjoy alcohol, limit your intake to two beers or two glasses of wine a day instead of drinking a six-pack or finishing off the entire bottle every night. Put hard liquor in the same category as eating in restaurants

We all know we should be eating fresh, wholesome food, but it isn't that easy when we are pummeled by deceptive advertising and surrounded on all sides by endless temptation. Living on a boat in remote places can remove you from that environment and make it easier to avoid processed food laden with chemicals, salts, and fats.

and enjoy it occasionally as a reward for some worthy accomplishment. And no, waking up in the morning is not an accomplishment, no matter how old you are.

The trick is to get back to eating wholesome basic food with as little drama as possible. This means buying fresh vegetables and fruits, meats from the butcher counter, and fish that still has a head (ask the guy behind the counter to cut it off if you are squeamish). Buy the family size of cereals and pastas and make your own sauces and dressings. Without being obsessive about it, cut out as much sugar, salt, and prepared food as you can.

Later on, we will have an entire chapter on the ideal galley and cooking arrangements for a retirement cruising boat, so there is a lot more to come on this subject. But stop eating junk and start eating good stuff now. We will discover the specifics of dining aboard later.

Step Three: Exercise. Then Exercise Some More

Don't run out and join a health club or buy an expensive exercise machine from the infomercials, just start walking to work or taking the stairs instead of the escalator every time you have a chance. Healthful exercise shouldn't be an obsession, any more than good eating is, but should become ingrained into your daily routine. Never overlook an opportunity to leave your car at home if there is a chance to walk to your destination. Don't take an elevator if there are stairs handy, and park on the outer edge of the parking lot when you must visit the mall.

Now buy a bicycle. A cheap beater from the recycle store is best because it will be hard to pedal, you will probably have to push it up hills, and you won't have the stress of worrying about it being stolen. (If you don't lock it up in most places, it will get stolen no matter how rough it looks, but who cares?) Now make bicycle riding a part of your daily routine, if it is only an early morning pedal around the block.

These first three steps in our ten-step plan to retiring on a boat are more important than all of the rest combined. If you can master them, you will have gone more than halfway to your goal even without completing the others. Not only will you have upgraded your health, sharpened your mental faculties, and improved the quality of your retirement years, you are very likely to have added significantly to the number of them you will have to enjoy. Now aren't you glad you bought this book?

Step Four: Change Your Attitude
Now quit your job and start living the unemployed life.

Okay, okay, don't really physically quit your job, just do it mentally with a change of attitude. If you are like the rest of us, your life has been dedicated to your career and advancement in it. Now that you are looking at retirement, you have either achieved your career goals or you haven't. At this point it doesn't matter because your working life, or at least your gainful employment, is nearing its end. Most people who retire on a boat report that doing so was more work than they had ever done before, so don't look forward to a life of leisure, but we will get back to that.

Ask yourself what you would do if you woke up one morning and found yourself without a job and with no prospects for one in sight, as has happened with so many of us since the 2008 recession. The first thing you might do is look at your expenses and start trimming the unnecessary ones. If you have a car payment (and who doesn't) you might sell the car to pay off the loan, then buy a cheap beater or even a motor scooter to get around on. (If you think you would look funny or if the neighbors would laugh at you for riding on a scooter, jump ahead to Step Five.) Living now the way you would if your income were eliminated or drastically reduced will help a lot in getting you aboard a boat, but you can take it even farther by associating with people who have a positive attitude.

Step Five: Change Your Friends
Seek out and cultivate (networking is the buzzword for meeting people who can help you reach a goal) friends and acquaintances who think the way that you want to think. Associating with like-minded people will go a long way to help you retire as living-beneath-your-means frugal cruisers. A brief search of the Internet reveals dozens of organizations and forums dedicated to helping you reduce excess consumption. Once you locate one or two that mesh with your personal philosophy and lifestyle, they can be a huge help to keep you on the path to sensible frugality.

The website http://www.becomingminimalist.com is one of the more popular anti-consumer blogs and one of my favorites. It calls itself a minimalist site but it is a moderate one, and, although it says nothing about boats, it contains many nuggets of advice and example that are directly translatable to the frugal cruising life and basicism.

Step Six: Build Your Self-Confidence

Start gradually doing things you are already good at, and face up to mundane tasks that you would normally hire someone else to do for you. Take night classes in plumbing, cooking, electrical work, and carpentry; check for free how-to-do-it tutorials on YouTube.

Since earliest times, society has been organized into specialties. Farmers farmed, plumbers plumbed, and goldsmiths fashioned beautiful objects out of precious metals. In medieval society it was often illegal to do work outside your guild or trade, so we have been conditioned for a long time to phone a specialist when a sink gasket needs replacement or when it is time for an oil change in the family car.

This dependency on others has to change when we live on a boat. Everything we hire others to do while on the water is going to cost a lot more than for the same work we had done while on land. There are several good reasons for this and a lot of bad ones. Boatyards have chronically high overhead that must be recovered from a comparatively small market, but a lot of them also have a "charge-what-the-market-

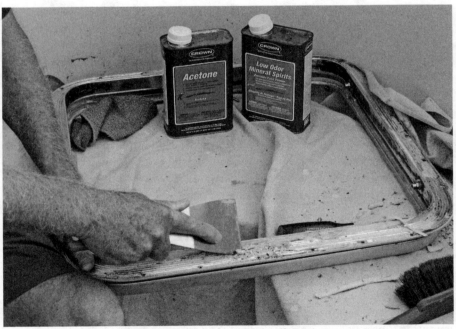

Removing, re-bedding, and reinstalling deck hatches and portlights is often essential to stopping leaks. It is a nasty, time-consuming job that in many boatyards will cost upward of $1,000 for each hatch. Doing it yourself costs nothing but a little time and the self-confidence that comes with knowing how do it.

will-bear" mentality that encourages them to size up each job and charge as much as they think they can get for the work. Transients, who are unlikely to be repeat customers, are obviously a bigger target for this practice than the local folks who trade at the yard regularly, which is one good reason for being skeptical about local recommendations for boat work.

Another reason for doing it yourself whenever you can is that doing your own maintenance and upgrades is the only way to ensure that you get the job done correctly. As you take on more and more of the do-it-yourself jobs, the skills you accumulate will build your self-confidence and make true self-reliance possible.

Step Seven: Stop Buying Stuff

We aren't ready to drop out of the consumer society, not just yet anyway, but we are getting close. Dropping out will have to wait until we get to Step Ten. Right now we need to stop buying stuff we don't need. Yes we already have tons of stuff lying around that we have no real use for, but let's not chuck it out in haste. Instead, let's try to stop adding to it, and the best way to do that is to just stop buying anything. Simply stop going to the store for a few days and see how you get on. Then, if it's working for you, keep on not going to the store for at least a month.

I have no way of knowing what your shopping habits are, but if you are like most Americans and other citizens of prosperous countries, you go shopping two or three times a week, and many of us go every day. So for this exercise, just stop going to stores. When you need something, see if there isn't something else that will do as well or just try to do without it.

It is unlikely that you can go for long without buying anything at all. For basic items like milk and bread, there should be a small dairy or convenience store within walking distance of where you live, so start doing that sort of shopping on foot and it will soon become a habit. Susan and I regularly walk or row the dinghy for a mile or more to do our grocery shopping and are disappointed when there are stores within range that don't require any effort to reach.

If you are faithful to this exercise, you will find that most of those trips to the store are just wasting your time and encouraging you to buy stuff you don't really need and probably don't even want, as the next step will clearly demonstrate.

Step Eight: Store Stuff You Aren't Using

Once you have weaned yourself off the shopping habit, take all your stuff, except for the most basic of basic items that you use every day, and pack it away in boxes. This is a big one and quite disruptive so don't take it lightly or start on it until you have mastered all seven of the preceding steps, especially the first.

Pack away most of your clothing, tools, kitchen gadgets, sports equipment, and anything else you treasure but don't necessarily use that often. Label the contents of each box carefully because you are bound to make a few mistakes and pack stuff you really do need. You will want to be able to retrieve these items without having to grovel through a mountain of mystery boxes.

This is a tough one, but one of the first things you should get out of sight is your television. It is best to simply put the thing away and stop watching broadcast shows of every kind, but if you are a TV addict like a lot of us are, you may not be able to cold-turkey this one. In this case, trade in your 60-inch flat screen for the smallest set you can see without eyestrain, and try to limit and gradually reduce the number of shows you watch.

One useful trick is to put the TV away in a closet or somewhere else not that easy to get to, then take it out when you must watch some particularly interesting show. You may quickly learn that the reward in entertainment you get from most broadcast programs isn't worth even the minimal effort it takes to retrieve the thing and plug it in, and you will go for a walk or read a book instead.

Although the Internet is coming on strong, TV is still the most effective medium for advertising the glamour products and high-end merchandise that we buy because we think it makes us cool. Cars and beer, two of the most important products that we purchase to boost self-image, are among the heaviest network advertisers, but there are many others. It is a statistical fact (as determined by my own highly scientific surveys) that the amount of money advertisers spend promoting their products is in near-perfect inverse proportion with the need we have for those products. And the advertising component of truly useless items, like exercise machines and designer-label clothing, can be as much as 90 percent of the cost of selling you the item.

Because we, as individuals and as a society, have been bombarded with millions of every sort of advertisement imaginable (and lots that are beyond imaginable) we don't have any way of knowing how much influence these things have on our buying decisions, so the best defense against this influence is to simply stop watching the ads.

As much as is practical, move the TV and all the boxes into a single room or into the garage where they are out of sight but still accessible. This will gradually wean you from the idea that all these physical things that have been cluttering up your life are important to it, but it will leave you a way out. Not everyone is suited to a cruising retirement, so by gradually reducing the number of your possessions as well as your living space, which we will cover next, you can back out at any time.

If you give all your stuff away and move onto a boat right away, you might find that you don't like it at all and that you have made a very expensive mistake. By keeping your stuff stored away and out of sight, you can gradually get used to the basic existence that translates so easily to life aboard a cruising boat.

Proceed cautiously as you peel away the layers of superfluous paraphernalia from your life. You must put away everything that you don't need while keeping everything that you do need. As we said before, the trick is to recognize the difference.

Once you have boxed up all your extra stuff, go about your life just as before. As soon as you miss something, refer to the above and carefully consider your real need for the item. If you decide that you really do need an item that is packed away (say you accidentally packed your toothbrush) then go get it. When you encounter something that you saved out but don't really need, simply add it to the items packed away.

Do this for a month, and if you are like most of us, you will be amazed at the volume of stuff that remains unused and stored in boxes. Once you get over the initial shock and find your groove, you will be moving more and more of your stuff into the boxes, even stuff you thought you could never live without. It is tough at first, but before long, your heart will leap with joy as each new useless item is discovered and relegated to cardboard obscurity. After a few months of doing this, most of us can't even remember many of the things we stored away.

Step Nine: Reduce Your Living Space

Once you have removed the most useless of your nonessential possessions from your immediate presence, you will find yourself with a lot of extra empty space. Start by closing off any unused rooms you might have, or use them to store all those boxes. Gradually move all the furniture that you don't use often into an unused room, as well as wall hangings, framed pictures, and knickknacks that are lying around.

Keep one or two decorative items for each room that remains. Decoration is a legitimate function that helps make our living space a home, so don't neglect it. Now try to arrange the furnishings you have left in a pleasant and relaxing manner. Read up a bit on *feng shui* for help with techniques of decorating in ways that please the good-luck dragon and require nothing but an imagination and a little guidance.

Continue to gradually reduce your living space as you continue to move unused items into storage boxes.

Step Ten: Now *Drop Out of the Consumer Society*

Most of us don't really want to "drop out" to the extent we become reclusive hermits. Instead, we will move to the very edge of our consumerist society where we can keep track of what is going on without having to actually participate in it. As we discussed before, we have done our part for consumerism and we can now, with a conscience clear of guilt or concern, move to the sidelines and let others carry on the traditions of overconsumption.

Rejecting consumerism may reduce our standard of living, perhaps a lot for some of us, but it will not compromise or reduce our basic needs or reduce our quality of life in any way. To the contrary, divesting our lives of excess material objects and the desire to possess them allows us to concentrate on relationships, enjoy our surroundings, and participate in the true sense of community that comes with real freedom.

Here I will apologize for the paucity of material in this chapter relating to boats and how to live on them. But getting past materialistic dependency and adjusting your

The collection of unneeded scraps of wood and boat parts on Vicarious *is constantly growing, and if left unchecked would eventually sink the boat. I must periodically take armloads to the dumpster. The embarrassing thing here is that this photo shows what was left over after I cleaned out the "useless" stuff.*

attitude to see the wonderful benefits of living a life unencumbered with physical things is essential to the rest of this book. If you have made it this far, you have done well, so let's get back on topic and talk about the choices that are yours to make when you adopt the cruising life for your retirement.

CRUISING WITH STYLE AND PURPOSE

I'll say this about Susan: I love her more than pepperoni pizza and pumpernickel and life itself, but she sure has difficulty grasping the big picture of the really important issues we face.

Throughout this book, we (where "we" is mostly me) are assuming you are not yet retired but are looking forward to it; you have limited experience messing around with boats; you have some sort of retirement income lined up but are not wealthy or overburdened with excess cash; your health is good for your age; your relationships with significant others are sound; and your intellectual acuity is keen enough to deal with abstract concepts like intellectual acuity.

But maybe none of this is true. Perhaps you are already retired; you were born and raised around boats; you have bags of money lying around; you are in the midst of a messy divorce; you are 100 pounds overweight and smoke two packs a day; and your intellectual acuity is less than acute. If so, don't put this book down just yet. I have written everything that follows to cover, as widely as possible, the entire spectrum of retired and potentially retired people who think they might want to retire on a cruising boat. To experienced sailors and cruisers, some of what follows might be a bit basic. But haul up the daggerboard and sail right over the shallow parts; you are bound to find a few nuggets of wisdom lurking in the depths.

If you are already retired and are living on a boat, great, but read on anyway. There is some sound advice in here and more than a few fascinating tales of adventure and nautical derring-do (some of which may even be true) that will appeal to cruisers of all ages and levels of experience.

Types of Retirement Cruising

One of the first things you should do (and have probably already done) is to decide just what type of cruising you want to do after you retire and where you want to do it. The options here are many, but once you factor in your experience, your expectations, the capabilities of your boat, and your financial resources, you can narrow them down considerably. For convenience, let's define our choices as sheltered cruising, coastal cruising, offshore cruising or voyaging, and bug-out cruising (see later in this chapter for a definition of bug-out cruising).

SHELTERED CRUISING

Sheltered cruising is the art of traveling in a boat from one location to another while never leaving the protection of a nearby land mass. Rivers, canals, lakes, and large bays with many sheltering islands lend themselves to this sort of boating, and it is by far the most popular way we have of cruising broad expanses of water without having to worry about the difficult or dangerous conditions often found offshore. Sheltered cruising can be enjoyed by just about anyone in just about any sort of boat just about anywhere there is a river, canal, or lake that covers enough geography to offer a selection of destinations.

There are thousands of miles of rivers, interconnected lakes, and canals in Europe and in the United States, attractive to retired cruisers of all skill levels. But cruising in sheltered waters will appeal especially to beginning cruisers with limited nautical experience and to older cruisers whose appetite for excitement has been sated by time and happenstance. Sheltered cruising is the easiest way to get a cruising retirement started with as little fuss and expense as possible. It offers the considerable advantage of acting as a classroom to novices who can pick up seafaring skills as they progress through scenic farmland and busy cities while experiencing a lifestyle both idyllic and accessible. For those of us new to boating, sheltered cruising can be a handy stepping-stone to the more advanced and difficult forms of moving about on a boat.

Canal Cruising

Some years ago, I watched an English cooking show that featured a celebrity chef named Rick, who, with a scraggly little dog named Chalky, meandered through the canals of Europe on a canal boat, sampling and analyzing the local viands as he went. I don't recall the name of the show, but it is a popular one fans will recognize right away. The series was shared at a potluck, and it instantly captivated the audience. Several cruisers there had experienced the European canal system, and one had lived aboard a canal boat in England for many years while he built a large catamaran. It was a fascinating show and left everyone watching with a desire to do the same. I am sure one or two actually did it.

The show made canal cruising seem easy, and although I have not experienced this sort of thing, I have met many people who have. I have yet to meet one who thought it was anything other than a marvelous experience. I understand, however, that it isn't a particularly economical way to see Europe, as there are canal fees, and fuel can be expensive. Renting canal boats has grown steadily in popularity over the years, and the rates in the summer season can be high. Most cruisers I have met who have cruised the canals of Europe have done it in their own sailboats, but there you have the added expense and nuisance of un-stepping and re-stepping the mast.

In the United States, canal cruising is limited to the Erie Canal system in New York and to sections of the Intracoastal Waterway (see pages 43–44), but the attraction of canals to the more cautious and elderly cruisers among us is obvious: with no chance of getting lost, or of dragging anchor in the night, or getting caught with too much sail up in a major blow, it is one of the most stress-free ways of traveling on a boat there can be.

The European canal system is a vast network of natural rivers and dug canals connected by locks and waterways, some of which date back to Roman times. Canal cruising is popular with cruisers in Europe looking for interesting places in protected waters, but beyond that, I won't be qualified to comment until we get there. Stay tuned.

Great Barrier Reef

In the southern hemisphere winter of 2000, we spent several months cruising through the Great Barrier Reef (GBR), and it was one of the most memorable trips we have ever undertaken. Officially, this massive expanse of coral and sand covers over 130,000 square miles and extends from Torres Straight in the north to Fraser Island in the south. In between there are thousands (about 3,000 depending on how you count them) of individual coral reefs and more than 900 islands. If a cruiser visited one of these islands a week, it would take nearly 20 years to visit them all.

All these islands and reefs make for some pretty spectacular cruising; nearly all of it is in sheltered waters. For sailors, the vast areas behind the reefs offer the unique combination of calm seas and steady, reliable winds. In most areas, the fetch is limited, so, even in strong winds, the waves never get a chance to build to more than a meter. That doesn't mean it doesn't get rough (nasty even) on occasion when the barometer drops and the wind rises, but you are nearly always within a few hours of a protected anchorage or, at worst, the calm waters in the lee of a reef or an island where riding out a storm can be a safe and satisfying experience.

Most of the GBR is included in the Great Barrier Reef Marine Park and is thus protected from overfishing by commercial interests and exploitation by the voracious tourist industry and from private development. This also means there are volumes of laws and regulations, and bureaucratic hoops to jump through, but the attractions of this vast area make dealing with the local authorities, taxing as it can sometimes be, well worth the effort.

Southeastern United States Watershed

The Tombigbee Watershed in the southeastern United States is a multi-billion-dollar Army Corps of Engineers boondoggle (Oops, there I go again. Change that to "economic development project") that includes hundreds of miles of navigable cruiser-friendly waterways accessible to anyone. If you enjoy leisurely boating through bucolic countryside with the ability to stop in small waterfront communities or visit large port cities or roam just about anywhere you please, then the Tombigbee and the associated Tennessee Valley Authority hydroelectric projects might be the answer to your retirement dreams. The Tombigbee is just a part of a larger

Never Underestimate Bureaucratic Foolishness

As an example of Orwellian mind control at its finest, take this incident we experienced on Lady Musgrave Island. There are many areas of the GBR that are off-limits to fishing of any kind, and Lady Musgrave is half fish sanctuary and half open to hook-and-line fishing. Scuba diving is permitted in the fish sanctuaries as well as everywhere else on the island, and spearfishing is legal in the areas open to fishing. However, spearguns can only be used while snorkeling and free diving; their use with scuba equipment is not allowed anywhere in the Marine Park.

I am opposed to spearfishing for sport with any kind of equipment. I think it is a barbaric, wasteful, and unsustainable form of harvesting fish. But, ever the hypocrite, I did keep a Hawaiian-sling type of spear for collecting a few bottom fish for dinner when hook and line were either inconvenient or (more often) unproductive.

On Lady Musgrave, I was informed by an aggressively officious park official that the Hawaiian sling on board our boat in the presence of scuba gear was prima-facie evidence of spearfishing with scuba. It was also grounds for our immediate arrest and the unconditional seizure and eventual forfeiture of *Sultana*. This seemed a bit harsh to my anarchic mind, and as much as I wanted to argue the point, I immediately got rid of the speargun and haven't had one aboard since. Later, another less regulation-bound official told me that this was nonsense. A speargun and scuba gear on board are fine as long as they aren't being used together. Either way, it is seldom worth the effort to argue with local officialdom, regardless of your occupation of the moral high ground.

When dealing with over-zealous government officials, I have always found servility is the best policy. No matter how outrageous their pronouncements or requirements or how ludicrous their position, I just smile and nod my head in agreement.

waterway that includes many of the Tennessee Valley Authority impoundments, the Mississippi River, the Great Lakes, the Erie Canal, the Hudson River, and the eastern Intracoastal Waterway.

The Great Loop

It is possible to do a giant circumnavigation of the entire eastern United States by cruising these rivers and canals with only a few forays into open water: one to get across the Great Lakes and another to transit the stretch of the Atlantic Ocean between the Hudson and Delaware Rivers. The thousands of cruisers who have completed this trip, as well as many thousands more who dream of doing it, call it "doing the loop," and wear the accomplishment as a well-earned badge of honor.

Because of its accessibility, the sheltered nature of 90 percent of the waters it uses, and the fact that it can be accomplished in bits and pieces over many years, the Great Loop is particularly popular with retired cruisers. In fact, while provisioning in Fort Myers, Florida, getting *Vicarious* ready to cross the Gulf of Mexico and the Caribbean Sea to the Panama Canal, we met an entertaining retired couple in a large Hatteras motor yacht (of the style called a long-range cruiser or LRC) who were celebrating their completion of the loop, which they had started a full ten years earlier. The trip took them that long because they needed to save up money to buy fuel for their behemoth of a boat before starting each leg.

The Intracoastal Waterway (ICW)

Cruisers familiar with the Great Loop know that about a quarter of the loop trip includes the Delaware and Chesapeake Bays and the system of rivers, bays, and canals that meanders down the Eastern Seaboard to Florida just inside the protection of the shoreline. This vast system of waterways is officially known as the Intracoastal Waterway (and informally as "the ditch"), and it is one of the most popular cruising grounds on earth.

The Intracoastal Waterway between the Delaware Bay and Key West, Florida, is almost entirely inside protected waters and wanders through some of the most beautiful and interesting geography in the United States. No wonder it is one of the most popular (possibly the most popular) cruising grounds on earth.

Technically, the Intracoastal Waterway stretches from Maine to Brownsville, Texas, but, for practical purposes, the inshore protected waters start at the mouth of the Delaware Bay. The protected portion of the waterway that formerly took cruisers through Barnegat Bay in New Jersey is no longer dredged, so it is now quite shallow and suitable only for shallow-draft boats. This leaves a long open-water passage from the Hudson River to Cape May, New Jersey, which excludes it from this sheltered category of cruising in protected waters and puts it into our next category: coastal cruising.

Inside Passage

Several years ago, while looking for a boat, we travelled the Inside Passage on a succession of car ferries from Hanes, Alaska, to Port Hardy, on the north end of Victoria Island in British Columbia. We stopped to look at several boats along the way, and, although we didn't find the vessel of our dreams, we did come away with a desire to return to this picturesque land of grizzly bears and planked salmon. In fact, as this is written, *Vicarious* is moored in Panama waiting to transit the canal for a trip north to the land of the midnight sun. Once there, we can more intimately explore some of the sheltered harbors and secluded anchorages that abound along the coast of British Columbia and Alaska, of which we could only get a brief glimpse as we steamed south on the ferries.

The Inside Passage offers protected cruising for nearly the entire distance from Seattle, Washington, to Kodiak Island, Alaska. There is one long stretch of open water to cross at the Gulf of Alaska and smaller sections at Queen Charlotte Sound, but, if open water is something you don't want to deal with, there is no reason to go that far north. The scenery, isolated anchoring, and outdoor living available just between Victoria, British Columbia, and Juneau, Alaska, is enough to keep any adventuresome cruiser busy for years.

Be warned, however: just because the Inside Passage is almost all protected waters, it isn't necessarily easy cruising. The dramatic tides and tidal currents make the timing of passages critical, especially in low-powered sailboats and production trawlers, which are the most popular craft for these waters. But don't let this scare you away from this magical land. Although the cruising here is different than you will find anywhere else on earth save the Bay of Fundy, the procedures for dealing with tides and extreme currents are easily learned and with experience will become automatic.

If cruising for days on end through majestic forests and isolated fjords; visiting remote fishing communities that harken back to the Gold Rush; tree-anchoring in clear water that may plunge to 300 feet just a few meters from shore; enjoying evening visits from deer, black bear, bald eagles, and waterfowl; or snagging a fat halibut or salmon for dinner, all while hardly seeing another boat, then the Inside Passage might be the place.

A disadvantage (or advantage, depending on your point of view) is the seasonal nature of the weather that far north. The southern portions of the Inside Passage are

If it is secluded cruising you crave, along with the chance to commune with nature on a personal level, then the Inside Passage of British Columbia deserves your attention. No, it is not tropical; and, no, it is not necessarily easy sailing; and, yes, it is seasonal (gets bloody cold, really); but the chance to wear a woolly cap and the heavy foulies just reinforces the appeal for those few of us who grow weary of white sand beaches, tropical sunsets, and palm trees. (Speak for yourself, Nanook, says Susan, who rather likes to stay warm.)

actually quite temperate but still chilly enough to deter all but the hardiest cruisers from traveling in the winter months. There are several options for dealing with seasonal cruising: you can store your boat for the winter and go visit the kids for a few months, you can move the boat to Victoria or Seattle and spend the winter aboard while tied to a marina dock, or you can move the boat south to Panama or Mexico.

That last option, moving the boat south, entails a long and difficult offshore passage. Thus, many cruisers who yearn to spend the winter months in tropical climes but don't have the skills or desire to spend a month or so at sea have their boats delivered to the Sea of Cortez, Costa Rica, or Panama by professional delivery crews or as deck cargo on a ship. Sometimes the boat owners ride along on a crewed delivery, but more often they meet the boat at the destination. A delivery is not a cheap option but works for several of our more well-heeled friends. We even know of one intrepid cruiser with a medium-sized trawler who has his boat trucked overland from Port Townsend, Washington, to the Sea of Cortez every autumn, and back again in the spring. He has followed the same routine for years and has the exercise down to a science.

Here's a third option, available to those of us with piles of money lying around for which we have no other use. While in Cuba we met a young family from Texas who keep large fishing boats in Florida, Cuba, and Alaska, then travel by private plane to whichever location strikes their fancy. If the boat we saw in Cuba was an example of the others, the annual maintenance would be well over a million dollars each, so again, this is not an option for the budget-minded cruisers among us.

COASTAL CRUISING

Cruising between locations via short or moderate sections of open ocean with the objective of quickly getting from one sheltered cruising area to another is among the most popular forms of retirement cruising open to us. The ability to make not-too-challenging overnight passages between desirable cruising locations will open vast opportunities to cruisers looking to expand their horizons.

For our purposes, let's confine coastal cruising to an area where you can sail off to attractive and interesting destinations without making a passage in the open ocean longer than 24 hours or farther than 100 miles.

To those of us who have never experienced sailing in a small craft out of sight of land or motoring through a pitch-black night with no visual reference outside the boat's cockpit or pilothouse, the first offshore passage can be nerve-racking and stressful.

It is best to build up to your first excursion into the deep blue gradually. Start with long day-trips in good weather that eventually lead to overnight excursions to

The coast of Maine is a labyrinth of isolated islands, quiet anchorages, and spectacular scenery where a cruising boat can wander for years and never anchor in the same place twice. The summer is short here, and the cruising lasts from mid-June into October; then full-time cruisers need to find somewhere else to go or something else to do.

Weather Skills

One important skill for a coastal cruiser to develop is the interpretation of weather systems using the many tools available to amateur weather forecasters. Weather-interpretation skills are important for all forms of boating, of course, but the better you are at reading weather maps, GRIB charts, and radar images, the more safe and enjoyable your coastal cruising will be.

We will talk more about weather in later chapters, but start now by paying attention to the forecasters and prognosticators available through your local media. To quickly develop an understanding of weather systems, make a review of all the available weather tools a part of your daily routine. Even if you are still working and have years to go until you are ready to shove off on your retirement adventure, make a daily perusal of your local weather maps and GRIB charts one of the first things you do in the morning. Become intimate with isobars, highs, lows, ridges, troughs, occlusions, upper-air flow, and tropical depressions. Sharpen your nautical-chart-reading skills, then try to interpret how the information you retrieve from weather sources, such as wave heights and intervals, prevailing tidal and ocean currents (learn the difference between the two), high- and low-water intervals, and the phases of the moon, is going to affect specific sailing conditions.

Bad weather is as much a part of the cruising life as sunsets and mosquitoes. Knowing how to interpret weather maps, radar images, and broadcast weather reports is an important skill for all boaters, but it becomes critical as you become a cruiser.

your favorite anchorages in protected waters. Read all you can on seamanship and boat handling, search YouTube and the online forums for advice to beginners, and make friends with anyone at your local boatyard or yacht club who has firsthand offshore experience. Then practice everything you have learned every chance you get, while keeping in mind not everything with boats works the same way for everyone. You need to sort these things out for yourself to find just what works for you and what doesn't.

There are a great many areas in the world suitable for coastal cruising and available to anyone who wants the adventure of limited offshore travel without spending days on end out of sight of land. The Northeast Coast of North America from Long Island Sound to Nova Scotia is popular with seasonal cruisers; the Aegean

Sea between Greece and Turkey and the Adriatic Sea between Italy and Croatia are favorite spots with Mediterranean retirees; and the Fijian and Tongan archipelagoes are a more distant and adventuresome option.

I am not familiar with all of these areas, but here is a more detailed discussion of my favorites. Coastal cruisers who want to visit distant lands that require more than an overnight passage are among the heaviest users of temporary crew and delivery captains. If you want to go somewhere far away and aren't confident in your ability to get there safely, a delivery captain or professional crew is the logical answer. If your boat is insured, your insurer may require you to hire a professional (or recruit a skilled amateur) before you are offered coverage on any challenging passage. This can happen regardless of your skill and experience, which is just one reason many cruisers choose to go without insurance.

There are many areas of the world where coastal cruising is the most popular form of boating for retirees and elderly sailors. Here are a few of our favorites.

Northeast Coast of North America

Susan and I have probably spent more time on the water in this part of the world than all the others combined. In the introduction, I regaled readers with a summary of our early nautical adventuring as we sailed our tiny boat to ports far from our home base in Ipswich, Massachusetts. In all the years I worked for the Telephone Company in Boston, I would look forward to each year's cruise up the coast of Maine

The entire East Coast of the United States and the Maritime Provinces of Canada is one giant coastal cruising ground. There are only two or three stretches of water that aren't navigable within our arbitrary 24-hour offshore limit, and even these are manageable in good weather during the sailing season. Hundreds of sheltered anchorages all along the coast make day hopping from Halifax to Key West a fascinating (if somewhat slow) way to travel. So who's in a hurry?

with an anticipation that made the rest of the year seem to drag by in slow motion.

Sometimes these trips were only for a week or two, but, later on, as I accumulated more vacation time, we were able to extend our northward forays to a month or more. These extended trips took us to wonderful places in Canada, places such as Grand Manan Island with its spectacular cliffs and bird colonies; the Bay of Fundy with its challenging tides and currents; and the quiet coves and ports around Saint Andrews, New Brunswick, where Susan's ancestors first settled.

If we stick with our definition of costal cruising as an area where you can sail off to attractive and interesting destinations without making a passage longer than 24 hours or 100 miles, the entire East Coast of the United States qualifies nicely. The long stretch from Sandy Hook Light to the Cape May Canal can be broken up with a stop at Atlantic City. But, once south of the Chesapeake Bay, you are into either the shelter of the Intracoastal Waterway, which we discussed above, or you are outside, where you are definitely in an offshore environment.

The Bahamas

The vast and sparsely settled archipelago of the Bahamas is another of the most popular cruising areas on earth. Every year, immediately after the threat of hurricanes subsides to a manageable level, thousands of snowbirds from the United States and Canada throng south to spend the winter months baking in the endless sunshine, snorkeling for pirate treasure, and drinking horrible rum concoctions out of coconut shells. Joining them a bit later in the season is the annual migration of boats from Europe with cruisers coming from Scandinavia, Turkey, and everywhere in between.

The Commonwealth of the Bahamas covers nearly 200,000 square miles, which would make it nearly as big as Florida if it had any dirt, which it doesn't. It does have sand and coral, however, and little clumps push up through the surface of the Atlantic Ocean in more than 700 places, making for a system of islands, shallow bays, secluded harbors, and private getaways unrivaled anywhere else on earth. When you couple this with a friendly, welcoming people, a tolerant bureaucracy, wonderful weather, and reasonable fees for visas and cruising permits, it is no wonder half of all the cruisers in the world congregate here.

If it weren't for the difficulty of getting there, the Bahamas in its entirety would be classified as sheltered cruising because most of the islands are close together and accessible with an easy day sail. But the 50-mile stretch of water between Miami and Bimini puts this trip firmly into the coastal category, in spite of the short distance. The only way to get to the Bahamas from the United States is across the Gulf Stream. Stories of fright and terror reverberate throughout the oceanfront bars as each autumn brings a new crop of novice cruisers who try the trip without regard to the weather and wind reports. In dozens of ports up and down the Florida coast, the more experienced cruisers can be found, waiting for the perfect and quite rare southerly to flatten out the tumultuous waters of the Stream so they can make a fast and peaceful crossing.

You would think with the concentration of cruisers from half the world the Bahamas would be crowded, and you would be right. The major ports of Nassau, Freeport, and half-a-dozen other population centers are jammed with cruising boats from around the world, with the major marinas booked up years in advance. So if your kind of cruising involves shore power, air-conditioning, and a swim-up bar, then, yes, the Bahamas are crowded. But if you want to get away from the crowds and yearn for a quiet anchorage where you can commune with the dolphins and fishes (and maybe the aquatic pigs of the Exuma Cays) while enjoying the good life in a more solitary and relaxed manner, then the Bahamas are not crowded at all. Remember, there are more than 700 islands available to the cruiser in one form or another, and only a handful of them are inhabited. The rest are visited by fishermen and the occasional cruising boat and never see anything like a shore-power cord.

Most of the cruisers who don't end up in marinas spend the season wandering from one spectacular anchorage to another, and there are dozens of them. This means you will have a constant turnover in neighbors and lots of new friends. The camaraderie among those itinerant cruisers is palpable; it won't be long before you recognize most of the new arrivals as soon as they heave into view. In the most popular anchorages, you can count on a potluck or a round of sundowners on the beach, but if it is seclusion you crave rather than a party, there are plenty of anchorages where you will only see one or two other boats.

One invention of the Bahamian cruisers that has caught on in other areas is the sunset raft-up: a floating cocktail party with anywhere from two or three to several dozen dinghies that tie themselves together in a giant flotilla and drift about the anchorage swapping snacks, drinks, and improbable stories. Usually one dinghy with a small outboard is delegated the responsibility of guiding the raft-up away from moored boats and other obstacles and making sure the whole mob doesn't drift out to sea. Like the designated driver of shoreside parties, the designated floater needs to keep a reasonably clear head while the rest of the raft gives itself over to revelry and relaxing oblivion while watching the sun plunge ever so slowly into tomorrow.

Eastern Caribbean

Once you are in the Bahamas and have worked your way down the chain of islands to the Turks and Caicos (the southernmost islands in the Bahamian archipelago), it is a short hop to one of several available harbors in Haiti or the Dominican Republic. This crossing can be tricky, with large seas and squally conditions, so many novice sailors without open-water experience hire a professional crew for the two-day passage.

Once in the Dominican Republic, however, you are safely back in the realm of the coastal cruiser with dozens of possible destinations within 100 miles all the way to South America. The western coast of Puerto Rico is an easy overnight when the conditions are right, and then you can make the hop to the Virgin Islands. These are both passages against the prevailing trade winds and can be awkward, but, once in the Virgins, and excepting the notorious passage between the British Virgin Islands and Sint Maarten, the entire eastern Caribbean is just a series of short broad reaches away.

One popular misconception among new cruisers and old cruisers who have never been there is that because passages in the eastern Caribbean are short they are easy. But it just ain't so. True, most passages here, as everywhere else, can be a cakewalk when the winds and waves cooperate, but, when they don't, watch out. With the prevailing trades blowing a steady 15 to 20 knots, often shallow water, and contrary currents, seas can build quickly to five or six feet with a short interval that makes for unpleasant if not dangerous conditions. In all the thousands of miles we have travelled in *Sultana* and in *Vicarious*, the only time we were ever pooped was in the Caribbean, and that was on a short day-passage between two neighboring islands. (Getting pooped happens when a following sea breaks into the cockpit. It can be a frightening experience, and it is the reason cruising boats need small, quick-draining cockpits and a bridge deck or lockable drop boards.)

Western Caribbean

There are profound differences between the western Caribbean and the eastern. Getting there is a bit more difficult, for one thing, as the most popular route for Americans is across the Gulf of Mexico from Florida, or south from Galveston, Texas. This usually involves a four- or-five-day sail in conditions that can be squally and unpleasant. Here again, the popular way for cruisers unfamiliar with offshore travel to do the trip is with a professional crew. In extreme cases, many American cruisers who have a little extra cash and are not comfortable with stopping in Cuba will have their boats delivered to Mexico.

Boats from Canada and Europe that are bound for Mexico usually stop in Florida or the Bahamas, then move southwest to Havana. From there it is an easy daysail between anchorages to Cabo San Antonio on the far western tip of Cuba (among the most remote harbors in the Caribbean) before making the 125-mile jump across the Yucatan Channel to Mexico.

There is also a profound cultural difference between the island peoples of the eastern Caribbean and the land-based population of the western Caribbean. The eastern islanders are justifiably proud of their separate identity and wear their African heritage as a badge of honor. There are also cultural differences between neighboring islands that are more pronounced than those of the people in neighboring countries bordering the western Caribbean. The equally proud mestizo people of Central America are of Spanish, African, and Native American descent with just enough of every other nationality mixed in to flavor the pot. The one thing they have in common is their friendly, relaxed attitude and a willingness to accept the intrusion of wandering yachties with grace and humor.

The passage across the Gulf of Mexico can be a tough one, but once there you are in another cruising paradise. The most popular first stop in Mexico is Isla

Isla Mujeres is often the first stop for boats leaving the United States for Mexico and the western Caribbean. This little island stands in stark contrast to the tacky excesses of the Cancún tourist mecca just across the bay.

Mujeres, an island less than five miles long and only a 30-minute ferry ride from the frenetic tourist town of Cancún. Both Cancún and Isla Mujeres are tourist destinations, but where Cancún is a place for feeding-frenzy shopping and opulent resorts, Isla Mujeres is a place for backpackers and low-key travelers. Instead of looking for tax-free Louis Vuitton or Cartier, visitors here are looking for a quiet piña colada on the beach or a meander through narrow streets lined with vendors selling their palm-frond sombreros and hand-wrought jewelry from sidewalk pushcarts or hole-in-the-wall tiendas.

Isla Mujeres sports a half-dozen quality marinas with facilities that range from the basic to the posh, and there is a spacious anchorage with enough room for 100 or so boats. It is a tourist destination, though, and as such it is expensive. The last time we visited, the engine blew a water hose coming into the harbor. (Someone had failed to check the hose clamps. All the evidence pointed to Nelson, the dog, as the culprit.) So we found ourselves towed to the dock at the Villa Varillio resort and marina, definitely on the posh end of the luxury scale.

From Isla Mujeres all the way south to Isla Guanaja off the north coast of Honduras there are more than 500 miles of coastal cruising with dozens of harbors and gunkholes that make daysailing the entire distance an attractive option. To go

When circumstance found us stranded for three months at the posh Villa Varillio Resort in Isla Mujeres, Mexico, we decided to make the best of it. It was tough going, but the huge pool, swim-up bar, concierge service, unlimited free ice, giant screen television for the 2014 FIFA World Cup finals, attentive dock service, and general ambience of luxury made the stay bearable. That we were able to survive with our basicist standards intact says volumes about the resilient nature of cruisers.

beyond Guanaja requires a tricky offshore passage of more than 300 upwind miles through treacherous reefs, shoals, and pirates to Isla Providencia off the coast of Nicaragua, not a passage recommended for novice cruisers.

By far the most popular destination for cruisers who take this route south from Isla Mujeres is the Rio Dulce in Guatemala, where hundreds of boats congregate each year to wait out the hurricane season. The Rio (as it is called by most everyone who has been there) is a destination in itself, with secure harbors, lots of attractions, and reliable marinas where one feels safe leaving a boat for a month or a year while flying off to attend to other things. The Rio is also famous for reasonable prices, almost-honest officials, and an active cruising community that is the epitome of the cruisers' lifestyle.

While the route south from Isla Mujeres is an easy one, there is a prevailing northerly current that can run up to three knots, especially just north of Isla Cozumel. One tactic to avoid this is to hug the eastern shore of Mexico to take advantage of the significant counter-currents that extend out several miles offshore. If you try this, keep in mind the prevailing northeast trade wind that can quickly build to put you against a dangerous lee shore. There are enough protected anchorages to provide an emergency duck-in spot when needed, but diligence is the watchword anywhere along this coast.

Panama

As popular as Panama is with cruisers from around the world, it remains an undis-covered cruisers' paradise. This is because most boats traveling there are intent on getting through the canal. After a brief visit to the San Blas Islands in the Caribbean to buy the obligatory molas from the native Kuna Indians or an overnight stop in the Las Perlas islands on the Pacific side, they are through the canal and away. This is a shame, because Panama offers one of the most attractive contiguous cruising areas in the world.

In the post-Noriega years just before and immediately after the American handover of the canal in 1999, Panama accumulated a terrible and well-justified reputation for crime, corruption, and governmental malaise caused mostly by its position midway on the Colombia-to-United States drug route and a legacy of complacency with the infamous Medellín cartel. However, in the past decade or so Panama has made great strides to clean up its act and is now the most prosperous country south of the Texas border. With a much-improved infrastructure, reduced (but not eliminated) corruption among officials, a stable currency (the Balboa is

The vast cruising grounds of Panama offer spectacular cruising opportunities on both the Caribbean and Pacific coasts. With nearly endless anchoring options, friendly and welcoming local people, safe harbors, many full-service marinas with skilled workers, a mild (but sometimes very hot) climate well removed from any threat of hurricanes, and a big ditch to take you from one ocean to another, it is remarkable that more cruisers don't venture here.

pegged to the U.S. dollar), and nearly safe streets (except in Colón, where even a daytime visit can still be a life-threatening experience), Panama is one of the most desirable cruising destinations in South and Central America.

The cruising territories in Panama are vast. From the remote Bocas del Toro on the north end of the Caribbean side to the numerous and varied ports in the Archipelago de las Perlas on the Pacific, and from the variegated north Pacific coast all the way to the Costa Rican border, there are dozens of anchorages and marinas, all within a daysail of each other. With the exception of the long haul from Bocas del Toro to the entrance to the canal, it is possible to sail for years here without the necessity of a difficult offshore passage. The weather is better than most areas in the Caribbean, and oddly it can be a bit cooler than Mexico even though it is a thousand miles to the south. There are never any hurricanes, and, because Panama is south of the trade winds, gentle breezes box the compass for most of the year. Naturally there are some occasional squalls and spectacular thunder and lightning storms, but they just serve to liven things up a bit.

Tonga and Fiji

Most cruisers visiting Tonga and Fiji come from Australia, New Zealand, North America, or Europe, and getting there requires anywhere from a week to a year of offshore travel. Thus, inclusion here in the coastal cruising section may seem a bit odd. But the two countries lie only 400 miles apart, and together they have nearly a thousand separate islands, all within an easy daysail of each other. Once a cruiser arrives in either country, it is possible to sail for years and never visit the same island twice. Sailing conditions here are affected by strong and reliable southwest trade winds all during the southern winter sailing season, which runs from April to November. The cyclone season generally runs between November and March, with an average of five named cyclones each year. (A cyclone, as most of us know, is just a backward hurricane. See sidebar page 57.)

TONGA

Ironically, the Kingdom of Tonga is smaller than Fiji by about half but supports almost as many lovely and isolated anchorages all along its 800-kilometer (500-mile) length. Of the 176 islands officially constituting the Kingdom of Tonga (the only constitutional monarchy in the Pacific), only 52 are inhabited, and of the 700,000 square kilometers of the earth's surface claimed by Tonga, only 750 are solid enough to walk on. All the rest of that vast area is lovely clear green water studded generously with vibrant coral reefs, thundering volcanoes, and quiet anchorages. The trade winds are reliable and steady all through the winter sailing season, with 15 to 20 knots from the southeast predictable 80 percent of the time, the water is as clear as a new idea, and the sea life is prolific. This is a calving ground for humpback whales, and they are a common sight all through the early sailing season until about November, when they head back to the Antarctic.

Tonga is divided into three main island groups: the flat and sandy Tongatapu group in the south, where 80 percent of the population lives; the volcanic Ha'apai group roughly in the middle; and the coral-based Vava'u group in the north. Officially, there is a fourth island group in the far north: the seldom visited volcanic Niuas group with two islands and a permanent population of about 1,000 people. Niuas has no facilities for checking into the country, so to visit there one must sail to Vava'u, then return after completing the entrance formalities. Thus, not many cruisers bother with it, which, in my experience, can be a good reason to go there.

The Vava'u island group is home to a large fleet of charter boats that operates out of Neiafu Harbor on Vava'u Island, part of the massive Moorings worldwide charter fleet. Altogether there are abut 50 islands in this group and at least as many attractive anchorages, most of which are well-protected and comfortable. If you stop in at the Moorings office, they will give you a copy of the same map they issue to their charter customers with 40 numbered anchorages listed along with anchoring instructions and directions for getting through the fringing reefs.

Less than a day's sail south of Vava'u, the Ha'apai Islands cluster in volcanic splendor around the main island of Lifuka. Although there are more than 50 separate islands in the Ha'apai group (the actual number depends on what you call an island), there are far fewer natural harbors and safe anchorages here, mostly because of the group's volcanic origins. Volcanos just don't make good harbors like coral atolls do. But even though you may have to deep-water anchor in the lee of an island without the protection of a surrounding reef, the difference in topography and the contrast with the rest of Tonga is worth the effort all by itself. Where the islands of Vava'u are low coral atolls with sandy beaches, the lava and basalt Ha'apai islands tower to spectacular heights. The highest point in Tonga is on the tiny island of Kao, which shoots to over 1,000 meters right out of the ocean. There is no natural harbor on Kao, but it is worthwhile going a bit out of your way to sail by it just to observe the beauty of the soaring peaks.

The Ha'apaiislands are rural and sparsely populated. Most of the 6,000 people who live here congregate in Pangai on the main island of Lifuka, leaving the rest to a few farmers, orchardists, and fishermen. When we visited in 1993, the volcano at Metis Shoal was active. As we sailed by on a dark night we could see the glow of the eruption from 30 kilometers (18.64 miles) away like the nighttime luminescence of a big city looming just over the horizon. As we sailed closer, we could see clearly the fiery rivers of lava as they flowed into the sea.

Another daysail south from Ha'apai is the main island of Tongatapu, the largest and most populated island in Tonga, and home of the capital, Nuku'alofa, where the majority of Tongans make their home. I imagine Tongatapu has its share of attractions for touring sailboats, but we didn't discover any. The island is a flat, featureless plateau with little to recommend it except for the capital city of Nuku'alofa. Most of the cruisers who come here are either leaving the country on their way south to New Zealand or Australia, or entering to visit the two spectacular island groups to the north.

Typhoon, Hurricane, or Cyclone?

There is some understandable confusion among cruisers as to the difference between a typhoon, a cyclone, and a hurricane. There needn't be, because they are essentially the same thing. All three are tropical storms created when high-pressure air is sucked into a low-pressure zone with an extreme differential between the high and low pressures. The moving air is forced by the friction between the air mass and the surface of the earth (the Coriolis effect) into a swirling action as it rushes to fill the vacuum of the low. In the northern hemisphere, this results in a counterclockwise rotation of the air, and just the reverse in the southern hemisphere. What these storms are called depends on where you are rather than on any distinguishing characteristics of the air masses. They are hurricanes in the Atlantic, Caribbean, and eastern Pacific; typhoons in the western Pacific and in the Indian Ocean; and cyclones in the southern Indian Ocean, southwest Pacific, and Tasman Sea.

By international covenant, when the sustained winds of a tropical storm reach 63 kilometers per hour (39 miles per hour), it is assigned a name by the World Meteorological Association in Geneva, Switzerland, and classed as a tropical storm. When sustained winds reach 119 kilometers per hour (74 miles per hour), the storm is promoted to a hurricane, typhoon, tropical cyclone, or cyclone, and assigned a class from one to five depending on the strength of the winds. The strongest class, Class Five, has winds in excess of 249 kilometers per hour (155 miles per hour).

Just because a storm has strong winds doesn't qualify it as a cyclone, typhoon, or hurricane. Even though the weather bomb known as the perfect storm of 1991 (the one they made into a movie starring George Clooney) registered 78-mile-per-hour winds in Chatham, Massachusetts, and did hundreds of millions of dollars in damage, it never qualified as a named hurricane. Without that characteristic circular flow of air (clockwise in the southern hemisphere, counterclockwise in the northern), it is just a plain old storm, no matter how strongly the winds blow.

FIJI

Getting from Tonga to Fiji is more than 500 miles of downwind sailing through poorly charted reefs and islands, so this passage is not something for inexperienced cruisers (or anyone faint of heart) to try. But if you have the skills (be honest and don't kid yourself, because an inflated ego can get seriously deflated by even a small reef) or can afford to hire a skilled crew, this will be a trip you will remember the rest of your life. Actually this passage is one where taking on professional crew or a delivery captain can make a lot of sense even if you could do the trip by yourself.

Once in Fijian waters coming from Tonga, the closest check-in port is Savusavu on the island of Vanua Levu. Boats are forced to sail past numerous beautiful islands with attractive anchorages, because stopping at any of the islands in the Lau Group before checking in is strictly forbidden. Drug smuggling here is a major problem, so entering yachts are closely monitored by the Fijian navy. Transgressions are treated harshly, and even emergency stops can get you into a lot of hot water.

Fiji covers more than 194,000 square kilometers (75,000 square miles) of the surface of the earth but only 10 percent is dry land. There are 322 islands in Fiji, divided up into four major groups. The two biggest islands are Viti Levu, which hosts the capital city of Suva and more than 75 percent of the 900,000-strong population, and Vanua Levu, home to Lambassa and Savusavu. These three cities are the most popular check-in ports. The only other places where you can check in are Levuka on Ovalau and Oinafa on Rotuma. We found the officials at Savusavu to be much more agreeable than in Suva but have no experience with the others.

Fiji is a wonderful place to cruise, with easy less-than-a-day passages between dozens of lovely anchorages. The northern islands have some of the best scuba diving and snorkeling in the world. But in spite of all this, Fiji remains a troubled paradise. For a generation, leadership has been determined by coup and rigged elections. The racial stress between the indigenous Fijians and the large Indian population is exacerbated by cultural polarization, even though many Indian families have been Fijian for four generations or more. The political situation is in constant flux, and the officials often seem to be working from separate sets of rules. What seems to be OK on one island can get you a big fine on another.

Be particularly careful if you plan to bring a pet to Fiji, as the rules are draconian in the extreme. Pets aren't allowed ashore under any conditions, and a sizable bond that must be posted on check in is forfeited for the slightest infraction of the rules. It is always best to check noonsite (http://www.noonsite.com) and the most recent SSCA (Seven Seas Cruising Association) bulletins (http://www.ssca.org) for the latest local situation reports before entering any port where there is political and cultural turmoil; this is particularly true of Fiji.

There are many other areas in the world where the prudent retired voyager can meander for years without subjecting craft and crew to the terrors of the open sea. Except for the now-and-then overnight jaunt when it's time to move on to the next good part, the cautious cruiser can sail for a lifetime and never be out of sight of land. The Mediterranean Sea is full of such opportunities, as are the islands of the Philippine archipelago. I suspect that a major part of the appeal of the Eastern Asian countries is that the passages between anchorages are short and fast. But, alas, we have yet to visit these places, so I would be remiss in discussing them with you until I do get there.

OFFSHORE CRUISING

Where coastal cruising throws wide the doors to life on a boat, for some of us offshore cruising opens up life itself. There is nothing to compare to the feeling of freedom and spiritual renewal that comes from the limitless solitude that long-range travel on a boat offers. But not everyone wants to go for weeks or even months at a time without seeing another human except your travel companion; to be irretrievably dependent on your own resources without hope of assistance from the outside world; or to risk an unscheduled encounter with hurricanes, cyclones, typhoons, lightning strikes, plundering pirates, marauding sharks, derelict shipping containers, corrupt officials, and chowderheaded fellow cruisers from Miami with big boats and small brains.

No, not everyone is suited to offshore cruising. Most of us are far too practical to make the sacrifices in cash and comfort that sailing away from land in a small boat entails. Others among us aren't that adventurous, and cruising sheltered waters or coastal cruising is plenty enough to satisfy a lifetime of latent yearnings for travel and excitement. Voyaging off across the sea to distant lands also means leaving behind friends and family. To sail off knowing you won't be seeing loved ones for months or even years at a time is difficult for all of us; for many of us, not being there to watch the grandkids grow up is unthinkable.

And this is the way it should be. Where sheltered cruising and coastal cruising are decidedly normal activities, voyaging offshore is not, at least not if you are trying to do it on a limited budget like most of us are. (Here, to remind the reader, we are not talking about round-the-world adventures in a $2,000,000 boat tricked out with all the newest technology, or even in a $200,000 boat with outdated technology; that's another story for another book.)

While voyaging the oceans of the world is the ultimate form of the retired cruising life, it does take a lot more commitment in time and resources than either sheltered or coastal cruising. Crossing an ocean requires more in seamanship skills, experience, and training, of course, but it also demands a stronger boat (although not a larger or more expensive one) thoroughly equipped with gear and supplies sufficient to support vessel and crew in all sorts of weather and for long periods in areas where shopping malls are only rumors and repair facilities are scarce.

In previous sections of this chapter we visited a few areas of the world best suited to the type of cruising discussed, but we can't do that here. Ocean cruisers have sailed to just about every place on the globe that has water deep enough to let a keel clear the bottom. From the Arctic to the Antarctic, across every meridian, and up every river, cruising boats have penetrated into every navigable piece of water that exists, and, judging by some of the stories you hear in waterfront bars, a lot that don't. So if it is the exploration of new territory you are looking for, you are about three generations too late.

So, ocean cruisers can go anywhere there is enough water to float their boats, but that doesn't mean you should head off for the South China Sea or sail directly to the Ross Ice Shelf. There are many reasons certain areas of the world's oceans are more attractive to cruisers than others. The Mediterranean is more popular than the Bering Sea for obvious and easily understood reasons, and, for less obvious but equally valid reasons, the route from the Galapagos to French Polynesia is more heavily traveled than the route to the same destination from Hawaii.

World cruising destinations are determined by many factors. Politics is one, as exemplified by Venezuela, which was once a popular congregation point for cruisers from around the world. Now, with the current levels of crime and corruption, few even consider going there. The piracy in the Indian Ocean and the Arabian Sea have transformed this area into a no-go zone for all but the bravest among us (or the most foolish). Weather is another factor that can deter cruisers from visiting otherwise attractive areas. The Bering Sea was one somewhat silly example used above, but there are other areas such as the Philippines and the Sea of Japan that would be more attractive to cruisers if it weren't for the unpredictable nature and ferocity of the cyclones that rip these areas apart with distressing regularity.

For many decades, the bible for offshore cruisers and would-be ocean voyagers has been *World Cruising Routes* by Jimmy Cornell, first published in 1987 and now in its seventh edition. This remarkable book is a compilation of hundreds of years of data collected by the British Admiralty, artfully distilled and rendered readable for ordinary folks like you and me. If you are looking forward to long passages offshore once you get your retirement cruise under way, this book, along with a complete set of pilot charts, will become your guide to safe and successful passages.

BUG-OUT CRUISING

There is an interesting fad or movement (movement if you are a participant, fad if you aren't) that plays to the fears of a substantial number of us, that civilization is about to disappear in a fiery ball of flame, and humanity is about to lose forever all the essential shopping malls, Walmarts, Big Mac hamburger stands, and Taco Bells on which our society has become so dependent. Without McDonalds and KFC to feed us, famine and pestilence will spread across the land and turn our neighbors and friends into roving mobs of hunger-crazed maniacs whose only thought is to steal our food (and perhaps kill us, too). Our governments will respond by rounding up the few of us who have survived the initial disaster and herding us into concentration camps until a humane method of disposal can be worked out.

There are all sorts of specific scenarios that outline just how our society is destined to implode. Wikipedia (https://www.wikipedia.org/) lists 48 major categories of doomsday theories, from "gray goo" to World War III, and each main category has several sub-categories, each of which explains just how this apocalypse-real-soon event is going to come about. Theories range from wacko speculations about banks and insurance companies accumulating so much wealth that the rest of us couldn't afford a Whopper burger even if we could find one to more respectable and widely supported theories that waves of zombies will sweep ashore biting everyone (except bankers and insurance-company executives, of course) on the neck and turning us all into zombie trainees. There are dozens and dozens of these speculations. In fact, there are so many doomsday theories that the mathematical probability of one of them not happening soon is statistically nil. Cataclysmic annihilation is inevitable, so our job is to get used to it, then get ready for it.

The best way to prepare for the inevitable annihilation of society is by watching a few episodes of the reruns of *Doomsday Preppers* on the National Geographic Channel on YouTube. This entertaining show (I admit to only watching a few installments, but they certainly were entertaining) features personal profiles of dedicated preppers (that's what subscribers to the various apocalyptic scenarios who are preparing for the upcoming SHTF [you figure it out]events call themselves) detailing, for our edification, how they and their families are going to live through whatever catastrophic cataclysm they subscribe to and are spending all their money and most of their time prepping (getting ready) for it.

There are a few common threads that run through these interviews. Most of the preppers have a 10-year supply of canned spaghetti and ravioli, water and watermakers, a fuel stockpile, spare parts for the critical equipment, fishing gear, an average of eight guns for each prepper, and a few thousand rounds of ammo for each gun with different types of bullets for different situations ("yer holler points er fer yer close-in work an, yer FMJs er fer yer long-range stuff").

Most preppers also have their bug-out stuff. First is your bug-out bag with shelter, cooking gear, freeze-dried food for three days, a big scary knife, and about a jillion other things that will vary with the type of bugging out you plan to do. All this fits into a backpack that you carry with you as you head for the woods.

Next comes the bug-out vehicle with all of the above and lots of extra food and ammo. An old school bus, perhaps with the windows welded over with sheet steel, gun ports pointing every whichaway, and "guns don't kill people, bullets kill people" bumper stickers, seems to be the most popular bug-out vehicle. Using a school bus apparently keeps everything inconspicuous—especially with those welded-shut windows.

Last is the bug-out spot, which is a previously fortified and supplied bunker deep in the forest or in some long-forgotten mine shaft.

After watching a few of these videos on YouTube, I was a convinced that the world has the runs and is on its last roll of toilet paper. If we didn't want to end up with our throats ripped out by some decomposing ex-person with a personality disorder and bad teeth, Susan and I had better start putting together our bug-out kit.

I could hardly contain my excitement as I started to let Susan in on my plans. Most preppers agree that it is critical that you not tell anyone but your most trusted companions that you are a prepper (they say this right on national television, so it must be true) lest the starving hordes hear about it and target you in their first-wave attack.

I was halfway through describing to Susan what we needed in our bug-out bag when she raised her hand to stop me. "We already have bug-out bags. We have everything you describe in the shore bags we take on long hikes."

"Those aren't real bug-out bags," I answered, wondering why I hadn't thought of that. "They don't even have a .357 Magnum or any ammo." *(continued)*

The *Vicarious* Shore (Bug-out) Bag

The *Vicarious* shore bag (Susan refuses to call it our bug-out bag) is one step above a grab bag to be used if we were forced to abandon ship and one step below an ultralight backpacking kit. It has evolved over the years from our background hiking in New Zealand, Olympic National Park in Washington state, and in Alaska. Our experiences staying in basic accommodations in Central America have also influenced the items we carry in this kit, but the necessity of carrying it with us every time we left the boat for any extended length of time was driven home on a trip from the city of David (pronounced *da-veed*) , on the Pacific coast of Panama, to Almirante, a remote town in Chriqui Province of Panama.

I was recovering from an illness and felt that the normal six-hour bus trip over very bad roads would be a bit too much for my enfeebled physique to endure, so we had made reservations via the Internet to stay in a motel that we believed was near the halfway point. Before we got on the bus, I asked the driver if he knew where this motel was. He affirmed that he did and would drop us off at the appropriate spot. Sure enough, about three hours into the trip, the bus pulled over to the side of the road, and the driver indicated we were to get off. The only building was a small restaurant, more a snack bar really, surrounded by jungle. No one at the restaurant could speak English, so with my bumbling Spanish I tried to get directions to our hotel. After considerable back and forth, it became obvious that we were on the wrong road, and our hotel was some 30 miles away over the mountains. It was getting dark, there would be no more buses until the next day, and the only obvious place for us to stay the night was in a ramshackle shed at the back of the restaurant.

The prospect of a night in the equivalent of a garden shed was grim indeed, as we had nothing with us but a toilet kit and a change of clothes—the things you would normally take with you when going to a hotel.

But then Lady Luck once again came to our rescue, and we learned that the Jilguero Gardens backpackers' hostel was just a short walk up a steep, twisting mountain road. We were the only customers for the night, and it turned out to be such a lovely place, with sweeping mountain views, extensive, well attended gardens, and modern, barrack-style cabins, that we opted to extend our stay for an extra day.

That experience turned out well only because of our good fortune, but it had been a close call, and the dread of being caught out for a night in the jungle lingered. At that point we decided any time we were traveling away from the boat for even a single overnighter, we would have the amenities to maintain at least a basic level of comfort, build a fire if necessary, and indulge in a hot cup of tea. Since we already had most of the items we needed, either in our abandon-ship grab bag or in our lightweight hiking supplies, it was only a matter of compiling the items we felt appropriate into our shore bag.

Our shore kit is always in a state of evolution, with items being dropped or added as needed, but here are a few of the more important basic items (see the photograph):

1. An aluminum wind shield has numerous uses and is indispensable when using an alcohol camping stove in any kind of breeze.
2. Two lightweight cups for drinking. We tried titanium cups, because they are slightly lighter than these plastic ones, but they are unpleasant to drink from, especially for coffee and other hot beverages.
3. Two eight-inch titanium plates. These weigh only ounces and can double as a small frying pan with the use of the pot grabber (located between the coffee packets and the Hydrolite).
4. A small battery-operated headlamp to light the way after dark. And we have spare batteries, of course.
5. A Nalgene bottle carries the fuel for an alcohol stove, the next item on the list. We usually have this full of Everclear grain alcohol, which burns cleaner and hotter than denatured alcohol, and, because it is non-toxic, it can be used as an emergency disinfectant or to make an emergency sundowner cocktail. (This stuff is 190-proof corn liquor; drinking it undiluted would be an interesting way for you to entertain your friends.) Everclear is many times more expensive than denatured alcohol, but its versatility makes it worth the cost.

Vicarious's shore (bug-out) bag, which we carry with us on every long excursion away from the boat. It contains elementary tools and equipment we might need if we find ourselves stuck somewhere that lacks basic amenities. We developed these bags while hiking in the South Island of New Zealand, Olympic National Park in Washington state, and Denali Park in Alaska. With minor adjustments in a few esoteric items, like emergency clothing, they work everywhere we go.

6. A small alcohol stove. This one is made by Emberlit and can also be fueled by wood. The idea that we carry the alcohol stove just as an excuse to bring along the Everclear is, of course, ridiculous.

7. A 750-milliliter titanium pot, just the right size to heat water for two cups of tea or coffee.

8. Two small head nets for protection from mosquitoes and other biting insects. (Not shown is a bottle of insect repellent with a high DEET content. Yes, I know that DEET is mildly carcinogenic, but so can be insect bites, and nothing else seems to work.)

9. A LifeStraw emergency water filter for drinking any water from any source while traveling in remote areas. And, no, it won't work on salt water.

10. Twenty-five meters of stout cord, useful for too many things to list.

11. Two each knives and spoons. Again we tried the titanium ones but the real ones are well worth the slight increase in weight.

12. Several packs (one shown) of facial tissues. These pocket-sized packs are more handy than toilet paper and work better for other tissue needs. Don't go anywhere in South or Central America without a personal supply of tissues.

13. A Garmin eTrex 20 GPS with local maps loaded (and extra batteries, naturally).

14. A basic compass and the ability to use it properly. And, no, a GPS isn't a real substitute for a compass.

15. An assortment of instant coffee and hot chocolate in serving-sized packets, and tea bags.

16. Hydrolite emergency rehydration tablets are important anywhere in the tropics, especially any area subject to Montezuma's revenge (also called the cruisers' two-step).

17. Towels are often not supplied even in some upscale backpacker establishments, so these two microfiber towels can be essential kit.

18. Two emergency space blankets. These have never been needed, but in an emergency they could be rigged into a crude shelter. By cutting a hole for your head in the center, they could also be fashioned into a crude-but-effective rain poncho. I suspect if we ever do need these things, we will need them a lot.

19. This small Leatherman multitool has multiple uses (of course,) but the sharp knife is the most useful.

20. The Swedish fire stick is our emergency backup to forgetting a butane lighter or matches. These things work surpassingly well for starting a fire, but they do take a bit of practice.

21. A small salt and pepper shaker (hiding behind the titanium pot) goes with us everywhere, even into restaurants.

22. Not shown is my Ruger .357 Magnum and 1,000 rounds of ammo, in keeping with the principles I learned watching *Doomsday Preppers* on YouTube. That critical item is still under negotiation with Susan. (There is the matter of the legality of the thing anywhere outside of the United States, but these concerns are trivial when the importance of maintaining our "perimeter-defense standards" is considered.)

This entire kit weighs just over two pounds, including the carry bag we store it in, and fits into a package that is about 10 inches square. We often add packaged soups or some French bread and cheese, or other food items, when we know we will be picnicking on a beach, along a mountain trail, or in a backpacker facility that allows cooking. We have also tried lightweight dehydrated backpacking meals with mixed results.

There is a tendency to add things to this kit that might come in handy sometime but which we don't really need. Extra items add to the weight and bulk. The more the kit weighs and the bigger it becomes, the less likely you will be to take it with you. So, as with life itself, the important thing is to keep it small and simple and easy to manage.

"And we don't need a bug-out vehicle because, for one, we don't even own a car, and, for two, *Vicarious* is already our bug-out vehicle."

"Aw yeah, but . . . ," I countered glibly.

"And for a bug-out spot, we have the entire Pacific Ocean. We always keep enough supplies for six months, and what sort of starving hordes would ever think to look for us halfway between Hawaii and Homer, Alaska?"

I'll say this about Susan: I love her more than pepperoni pizza and pumpernickel and life itself, but she sure has difficulty grasping the big picture of the really important issues we face. Her comments did get me to wondering, though: do you think zombies can swim?

The type of retirement cruising you decide to undertake depends on many things: Money is among the most important, as is your tolerance for a lifestyle many will regard as a bit eccentric if not downright odd. Your health is one we will discuss in a latter chapter, and your mental attitude is another. Familial relationships, business commitments, self-confidence, nautical expertise, the ability to make your own decisions, fears and phobias, and a host of other factors are all germane to a successful retirement cruise. But the most important decision that must be made is the decision to go. Once you cross that meridian, where you cruise and how you do it becomes incidental.

With all that in mind, let's next talk about what kinds of boats are recommended for the type of cruising you want to do, where to find good deals on good boats, then what to do with them after you find them.

HOW TO BUY A CRUISING BOAT

*The more stuff you don't have on your boat, the more time and
money you won't spend buying it, installing it, maintaining it,
cursing it, regretting it, and removing it after you finally get sick of it.*

START HERE: I have said it before and I will repeat it here: the type of boat you choose to fulfill your retirement cruising ambitions isn't nearly as important as are other critical considerations. Your mental state, physical health, domestic circumstances, financial situation, and your ability to make your own decisions are all more consequential than the size and style of your yacht. In fact, the retired cruising life is a lifestyle unto its own, and the principles behind living it successfully don't depend on a boat at all. It is just as easy to live this way on land far from the sea as it is on a yacht. But this is a book about retiring on a boat, not in a shack in a desert or a log cabin in the wilderness, so let us proceed to find a sturdy and dependable craft that will allow us to do just that.

Of course you may already have a boat on which you are planning to spend your post-employed life. If so, great, don't sell it and run out to buy another based solely on what follows. Most boats that are big enough to be comfortable and accommodate basic facilities like a toilet and galley can be used to live aboard. Even if your boat isn't suitable for the type of cruising you plan to do, don't trade it in just yet. Wait until you digest the rest of this chapter and do a lot of supplemental reading and research before sticking your toe into the used-boat ocean. Buying a boat is expensive by definition and stressful; buying the wrong boat can be a financial nightmare from which you may wake to find your retirement plans in tatters, so proceed cautiously.

Types of Cruising Boats

While just about any boat can work as a retirement cruiser, some boats work better for certain types of cruising than others. Cruising the canals of Europe, for example, in a 40-foot ketch is possible, and many have done it, but doing the same trip in a boat designed just for canal cruising can make it a more enjoyable experience, as anyone who has struggled to travel with unstepped masts and a tangle of rigging lashed to the deck can confirm. Canal boats work best for canal cruising, trawlers work well for sheltered and coastal cruising, and sailboats work best for more ambitious coastal cruising and offshore voyaging. Let's take a look at each of these and review a few other considerations such as size and price.

SIZE

One of the most insidious traps in buying a retirement cruising boat is size. Americans especially like large yachts, but none of us is immune to the big-boat virus. Big boats are impressive, they communicate the message that the owner is a person of importance and consequence, and they play to the human ego like a diva delivering an aria in *Rigoletto*. Spacious boats can be more comfortable than smaller, cramped ones, and they will usually have much more storage space to squirrel away supplies, spare parts, and toys such as bicycles, kayaks, and windsurfers. But large size comes with large penalties. Big boats are more difficult to handle safely than small boats, and they are limited by draft and waterline length in the harbors and anchorages they can enter. The biggest disadvantage of big boats is they are too big for an average retired couple to operate comfortably, which often results in the boat being tied to a dock in some marina where the owners would rather not be. The bigger the boat, the harder it is to move, and the harder a boat is to move, the less often the owners will move it.

Big boats mean big problems, but resisting the temptation to move up in size solely to gain the prestige of owning a large yacht and to bask in the perceived admiration of our fellow cruisers can be a tough boot for an old dog to chew.

Determining the right size of boat for you can be difficult; it is as much of an emotional decision as a practical one. No matter how much we try to deny it, most of us fear if we show up in a small boat, people will laugh at us. A big boat becomes a prestige thing and an expression of our self-worth and value to society. A little boat, on the other hand, tells all that we are a low-class loser who can't come up with the down payment on a decent-sized yacht. It's no wonder many of us end up buying more boat than we need to do the job, and a lot of us buy boats that are too big to do the job at all.

When we tell folks about our several passages through the Caloosahatchee River and Lake Okeechobee, in Florida, one of our favorite spots on earth, an astonishing number tell us they always wanted to do that trip but their mast is too high to fit under the bridges or their keel is too deep to clear the shallow spots. Likewise, there are a large number of boats each year that want to get into the Rio Dulce in Guatemala but find they must forgo this, one of the most popular destinations in the western Caribbean, because they can't get over the sandbar that guards the entrance. And, while securely anchored in the cozy harbor on Atutaki in the Cook Islands, we watched in amusement as the mega-yachts anchored a mile offshore, risking an open roadstead just so they could spend a few worried hours on this island version of the Garden of Eden.

There is no way anyone can tell you what size boat you should buy for a retirement cruise; there are simply too many variables in your needs and lifestyle afloat to even hazard a guess. When Susan and I started looking for a boat for this last chapter in our cruising lives, we set an arbitrary figure of 40 feet on deck as the maximum we would consider. Forty feet is quite a large boat for two elderly people to handle alone, but we rationalized we had a lot of experience and would be able to make modifications to make the boat easier to sail. But as we looked at different boats we came to appreciate the smaller ones for their cozy comfort and ease of maneuvering that was lost as a boat increased in size. The boat we ended up with, *Vicarious*, is 37 feet long on deck and 32 feet on the waterline. It's still a large boat for two old folks and a dog, but a comfortable one for us. After three years living on her, we wouldn't trade her for anything, smaller or bigger. Throughout the rest of this book, I will try to help you zero in on just the perfect craft for your lifestyle, budget, and plans.

The next big decision you must make after size is cost; deciding how much you should spend on a boat can be a bugbear for sure, but don't forget to consider the operating costs before you decide to buy.

INITIAL PRICE AND COSTS

Buying a boat is a traumatic adventure into the unknown for most of us. It is a lot like buying a house, and, for many of us, it is buying a house. It doesn't happen that often, for one thing, so it isn't something you can practice doing until you get good at it. I have made the journey across the rickety bridge to boat ownership seven times, but that is spread over 50 years. That means, on average, I buy a boat every

The STUPOR Index

Boat owners are fond of all sorts of ratios and indices: there is the length-to-weight ratio, which is a sort of body-mass index for things that float; the AVS (Angle of Variable Stability) factor , which determines when your boat is about to turn over and drown you; and the hull-speed-to-waterline-length ratio, which demonstrates how easy it is to express a simple concept in a complicated way. My favorite is the STUPOR Index, which measures the effect a big boat can have on your purchasing decisions and financial health.

Simply stated, the STUPOR Index (a convenient acronym for Starting-to-Ultimate-Price-Obfuscation Ratio) is the original cost of buying and operating a boat, exponential to the displacement of the boat times the waterline length divided by the reciprocal of your net worth, which gives you the maximum number of years you can expect to run your new boat before you are forced into bankruptcy. In basic algorithmic notation we all understand, the STUPOR Index is thus:

$$X^2 + Y^2 = Z^2$$

Which using standard mathematical reduction logic simplifies to:

$$\frac{\text{åß}\partial f \copyright \; \Delta° \neg \dots \text{æ}\Omega \approx \text{ç} \sqrt{\int\,}^{-}\mu \leq (z \div a)}{\text{£} \div \$^{\text{™}}} = \sqrt{Z}$$

As you can see by plugging in your own numbers and working out the solution, the STUPOR Index clearly shows how spending a little more on your initial purchase of a boat can easily increase the future costs, and how those costs will rapidly escalate to the point where you are broke.

Interestingly, the STUPOR Index is used by legions of affluent yacht buyers to justify spending more on a boat than is economically wise, and it is the primary tool of the boat-show sales forces to get your autograph next to the "sign here" sticky tab on a new-boat contract.

seven years, which is enough time for the used-boat market to change completely. Susan and I owned *Sultana* for more than 20 years, and the market in 2013, with boats by the hundreds available everywhere we looked, bore little resemblance to the go-go sellers' market of 1993, when good boats at a decent price were few in number and far apart.

Purchase Price

The first consideration on your boat-buying quest must be purchase price, and you should determine the maximum you want to pay before you ever look at a boat or even decide what type of boat you will be looking for. Paying too much for a boat or paying more than you initially planned is so common among boat buyers that the experienced brokers count on it. When you tell a broker your maximum price is $50,000, he or she will automatically start showing you $75,000 boats. Part of this is the accepted fact few sellers expect to get their asking price, so they allow a healthy margin for negotiation. But the broker also knows if you can be shown a boat that twitches the right strings, he or she can have you dancing like a puppet and digging deeper than you ever thought possible, trying to come up with the cash for some amazing bargain that always seems to pop up out of nowhere.

There are two ways to handle this inflated asking price and combat the urge to pay more than you want to pay. You can refuse to look at anything priced higher than your maximum, which risks making the broker think you are an inflexible jerk. Or you can deflate your maximum to compensate for the inflated asking price. This may seem like a silly game, because that is what it is, but your willingness to play the game will make the broker's job a lot easier and hasten the day when you sail away in your new yacht. So when you approach a broker, have two figures in mind: the first is the maximum you tell the broker you will pay for a boat, and the second is the amount you are really prepared to spend. The broker will know your maximum is really your starting price and will try to match it to the lowest price the seller will accept. Of course you realize the broker is expecting you to make a lower offer than the asking price, and you, naturally, know the seller is going to be happy with less than the asking price. The hard part for the buyer is to find out what that lower number is, and the hard part for the broker is to discover what your upper number is. The game that determines these figures is called *Low Bid Refusal*, and it works like this:

You know the seller is asking $50,000 for a boat you think you would like, so you say something like, "Gee, sort of a nice boat, but 50 grand is a lot. I might go 35 for a quick deal." To which the broker is required to respond, "I don't think you will find a boat like this for anywhere near that, but I will run it by the seller."

Several hours later, the broker rings to say, "The seller says he will consider $47,500 if we can wrap it up before the end of the month." To which you reply, "My wife doesn't like the color of the cockpit cushions. If you can get them recovered in a nicer fabric, I might be able to go $37,500, but he will have to throw in the dinghy."

The next day the broker calls with the final counter offer (which is never the final counter offer): "OK, the seller has dropped the price to $45,000 with new cockpit cushions but no dinghy; final offer, and he wants an answer today," to which you reply in a disappointed voice, "Aww, too bad. I was looking forward to buying that boat. What else ya got in that price range?" To which the broker replies, "We are pretty close here. Let me make one more try. If I cut my commission by half, could you go to $40,000?" To which you reply, "Maybe, but it would be conditional on a sea trial and a survey, and I still want that dinghy."

Twenty minutes later the now-animated broker calls back with the good news: "Well it looks like you wore the guy out. The seller has completely caved. You can have the boat for only $42,500 including new cockpit cushions, and the dinghy is yours."

Later that night as you and your significant other celebrate, you try to stifle your smug expression of triumph as you say, "I can't believe the guy sold us that boat for only forty-two five. It's the perfect boat for us. I would have been happy to pay his asking price if he had held out for it." To which your SO replies in an admiring voice, "Oh, Ashley (assuming your name is Ashley, of course), you are the most persuasive person I have ever met. When you want something, you just go for it until it is yours." To which, if you are smart, you reply, "That's how I got you, isn't it Snookums."

Meanwhile, in a dimly lit bar across town, the broker and the seller are enjoying a celebratory cocktail. The seller says, "Well, Angelina (many boat brokers are named Angelina, unless they're blokes, in which case they are named Chuck), I can't believe how you pulled it off. Getting $42,500 for that albatross was brilliant salesmanship. With no offers in six months, I was ready to take the guy's $35,000 just to be rid of it. How did you do it?"

"The key was the dinghy," Angelina answers authoritatively. "Letting a buyer think he is getting something for free will do it every time."

"Well it was a major deal for me, and I owe you big time."

"That's what brokers are for," says Angelina. "Selling boats is like squeezing a turnip. You got to know just how much juice you can get before the whole thing turns to mush in your hand."

"You know," says the seller, "they say the second happiest day of your life is when you buy a boat. Do you know what the happiest day is?"

"Nooooo . . . , that's a tough one; enlighten me."

"The day you sell it. Haw, haw, haw . . ."

"Ha, ha, ha . . . Gee, I never heard *that* one before. Now, if you are wondering what to do with that 40 grand I just got for you, I have an amazing deal on a pristine Hinckley sloop—the seller really needs it gone, and it comes with a free . . ."

Operating Costs

While most of us will agonize over the purchase price of a boat for weeks or months before we get to our final offer and close a deal, many of us don't pay much attention to the money we will expend on running the thing once we get it. Operating costs can be even more important than the up-front price of your new extravagance, and they can empty your kitty in an astonishingly short period of time.

Operating costs include all the many items that will regularly cost you money for as long as you own the boat. Insurance can be a big one; fuel costs get more important with every tick of the diesel-price clock; routine maintenance, such as oil changes, varnishing and painting, sail repair and replacement, never stops coming, and the price never goes down. Dockage and mooring fees happen every month, and some hundreds of other little costs and expenses continually pop up like the dandelions on the new-mown lawn did back when you worried about that sort of thing.

Novice boat buyers, especially, tend to ignore or underestimate how much cash they will have to part with to keep their new floating palace a floating palace, but we are all susceptible to the disease. There is a lot of bad advice on boat buying available everywhere you turn, from greedy brokers who just like to sell boats to legions of self-proclaimed experts tooting their horns at boat shows, in yacht clubs, and on the Internet. You need to ignore all of it.

Another 10-Step Plan: Buying a Boat

Back in Chapter Two, we discovered a 10-step plan to help you drop out of the consumer society. It's the easiest way to free up your life and your finances enough to enjoy the true freedom retirement cruising offers. Obviously, the plan worked because here you are at Chapter Four already. With that success in mind, let's come up with another 10-step strategy for selecting the perfect boat for your retirement.

STEP ONE: REREAD CHAPTER TWO
Before you go any farther, go back and reread Chapter Two. If you have already reread it, reread it again—it is that important. The entire second chapter demonstrates how you can increase the quality of your life in ways you can only imagine: By getting rid of the unneeded stuff that acts like an anvil chained to your neck and keeps you anchored in the harbor of conventionalism, you can escape to the open sea and discover a world of freedom you never dreamed existed.

Pay particular attention to steps four and five in the first ten-step plan. If you can change your attitude about what you perceive others to perceive about you and can surround yourself with like-minded friends, you will be on your way to a cruising retirement long before you look at your first boat.

It is critical that once you start shopping for a boat, you are not influenced by what you think others will think of you for buying it. You need to find the perfect craft for you and anyone going with you, and what others think of it and of you for buying it doesn't matter at all.

STEP TWO: REALIZE YOU ARE NOT INVESTING IN AN ASSET
In the accounting world, an asset is some form of property that generates income or increases in value and makes you money. If you own a house, for example, it is an asset because it saves you from paying rent, and it can appreciate in value over time. Your car, on the other hand, is going to cost you a lot of money to own and is a liability, no matter how much it is worth or how much you paid for it. (On a business ledger, things like cars may be listed as assets to take advantage of depreciation, but because the net effect on the bottom line is decidedly negative, they are in fact liabilities.)

Likewise an investment is an expenditure of money you can realistically expect will return, over time, more money than you spend on it. And, as many of us think of a boat as an asset, even more of us will speak of our boat-buying as an investment.

It is quite natural that we who live on boats as our only home like to consider it as both an investment and an asset, the same as our house was back when we lived on land. But this is a mistake. Boats, no matter how you configure your purchase, are a cash drain on your cruising kitty. If you can get it lodged securely in your head that boats are neither investments nor assets, you will have gone a long way to keeping your foot out of the bear trap of overindulgence that is the ruin of many retirement plans afloat.

STEP THREE: PICK A PRICE

Spend a little time with a pencil, paper, and a calculator to work out a realistic amount you can spend on a boat. You will need two numbers, as discussed above: one for the purchase price and another for the annual operating costs. Try to be conservative here because the more of your cash that stays in your pocket and isn't spent on a boat, the happier your cruising days will be.

I feel anyone who is going to live full-time on a boat as their only home can spend up to 20 percent of their net worth on the purchase price. Any more than that and you are in danger of becoming boat poor, a condition like being house poor but many times worse. (To compute your net worth, add up the actual value [the amount you can realistically sell an item for, not the amount you paid for it] of all the things you own, add your cash, and then deduct all your debts. Be honest here, and if you must estimate a number, make it a conservative one.)

That means if you have a realistic net worth of $250,000, you should safely be able to pay $50,000 for a boat. But be careful here as well. Any boat you buy will have commissioning costs in addition to the amount you pay to the seller, and those should be considered a part of the purchase price. A good survey is $1,000 or more, and there are always a few repairs and upgrades you should make, such as a new VHF radio or repairs to deck leaks that need to be made before you move aboard. These repairs and upgrades are hard to estimate, because many items will be overlooked by both you and the surveyor (it always happens, so get used to it), so deduct another 20 percent from your maximum purchase price to pay for them. That means for a $50,000 purchase price, you need to hold back $10,000 for commissioning and contingencies, leaving a maximum of $40,000 you will pay to the seller.

You are setting down your maximum purchase price here, but keep in mind that operating costs are going to be a factor after you decide what type of cruising you plan to do and the boat you are going to do it in. We haven't discussed either of these yet, but, don't worry, we will get there soon enough. Right now, coming to terms with the portion of your net worth you can safely devote to a boat is the important first step.

If you aren't going to live on your boat full-time and are planning to cruise part of the year and do something else with the rest of your time (a popular option with retired cruisers) you should never pay more than 10 percent of your net worth for a boat. That means with a $250,000 net worth, your maximum offer to the seller should be no more than $20,000 after deducting the 20 percent for commissioning and contingency.

The reasons you should not pay as much for a part-time cruising boat as you would pay for one you will call your home are quite simple. Boats used part-time can cost more to maintain than full-time boats, because leaving a boat in storage, no matter how secure and weatherproof, can be harder on the boat than using it. Corrosion can easily get started without being noticed and can escalate until fixing it is expensive. Unused electronics deteriorate quickly, especially if there is any trace of condensation present, and soft goods, such as upholstery, sails, and interior spaces, can go over to mildew and mold in a single season.

Another reason for committing a smaller portion of your net worth to a part-time boat is while you are not using it, you are doing something else, and that something else is probably going to cost money. One favorite scenario with retired cruisers is to travel the world in a boat for part of the year, then switch to an RV while the boat is in storage. The expense of an RV is about the same as for a boat, so the 10-percent rule should prevail there also. Interestingly, RV buyers seem to be even more inclined than boaters to buy bigger than they need, just for the prestige of owning a bigger camper than the guy on the adjacent hookup.

Once you decide on the maximum amount you can pay for a boat, stick with it. No matter what price range you are looking at, you are bound to come across a few beautiful boats at ridiculously low prices for only $10,000 or $20,000 more than you are prepared to pay. The broker may even offer an attractive financing deal to put you in the more expensive boat, but if you can resist the temptation to go over your predetermined limit, your retirement cruise will be a happier one.

STEP FOUR: DETERMINE OPERATING COSTS

Operating costs are harder to calculate for any boat when you don't have a history of experience to base them on. The previous owner may have extensive data available that can be considered, but operating costs fluctuate wildly with how a boat is used, and there is no guarantee you will use it as the previous owner did. Operating costs are usually higher for the first year or so you own a boat, because it takes about that long for a new owner to become familiar with the complex systems that make a modern cruising boat work. The more you become familiar with your boat, the less time and money it will take to keep afloat and headed in the right direction.

Certain operating costs, such as insurance, storage, and dockage, can be determined easily by soliciting a quote from the people providing these services. Other costs, such as fuel, scheduled engine maintenance, and general repairs, aren't so easy to estimate. Fuel is particularly important for any type of powerboat, and, the bigger the engines, the more important it becomes. Fuel prices fluctuate in an unpredictable manner: they are at a five-year low now, but the long-term trend is always upward. And fuel consumption is dependent on how the boat is run, how clean the bottom is, and how fast you go.

It is easy to say you plan to run your new engine (or engines) at the most economical speed, but trying to run a big sportfisherman with two 500-horse engines in the barn at an efficient speed is nothing short of agony; for many of us, it is nothing short of impossible. Operating a powerful boat at an efficient speed is just like driving a car on the interstate for a long distance at idle. After an hour or so of crawling along, there is a huge temptation to stomp on it, fuel cost be damned.

The best you can do with these unknown expenses for any new-to-you boat is to make an educated guess at what you can expect to spend on them. This is difficult when you haven't even selected a type of boat yet, but try to come up with a realistic figure for an amount you can realistically afford for the monthly and annual costs of running any boat you are planning to buy. Do this before you make even an exploratory offer. Then, when you come up with a figure, double it if you have a lot of experience around boats; if you don't have a lot if experience with boats, quadruple it.

Don't forget to include a depreciation of 10 percent a year (a bit more for a newer boat and a bit less for an older one) in your annual outlay. And remember: if you egregiously overestimate the operating costs (an event that happens about as often as a total eclipse of the sun), you will have a pleasant surprise waiting for you at accounting time; if you drastically underestimate your costs (as almost all of us do, every time we do it), your surprise will be less than pleasant in direct proportion to the amount of your deficit. The number of novice boat owners who have had their lives altered, if not ruined, by the unanticipated operating costs of a too-expensive boat purchased on a whim is impossible to calculate, but I can guarantee there have been a lot of us.

Once you have a realistic figure for how much you can comfortably spend on the purchase of a boat, and an estimate of what you can spend to run it, it is time to start looking at boats. But first, decide what kind of cruising you plan to do.

STEP FIVE: YOUR CRUISING STYLE

Back in Chapter Three we talked about the different types of cruising and cruising styles available to anyone wanting to retire on a boat. After dividing our options into three tidy categories—sheltered cruising, coastal cruising, and offshore voyaging (ignoring bugout cruising for now)—we continued with a discussion of each as if they were different worlds. This is a handy way to gain initial understanding of the diversity of the retired cruising lifestyle, but it falls short of describing the reality. Few cruisers, retired or otherwise, restrict their boating to one or another particular style. Most embrace two and sometimes all three, without even realizing when they move from one to another.

Beginning cruisers who want to eventually cross oceans to distant lands are well advised to start with small, easily achieved goals in sheltered waters. I spent much of my early childhood and the first few years as a young adult in Maryland near enough to the Chesapeake Bay to enjoy an occasional trip in boats belonging to friends and family. My first overnight ever was aboard a 24-foot outboard powerboat that my boss at the time (I was a freshman at the University of Maryland and worked part-time for a local drug store) had taken out for an afternoon of fishing. When the weather turned bad, we were forced into the shelter of Poplar Island, where we spent an unscheduled overnight while the lightning flashed and the wind howled.

Years later, when Susan and I bought our first sailboat, we spent many weekends in the anchorages around Ipswich and Cape Ann in Massachusetts. Over the years, we took progressively longer and more daring trips until we were familiar with the entire coast of New England and eastern Canada from Block Island to Halifax. At no point did we make a decision to begin coastal cruising or become ocean voyagers. It just happened. Most of the time we were cruising we were in all three categories. Nevertheless, you should decide how extensive you would like your planned retirement cruise to be, and plan for it now.

STEP SIX: YOUR CRUISING BOAT

OK, it's time to look for a boat, so let's get on with it. As you examine different designs and types of craft, try to concentrate on the design features and not the superficial window dressings with which savvy sellers doll up their offerings. The galley layout, for example, is much more important than the color of the cockpit cushions, but because changing the cushions is a simple task, you are stuck with the galley layout. A cramped, dark, unventilated galley will ensure that you don't do much cooking there. Likewise, the steering system, bulkhead location, ventilation, engine size and configuration, tankage, hull thickness, electrical system and capacity, and a hundred other permanent features that come with your boat are lots more important than the finish on the cabin sole or the color of the paint in the head. The condition of the engine and sails, the layout of the deck hardware, the size and age of the rigging (on sailboats), and the condition of the exterior finish are miles ahead of the age and condition of the chart plotter or radar or the number of life jackets on board. Try to look beyond the superficial façade, ignoring the gadgets and circumstances that are easy to correct and change while peering deeply into the very soul of your prospective purchase where, one by one, you can view the immutable bones.

The second consideration in selecting a boat for your retirement cruise, right behind your budget (discussed in Steps Three and Four), is the kind of cruising you plan to do (discussed in Step Five). If you think you will be content with staying in sheltered waters, that's one thing, but it's an entirely different thing if you might want to cross the Pacific or sail south to Tierra del Fuego. Let's revisit the different cruising styles with a few comments on appropriate craft for each.

Boats for Sheltered Cruising

Sheltered cruising requires only a boat with comfortable sleeping accommodations, a fundamental galley, and a functional and legal toilet. In many sheltered waters, the height of bridges you may encounter and the depth of the water you will be cruising through will need to be considered when choosing a boat. Maximum height on the Erie Canal, for example, is 20 feet, and its only 17 feet for other canals in the New York system. (All together, the New York Canal System has more than 500 miles of interconnected waterways, not counting Lake Erie, Lake Champlain, and the Finger Lakes.)

Just about any boat that is large enough to be comfortable and has room for a head and galley can be used for cruising canals and other forms of travel in sheltered waters. As a fully found offshore cruiser, Vicarious *felt a bit out of place motoring down the Dismal Swamp Canal in Virginia, but the trip was a highlight of our adventures along the East Coast of the United States.*

Even though sheltered cruising can be rewarding in any kind of boat, the most popular craft for inshore waters are small- to medium-sized powerboats. Trawlers lead the pack because of their spacious accommodations and superior fuel economy. Small sailboats are also popular with inshore cruisers, but unpredictable, shifting winds and frequent dead spots in the lee of hills can make trying to sail in rivers and small lakes frustrating. Motoring in a small sailboat with its typically smaller engine and inefficient prop can also be tedious. Larger lakes and spacious sheltered waters with many small islands, like the Bahamas or the Great Barrier Reef, lend themselves very well to sailboats of any size, as bridge height is not a concern, and water depth is manageable for all but the biggest craft.

Boats for Coastal Cruising

Both sailboats and powerboats are popular choices for coastal cruising, with the proportion in the United States, Bahamas, and Canada being about 50-50. Sailboats are a more popular choice in the Mediterranean, the Caribbean, and in the South Pacific, at least partly because of the higher fuel prices, but also because the distances between anchorages and marinas tend to be longer. The fuel cost of cruising long distances can be onerous even in the most economical boats.

If you are considering coastal cruising, the choice between doing it in a powerboat or a sailboat can be troublesome. You may hear the claim, usually from self-delusional powerboaters, that a powerboat costs no more to run than a sailboat because the cost of the sails and rigging offsets the cost of fuel. That may have been true two decades ago when you could fill your tank with 50 cents a gallon diesel fuel, but today, even with the low price of fuel, you are going to pay much more. As this goes to press, fuel prices are at a five-year low because of a massive glut in the world supply of crude oil. The last time we filled up *Vicarious*, (in Golfito, Costa Rica) diesel fuel cost $2.75 a gallon. That's down from $4.50 a gallon just a year ago. Prices are predicted to stay low for the foreseeable future, but you can guarantee that at some point they will start back up, and you should plan accordingly. The consideration of fuel price and the hourly fuel consumption of your engine or engines should be a prime factor if you are thinking of buying a powerboat in which to cruise for any distance.

Once you start looking, you will see hundreds of boats for sale with big, powerful diesel engines. These boats were designed and built in the days of super-cheap fuel and are now available for a fraction of their asking price of just a few years ago. But be careful. A 40-foot sportfisherman might have twin 500-horsepower engines and a 1,000-gallon fuel tank. It is going to cost the lucky owner of this beast $2,500 bucks to fill 'er up, and that will be gone in abut 10 hours if the boat is operated at its optimum speed. Even at its most economical speed, you will be ready for another fuel stop in less than 100 hours. As we mentioned before, driving a big, powerful boat built to honk along at 25 or 30 knots is pure agony when you attempt to idle along at 10 knots.

Many coastal cruisers who travel in powerboats compensate for the costs of fuel by making shorter passages between anchorages and staying put longer than they did in the past. This strategy can work quite well, and it will improve the quality of your cruising. If you spend less time motoring between stops and spend more time in port, you are bound to learn to relax more and see more of the world around you, and, after all, that's what cruising is about.

More and more, coastal cruisers are turning to sailboats as the most economical and comfortable craft to pursue their dreams, whereas just a few years ago powerboats were coming on strong for making short ocean passages. Here again, the switch

This lovely little Mariner ketch is a bit light for serious offshore voyaging but would be perfectly safe for short jaunts into the open ocean when the weather cooperates. This degree of seaworthiness makes it an ideal coastal cruiser: fun to sail and a comfortable liveaboard for two people.

to sail is driven by the price of fuel. Even if you spend most of your passage time under power, the smaller, more efficient engines popular in sailboats mean you will spend less for fuel than in a powerboat.

But powerboats are far from dead. There are a lot of advantages in choosing a powerboat over a sailboat for your retirement cruising, and a medium-sized trawler with a single small diesel engine can offer reasonable economy even with expensive fuel. A 36-foot Grand Banks with a 125-horsepower Ford Lehman engine, for example, can chug along at six knots while burning a bit over two gallons of fuel an hour. The downside of this economy for the buyer is the demand for efficient powerboats is increasing, so a single-engine trawler at a reasonable price may be hard to find.

Then there is the logic, often bordering on rationalization, that the money saved on buying a 20-year-old sportfisherman with two 500-horsepower engines over a trawler of equivalent size with a single 125-horsepower engine can buy a lot of fuel. This may be true, but when the next upward bump in fuel prices comes along, as it surely will, these dinosaurs will lose even more of their value. Eventually the entire fleet will become floating condos tied permanently to the dock, going nowhere.

Boats for Offshore Cruising
Where just about any boat that is safe, seaworthy, and fitted out with basic amenities can be suitable for sheltered and coastal cruising, offshore boats require certain standards that set them apart from your average weekender. Rugged construction, an easily managed rig, sea-kindly motion in big waves and swells, commodious storage and tankage, and narrow beam with round bilges are a few of the qualities you will be pondering when you consider buying an offshore cruising boat. You may also decide to spring for a few items of esoteric gear most near-shore sailors needn't consider. (See Sidebar pages 82–83.)

I could write several long chapters to advise prospective retirees who yearn to venture out of the sight of land on how to buy a boat to do it in, but I'm not going to bother. For one thing it would take up most of the rest of this book, a disproportionate share since the majority of retired cruisers choose to stay coastal or inshore. And, for another thing, there are already about a dozen good books out there on the subject. For starters, you should pick up a copy of *The Seaworthy Offshore Sailboat*, by John Vigor (International Marine, 1999, 2001). Here is an authoritative, easily read treatment of a complicated and sometimes contentious subject by an author with extensive experience who, as a journalist, treats the writer's craft with a level of respect unusual for this sort of book.

Referring you to another author may seem like a classic cop-out, and it is, but I would admonish the reader to not try offshore sailing in anything but a boat meeting all of Mr. Vigor's criteria. A shocking number of inadequate boats are taken onto the ocean by poorly prepared crews, and the fact that the majority of them seem to suffer no ill effects encourages others to do the same. But appearances of impunity can be deceiving.

For over 30 years I have been informally keeping track of the reasons new offshore cruisers give it up after only a short time, often after a single trip. One of the top cruise killers is traveling offshore in a lightweight production boat that is better suited to coastal cruising. Sailing across an ocean in a small boat is one of the most relaxing and satisfying pastimes there is, but it has to be done right in the right kind of vessel, and with the self confidence that only comes with experience. Nothing kills the enthusiasm of a new cruiser quicker than a night spent cowering in fear while riding out even a moderate blow at sea in a boat with squirrely handling and a cruel sea motion, and with improperly secured stores flying about the cabin like a swarm of bats leaving a cave at dusk.

If you are interested in cruising across an ocean in a powerboat, I would refer you to *Voyaging Under Power*, Fourth Edition, by Robert P. Beebe and Denis Umstot (International Marine, 2013), and to *The Troller Yacht Book,* Second Edition, by George Buehler (International Marine, 2011). Both these books treat offshore cruising under power in a readable and sensible manner. But be forewarned: if you are considering an offshore retirement cruise in a powerboat, you will need a lot of cash in the bank. A 10-year-old Nordhaven 40, a classic offshore cruiser, will cost the better part of half a million bucks to buy, and, even with an economical 120-horsepower diesel in the engine room, it is going to cost about five grand, at today's fuel prices, just to fill the tanks.

Of course there are powerboats available that don't cost this much, but realize that the Grand Banks 36, which will take you to the Channel Islands in safety and comfort, isn't going to make it to Hawaii. That trip is going to require a much stronger boat, piles of money for fuel, and lots of specialized equipment (like roll stabilizers) that is expensive to buy and difficult to operate.

Among my favorite boat designs is George Buehler's Diesel Duck. It is one of the most economical and seaworthy offshore powerboats available, but the lowest price I have ever seen listed is $250,000. That means, using our formula of 20 percent of net worth for a rational boat purchase in Step Three above, I would need $1,500,000 to justify purchasing such a boat as a full-time retirement home. If I only planned to cruise part-time, my net worth for a rational purchase goes up to $3,000,000. Now obviously there are a lot of people who have more than $3,000,000 in the bank and can easily afford a quarter-million for a yacht. But I don't and I can't, so we will leave further discussion of offshore powerboat cruising to Robert and George while we do our offshore boat shopping at slightly less lofty altitudes.

STEP SEVEN: MAKE SURE YOU ARE READY, THEN MAKE SURE YOU ARE SURE

OK, now you have a good idea what type of cruising you want to do in your retirement years, you have a rough idea of where you want to do it, and you have some positive vibes about the boat you want to do it in, but don't commit yourself

(Continued)

The Curse of Gadget Obsession

Cruisers love gadgets. Whether your retirement cruise takes you to the middle of the Pacific Ocean or across to the opposite shore of a lake in Nebraska makes little difference. Marketing forces and the pervasive influences of our consumer culture have been programming us since birth to spend most of our lives accumulating the resources to buy stuff we don't need and often don't even want. Resisting the impulse to purchase items we can do without becomes increasingly difficult as the amount of cash we have available for trivial expenditures increases.

There is in most of us a tendency, carefully orchestrated by advertisers and the popular boating press, to rationalize the purchase of unneeded items by working it into our minds that the item is important or even essential. Popular objects of this fantasy are watermakers; generators; overcomplicated chart plotters that interface with depth sounders, radar, GPS, weather fax, water temperature, and just about every other type of data imaginable; air conditioners; life rafts; personal-locator beacons that attach to a life vest; and even dedicated popcorn makers, bread machines, and vacuum baggers.

This list could go on forever, and it is growing steadily as inventors and corporate marketing departments struggle to come up with new stuff we can't do without or to reconfigure the old stuff so it looks like new stuff. Some of these must-have items are truly miraculous: chart plotters are stunningly complex electronic sensations, water makers take mechanical precision to levels only imagined just a few years ago, and we now have powerful generators so quiet the next boat in the anchorage won't know you are running one.

Unfortunately, as each new marvel is introduced, the cost is increasingly onerous. True, the price of many items comes down drastically after new items become popular, but the true cost invariably increases. The purchase price is often minor when the cost of installation, maintenance, time, lost storage or deck space, and aggravation when the thing doesn't work properly are all considered. Some items, like a multifunctional chart plotter or an electronic autopilot, can even be dangerous when our dependency on them becomes complete and we have nowhere to turn when they fail.

The captain of a well-equipped catamaran in Panama recently said to me, regarding his expenditure of many thousands of dollars on a new marine air conditioner, "Hey, I have the money. Why shouldn't I be comfortable?" Nothing I could have said would have changed this cruiser's mind, so I changed the subject. But I could have pointed out several reasons not to indulge in air-conditioning on a boat in which you intend to go places, no matter how much money you have. For one thing, air-conditioning is addictive; once you have it, a trip outside of your custom cockpit enclosure in the heat of the day becomes much more uncomfortable than when you are acclimated to the ambient temperature. The danger is you will become so accustomed to air-conditioning you will only reluctantly go outside, ever. Cruising should be an outdoor activity. If you are going to spend your retirement years indoors, you might as well stay in Poughkeepsie where you can keep an eye on the thermostat and get a lot more channels on your flat-screen TV.

The maintenance and depreciation of anything you add to your boat have to be considered in the overall cost, as does the environmental impact of the energy you are using to run the item. The necessity of an expensive and noisy generator and the valuable storage space you no longer have in your boat because of the bulky plant and ducting are all costs to consider after the purchase price is spent.

I don't mean to dwell on just air-conditioning here. The more unnecessary stuff you load onto your boat, the more your equipment inventory smothers the freedom most of us adopt the cruising life to enjoy. The more stuff you don't have on your boat, the more time and money you don't spend buying it, installing it, maintaining it, cursing it, regretting it, and removing it after you finally get sick of it, it becomes obsolete, or it just wears out.

The inventory of electronic gadgets aboard Vicarious *may seem excessive, but it's only about average for offshore cruisers. Susan claims I am obsessed with computers, which isn't true, but I do admit to having one or two more than we would need in a pinch.*

just yet. Step back and think it over once more before you rush out and buy a ·
boat. Reconsider everything that has brought you to this remarkable change-of-
life decision to sail east of the moon and enjoy your last few years and decades
aboard a traveling yacht.

Now's the time to go back to the beginning and review the whole pot of
stew, noodle by noodle. Reconsider your health and your wealth, and ponder
the likelihood of either changing drastically in the near future. Think about your
finances and reconfigure a realistic estimate of how long you can keep your kitty
purring without having to go back to work to revive it. Spend a lot of time with
your significant other and make doubly sure you both share the passion for a
comparatively austere life of toil and hardship in a home that is forever rocking
in the waves and nibbling away at your cash like a termite munching on a leg of
your rocking chair.

If you are honest and scrupulously analytical in this preretirement re-analysis
of your cruising fantasy, you will most assuredly decide not to do it. That's why there
are multitudes of retirees clogging the gated communities of Florida and Arizona for
each one of us swatting no-see-ums in some lonesome anchorage in some faraway
lagoon most civilized people can't even pronounce, much less desire to visit.

The sad fact is for every hundred of us approaching retirement who dream
about spending our *après-travail* life on a boat, fewer than one of us will ever do
it. But maybe it isn't so sad after all. Think what it would be like if the situation
were reversed: anchorages around the world would be choked with boats moored
side by side so close together you could step from one to the other, and retirement
communities would have but a single house drifting alone on a sea of grass while
the lonely retirees sit among the stars watching the rabbits nibble the greens in
the garden. Now wouldn't that be awful?

The reason most older folks who think they want to retire on a boat never do
it is because they live in a world of reality forged on the anvil of common sense,
then tempered in the oven of responsibility: there is no room for such antisocial
behavior as robbing banks, stalking the streets in a raincoat, or wearing a polka-
dot tie with a striped shirt. Most of us are far too practical to get rid of all of our
carefully accumulated stuff, ignore our responsibilities to our families, communities,
and organizations, and disregard the need for reliable healthcare and safety. We
may want to chuck it all for the ephemeral, often illusionary, satisfaction of sailing
away in a boat, but most of us just can't bring ourselves to do it.

Thus, if you are ever going to realize this impossible dream of aquatic retirement,
you will need to be impractical, unrealistic, and a dreamer. Cruisers at any age are
a nation of frog-kissers and magic-bean buyers; we dream during the day and sleep
well at night. If you are a mature person with a healthy sense of responsibility, you
will probably, on close inspection of your plans, decide it isn't for you, but if you
are a bit unrealistic, a tad irresponsible, and have just a drop or two of rebel blood
coursing your veins, perhaps the cruising life is for you after all.

The distinction is—and this is important, so "look at me" (as my favorite Elmore Leonard character is wont to say)—while it is OK and even required for successful retired cruisers to be slightly off base, a bit unrealistic, and a lot optimistic, you can't be stupid about it. It's a lot like the tired old cliché about enjoying golf: you have to be smart enough to understand the rules but dumb enough to think they are important.

It comes down to a trade-off between stupid and practical, but if you are going to get it wrong, you will be way ahead if you err on the side of practical and not on the side of stupid. Practical people who make a mistake and decide against retirement cruising are seldom ever aware of their error—except, of course, for that wistful feeling that never goes away. However, stupid people who make a mistake and go cruising when they should have moved to the Happy Acres Assisted Living Center will find they have made a very painful and expensive blunder: one they are unlikely to forget, ever.

STEP EIGHT: OK, NOW YOU CAN BUY A BOAT

If you already have a boat, you can skip over this step, but I suggest you read it anyway, just to absorb the profundity it offers.

If you have survived Step Seven, congratulations and welcome to the cruising life. By now we have lost most of the other readers who are busy sorting through craigslist looking for RVs and retirement homes; we have become an exclusive little enclave of impractical romantics and unrepentant dreamers. So now is the time to move your deposit money into an accessible escrow account and start looking for a boat.

You have probably been casually looking at boats for some time now anyway, and you most likely know just what you want in a floating retirement home. But here I have to indulge in another massive-but-justified cop-out. I covered my particular (some would say peculiar) philosophy of buying a boat earlier in this 10-step plan, and in some detail in my prequel to this book, *The Cruising Life*, Second Edition, so I won't repeat it here.

But there are other reasons for avoiding the nitty-gritty of advice on how to go about buying your retirement vessel. Perhaps you are a wealthy person who wants to retire in a luxurious motor yacht, or perhaps you are a wage slave and want to use your carefully saved cash to buy the most practical and economical boat possible, or you might be in the middle: an average person with an average stash (kitty) looking for an average boat. There are about as many types and kinds of boats available to those of us wanting to become retired cruisers as there are types and kinds of retirees.

With this great diversity of suitable watercraft available to us and with this equally large diversity of retirees and potential retirees looking for them, it would be a prodigious task for any writer, much less a writer who has only owned seven boats, to offer up legitimate advice on how to buy the one just right for you. But my basic advice holds firm: try to find the smallest and least expensive (I hesitate to say "cheapest") boat that will do the job you expect of it and make your retirement cruise safe and comfortable. This may mean a $10,000,000 mega-yacht right off the showroom floor, or it might mean a $10,000 beater that is sound and functional, if a bit shabby in the appearance department, and nearly as old as you are.

A content retirement is possible on just about any size and shape of boat imaginable, as long as it is large enough to contain basic amenities that make you comfortable, small enough to be managed by elderly folks, and economical enough to not squeeze the life out of your beleaguered kitty.

Here the alert reader will notice our *10-Step Plan: Buying a Boat* has only eight steps. While this deficit is regrettable, it is not a cunning scam to deprive you of two steps, as it might seem. It's just that I feel it necessary to invoke my artistic license here. (It's valid until I reach the age of 75, when I will need an eye exam and to retake the road test.) I'm sure you will agree the phrase "eight-step plan" just doesn't have the poetic ring needed to retain the harmonic balance of the narrative, so I have opted out of the last two steps.

Sure, I could go back and reorder the steps so we end up with the full count, but we both have better things to do with the time left to us. At this point, I will admonish you to put aside your dismay (we all suffer losses from time to time) and carry on to buy just the right boat for you. If you like, you can also put this book aside and pick it up again once you are a certified boat owner.

In the next chapter we will investigate several possibilities for upgrades to just about any boat you end up with. These modifications will make your new/old boat more comfortable and easily managed for sailors of relentlessly advancing age (which, conveniently, is all of us).

AGE-PROOFING YOUR CRUISING BOAT

A satisfying life makes us eager to get up early in the morning to catch the sunrise, to move on to the next anchorage just to see what's there, to fully appreciate those blessings the Supreme Navigator has vested on us, and to not worry about those she hasn't.

OK, if you have been keeping up, you are now the proud owner of the retirement cruising boat of your dreams, or have made at least a close pass on what you have decided your perfect boat should look like. I can't even guess what type of boat you now have, how much it cost, or how big it is. But if you have taken my advice, it is as small and economical as you find acceptable, it is in good condition, and it is of a type that is suitable to the sort of cruising you are interested in.

If you haven't taken my advice and your new/old boat is something other than envisioned above, that's OK, too. As we have said several times, just about any boat will do the job as long as it is comfortable, seaworthy, and you are happy owning it. But because we are about to offer a broad spectrum of advice for adapting your new acquisition for cruising into retirement, we need to make some equally broad assumptions about the boat you have.

Let's imagine your sailboat or powerboat as having the following qualities:

1. You have bought a boat that is about 35 to 40 feet long on deck, and 34 feet or so on the waterline.
2. It is of rugged fiberglass construction and weighs about 15,000 pounds.
3. Your boat is 20 to 35 years old but has upgraded electronics, and the plumbing and electrical systems are in good condition.
4. If you have a powerboat, it has a single six-cylinder engine of about 125 horsepower. If you have a sailboat, it has a two, three, or four-cylinder engine of about 30 horsepower. In either case, the engine has survived a comprehensive survey and should not need major attention for the next few years
5. The inventory of equipment that was included in the purchase price of your new boat is adequate to get you going. Your dinghy; anchors, rodes, and chains; sails (if needed); docklines and fenders; Coast Guard–required

flares, horn, and PFDs; and other ancillary-but-essential items are in useable condition and will last until we get around to upgrading them in the next few chapters.

If your new/old boat is a lot different than imagined above, don't worry about it. Everything that follows works on just about every boat ever built, so let's get on with adapting this sucker to an average retired couple who aren't that old yet but aren't likely to be getting any younger. Our first consideration, and the most important, is safety.

Essential Safety Upgrades

Safety upgrades are the most important of all the modifications that I am going to recommend for any boat that is being used by elderly (or potentially elderly) folks. Older folks, like me, are more prone to injuries than we used to be. We aren't as resistant to bruises and abrasion because our skin is thinner and our blood is bloodier, our bones are brittle and tend to snap at inconvenient times, our stamina doesn't have the staying power it once did, our eyes and brains are both growing weaker, and on balance our balance doesn't balance like it used to. Although I have no hard data to support it, I believe injuries caused by accidents afloat are responsible for the premature end of more retirement cruises than all the other reasons combined (except just getting too old to continue).

Slips and falls are the most common accidents that befall retirees who live ashore in houses that aren't bouncing around like a sports-bar bull or rocking and rolling like an addle-brained teenager, so it is easy to conjecture that the accident statistics are much worse for those of us who live on boats. With that in mind, let's take a look at a few of the more obvious places that unsafe conditions can lurk, and try to discover ways to fix them. The outside of the boat is the most logical place to begin.

GET A HANDLE ON LIFELINES

A set of lifelines or solid safety rails was probably installed on your boat when you bought it, but unless it was used as a day-charter vessel in U.S. or Canadian waters, the lifelines are almost assuredly inadequate. Lifelines installed to industry standards and compliant with most offshore racing rules are only required to be two feet high, and there is no standard for the weight that a lifeline stanchion must support to be safe. Standards that do exist are on a sliding scale that increases as the boat size increases, which is silly. The boat isn't going to fall against the lifelines and flip into the drink, but you or I might, especially if the lifelines are inadequate. Our size or weight aren't going to change with the size and type of boat we buy, so these rules (like many such rules) make no sense at all.

This is one area where powerboats often have an advantage over sailboats. Many powerboats large enough for liveaboard cruising are built with solid welded safety rails that are often ruggedly installed. Sailboats, especially newer production models, are more likely to be fitted with flimsy lifelines that are little more than a token gesture toward a safety that doesn't exist.

All lifelines and safety rails should be strong enough to support your weight no matter what size of boat you have, so our first job to upgrade our new/old boat is to inspect the existing lifelines. Here's a handy checklist that you can follow, with items listed in a (sort of) logical order:

1. Make sure that all stanchions and pulpit/push-pit bases are installed with heavy backing plates on the inside of the hull. These bases are often hard to get to without tearing up the interior of your boat, but check as many as you can. If you don't find backing plates on the accessible ones, there won't be backing plates on any of them.

   Some boats, particularly those built in the sixties and seventies, have thick, overlapped hull-to-deck joints that are heavy enough to hold lifeline stanchions without backing plates, so, if you have an older, heavily built boat, check with a qualified rigger before planning any changes here.

2. While you are in there checking for backing plates, check for water leaks that indicate a failed seal around the stanchion base, and check the interior nuts on the mounting bolts for signs of corrosion. Red streaks emanating from the bolts are a sure sign of both leakage and corrosion.

3. Now go on deck and check the strength of the stanchions. The easiest way to do this is to grab one by the top and throw your weight against it like a sumo wrestler trying to tip over an opponent. A surprising number will bend quite easily. This grab-it-and-yank-it test can be a bit destructive, but if your stanchions are going to bend under your weight, this is the time to find out about it, not on some dark and stormy night while you are trying to reset an anchor or when you are climbing out of your dinghy after a few drinks ashore and find a sumo wrestler looking down at you. Stanchions, pulpits, and push-pits need to be a minimum of one-inch-thick, heavy-wall-316 stainless tubing no matter what size your boat is, and strong enough to withstand the weight of the heaviest person on board.

4. The bases on vulnerable stanchions, such as the ones on either side of gates and on fore-and-aft railings, should be reinforced with support brackets. Gate stanchions tend to be used as boarding aids and need extra strength to support the weight of people hauling against them as they climb onto the boat.

5. Stanchion height is the next item on our list. Standard top-wire height is 24 inches off the deck, which is fine for racing boats and boats crewed by youngsters, but a two-foot-high stanchion puts the wire right at knee level for a person of average build. That's the perfect height for a tripwire designed to flip any unwary elderly person who falls against it into the drink. The lifelines are 30 inches off the deck on *Vicarious*, which seems to

be just right as a compromise between total safety (unachievable without draconian measures) and a reasonable chance of any overboard adventures being stopped aborning.

Unfortunately, lifelines set to the best height for safety may look out of proportion, and they can interfere with sail handling, thus creating another safety issue. Like many things, lifeline height is subject to the owner's judgment and desires. The trick is to get them as high and as strong as is practical without affecting the safe operation of the rest of the boat. Lifeline strength, however, should not be a compromise, so set the height where you think best, but make sure the stanchions are strong enough to support the most clinically obese member of the crew.

OK, we are finished with the lifelines but now we want to check the pulpit and the push-pit. These are generally strong enough, but not always, so give them the old grab-it-and-yank-it test to check for strength. The height should be (but often isn't) the same as the lifelines. Boatbuilders today are fond of building pulpits and sometimes push-pit railings in two parts to provide a gap for boarding and exiting the boat through the bow or stern. This is a fine idea and allows convenient access when Med-moored or tied bow-on to a dock. But the design is inherently flimsy, and railings made this way need to be built with extra support, which they sometimes aren't.

Pay close attention to the welds that join the sections of stainless tubing. Push-pits and pulpits fabricated by a skilled welder should look like one piece with no visible evidence of a weld except a regular pattern on the bead. The bead on a good weld will look like an aerial shot of the waves washing ashore on a beach. All joints should be uniform and transition smoothly from one section to the next. Welds that show metal puddled during assembly or ones that have pits and craters should be inspected by a professional stainless fabricator. They might be OK, but only an experienced fabricator can tell for sure.

Finally, give the push-pit or pulpit on your boat an extra grab-it-and-yank-it test, just to make sure it will support your weight when you really need it to.

That's it for our preliminary lifeline inspection. The chances are good to excellent that if you have a sailboat, yours didn't pass muster; at least 80 percent of sailboats I have had contact with have substandard lifelines. Assuming yours does, too, your next decision is what to do about it. The job of upgrading lifelines can range from complete renewal of the entire system to simply replacing a few deteriorated components.

Elevating line height from the standard 24 inches can be a bit complicated, but it isn't beyond the capabilities of anyone with average mechanical skills and access to a welding shop. One resourceful lad I know in New Zealand solved the problem of low, flimsy stanchions by cutting of the tops off the existing thin-walled stanchions and inserting a smaller, heavy-wall tube that fit into the inside diameter

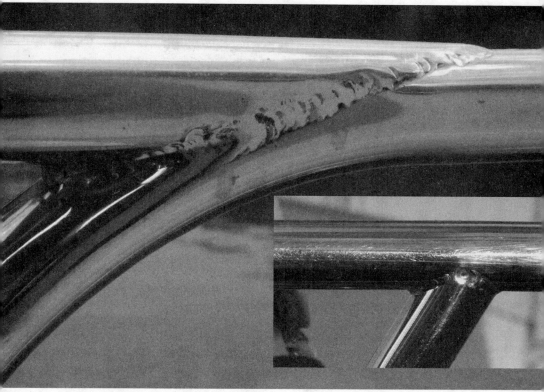

Here is an example of a poorly done weld in a stainless-steel safety rail. Note the pitting and the apparent lack of metal flow and penetration along the lower edge of the seam. This weld is weak and could unexpectedly fail, dumping an unwary crew member overboard. It needs to be redone by a competent welder. Compare the professional weld in the inset to the one above. Notice how the bead is applied evenly with full penetration on both sides. A proper weld in stainless will be stronger than the original material. A poorly done weld on safety equipment, such as handrails, is unacceptable.

of the existing stanchion and ran from the base to the desired height. A welder with a portable MIG machine came aboard and ran a bead around the overlapping joints. Our lad then drilled some holes, reinstalled the original wires, and the job was done in a few days without ever having to remove the stanchions. The stepped stanchions looked super sharp and were strong enough for even the heaviest grab-it-and-yank-it tester.

DECK SLIPS CAN BE DEADLY
Slippery decks undoubtedly cause more than their share of accidents, and the older we get and the more our sense of balance deteriorates, the more the slidey surfaces of our cabintops are a threat to our well-being. Long ago, sailors learned

to mix a handful of beach sand into the paint before laying it onto any surface that was likely to be trod upon. Beach sand still works just as well as it ever did, but unfortunately, it never worked all that well to begin with. We now have dozens of products designed to keep our Topsiders firmly in contact with our topsides, so we can leave the sand on the beach where it keeps the clams happy at high tide and safe from seagulls at low.

Nonskid is usually applied to any area on the top of a boat likely to be stepped upon, and, therefore, it gets a lot of wear. If your new/old boat was built more than a decade ago, it is probably ready to have the anti-slip material replaced, and this is something that you don't want to skimp on or delay. A slippery deck can end your cruising career quicker than a tuna can snap up a squid.

There are three basic types of nonskid material available:

1. Paint additives for nonskid have been around for about as long as deck paint. The plain old beach sand, mentioned above, was probably the first material added to paint to keep you from slip sliding away, but pulverized cork and walnut shells have also been popular over the years (and remain so with traditionalists who have the time to repaint their decks often), as well as ground-up old tires, and even, I am told by a reliable source, certain brands of kitty litter.

   Beach sand is still free, still available for the taking, and still doesn't work very well. Most (probably all) paint companies make proprietary additives from rubber, polymer beads, silica crystal (high-grade beach sand), and who knows what else, all designed to be mixed with deck paint. These additives come in a variety of grits—be careful here as the more aggressive grits can be hard on your bare feet and knees, especially silica—and are mixed with the paint immediately before brushing or spraying it on.

   The commercial additives I have used (Interlux Intergrip and a few others) all worked well and lasted for a few years before they needed to be renewed, which leads me to believe that they all have their good points and will do the job.

2. Deck nonskid appliqué material is not that common, but it deserves passing mention. One of the first was heavy canvas cloth that boatbuilders stuck to walkways and cabintops with paint. In the days of wooden boats, deckhouses and sometimes decks were waterproofed with painted canvas, but the weave was quite fine and filled with paint until the surface was smooth. An additional layer of coarse cloth was sometimes applied over this and stuck down with thinned deck paint so that the weave provided a nonslip surface. I have only seen this done on one boat (my 40-foot powerboat, *Duchess*, built in 1938), so I suspect it was never very popular. I have also heard of (but never seen) fish netting embedded in epoxy and painted over. This approach sounds good, but it would be rough on the knees and feet.

   The only commercial stick-on nonskid material that I know of is Treadmaster, a thick, rubbery material made in England and available with an incised diamond pattern or smooth. It can be glued to the deck, or you can get it with a simple peel-and-stick application. This stuff is very effective and, once stuck, it stays stuck for years. When it finally does come unstuck around the edges, however, it can't be easily re-glued, and (ironically) it's the devil's own job to remove it. Treadmaster is expensive when compared to alternate nonskid treatments, and it is not seen that often on the American side of the Atlantic. Treadmaster will also give your decks an industrial-flooring appearance that works well on replica tugboats, but that's not the look that all boat owners appreciate.

There is one other appliqué nonskid that deserves a quick look: faux teak decking is available from a number of sources and is seen often on new high-end powerboats and expensive sailboats. It is fabulous stuff, even though it doesn't look much like teak (or any other kind of wood) to me, and would be an excellent way to dress up an old boat. It is expensive, and application requires the services of a skilled professional. But what the heck, if you have the bucks, it might be worth a look.

3. Nonskid paints, of which there are a great many on the market, are rapidly taking over from paint additives as the most popular way to give traction to your deck. Proprietary deck paints with nonskid premixed are available from most marine paint companies. They come in many colors, and most are quite easy to apply. My favorite is Kiwi Grip, and I have used this product extensively on my last two boats. Kiwi Grip is a one-part latex paint so that it is water-soluble and needs no mixing, it rolls on easily (a special porous-plastic roller is supplied with each purchase), and it has admirable staying power. The last application on *Sultana* was 10 years old when we sold her and still looked like new. There are many other nonskid premixed deck paints that are equally as good, and perhaps even better, but lack of experience with them precludes comment. (Kiwi Grip is made in New Zealand, but it is available in the United States through Defender Industries and many other marine chandleries.)

Nonskid deck paint is one of the most important safety items on your boat, and it was most likely in a sad state when you moved aboard. Fortunately, worn-out slippery nonskid is as easy to fix as a few rolls of masking tape and a high-nap paint roller can make it, and it is as cheap as a handful of walnut shells or as expensive as your kitty can afford. Do it now, and get it out of the way so we can move on to other important safety concerns, such as keeping a clear deck.

Clear the Decks
Back in Chapter Three of *The Cruising Life,* Second Edition, I related how, when the Trefethen family finally sailed away from Marblehead and into Cape Cod Bay, the deck of *Sultana* looked like the bed of the pickup truck in the *Beverly Hillbillies* TV series. The only thing missing was Granny sitting in a rocking chair on top of the piles of stuff tied to the lifelines and handrails. I went on to relate how, while

The Prout Snowgoose Elite makes a fine cruising boat for those who favor catamarans and have a few extra bucks to spend (suitable ones usually go for over $100,000). This one, however, has so much stuff tied to the decks that it is riding four inches down in the stern. Sailing offshore with the decks so laden with extra gear, supplies, and equipment that it is hard to find a place to step is inefficient, dangerous, and foolish.

approaching Block Island at midnight in a gale, a large sail bag went by the boards and was lost forever. The point was, and still is, we never were able to figure out what was in that bag. It must have been important, or we wouldn't have packed it with such care. Whatever it was, we never missed any of it.

By the time we had crossed the Gulf of Mexico and were in Guatemala waiting for the hurricane season to blow over, we had tossed out or given away most of the other stuff cluttering up the decks, but we had replaced it with a higher grade of junk. We had a sailing rig for the dinghy tied to the cabintop handholds. Sarah, our daughter, had her windsurfer tied to the starboard lifelines; Phillip, our son, had his boogie board strapped to the port side; and Susan and I had our bicycles lashed to the pulpit (where they were sure to get a regular saltwater cleaning). Two large deck boxes were bolted to the deck aft of the cockpit: one for a gasoline generator we never used and the other for spare dock lines. Never mind that our spare lines could secure every boat in the Rio Dulce with enough left over to tie up the Gloucester fishing fleet. A 100-pound Danforth (our storm anchor) was secured in chocks to the foredeck, along with our regular 60-pound Bruce and a 35-pound CQR lunch hook. Even after more than a year of living aboard, the decks of *Sultana* made Jed Clampett's pickup look tidy.

Three years later, when we got to New Zealand, the boogie board, the windsurfer (sorry, kids), the sailing rig, the bicycles, and the storm anchor were gone. It isn't that we didn't want to keep these things, it's just that we gradually realized they took up more room than they were worth. Phillip sold his boogie board to a friend on another boat, the sailing rig was lost with the dinghy when someone failed to secure the painter, the bicycles just rusted away, and I'm not sure what Sarah did with her windsurfer. I would have liked to keep the big Danforth, but the likelihood of tripping over it and breaking an ankle while working sails on the foredeck was a bigger worry than getting caught in a hurricane. The prospect of a broken bone was a lot more scary when sailing hundreds of miles from the nearest medical help. So we gave the big anchor to a grateful fishing-boat captain in Pago Pago.

It wasn't until we left New Zealand for Fiji in 1999 that we had the renovated *Sultana*'s decks cleared of all clutter—almost. The big rollup inflatable dinghy was secured to padeyes on the foredeck, two boat hooks and a fishing rod were lashed in a way that didn't interfere with using the handholds, and four five-gallon jerry cans were lashed to the bulwarks amidships where they were the least likely to be in the way. Other than those few items, the decks were clear, and it was wonderful. Working the decks no longer involved running an obstacle course of irrelevant gear lashed here and there, usually right where your foot wanted to step while tucking in a reef or where your butt needed to sit while freeing a back-winded jib-furling line.

The feeling of liberation from the tyranny of clutter and from the fear of tripping over things stowed where they shouldn't be stowed was palpable, and I resolved to never again sail on a boat with messy decks. Now everything that comes aboard *Vicarious* has to pass the "bloody-thing" test: if we don't know where we are going to put the bloody thing, we don't buy it until we figure it out.

A corollary to the bloody-thing test is the "stupid-thing" test. If we already have the stupid thing and can't find a not-on-deck place to put it, out it goes. Friends thought it a bit odd when we rolled up the elaborate and expensive cockpit enclosure that came with *Vicarious* when we bought her and dragged it to the recycle center. The cover was a work of the canvas-fabricator's art. It had more zippers than Fonzie's jacket and enough hook-and-loop fasteners to outfit a manned lunar lander. But, while the cover was designed to be left installed with the boat under way, it offered too much windage for offshore, and it blocked the view of the sails from the cockpit, forcing the watch to stick his or her head out over the lifelines just to check the windicator. This was dangerous and inconvenient, as we spend a lot of time offshore. This meant the cumbersome cover had to be removed for each passage and stowed, and the only place it would stow was on the pilothouse roof lashed to the handrails. "Unacceptable!" screamed the results of the stupid-thing test, so out it went.

Now, when we need to cover the cockpit while at anchor, which is most of the time, we rig a simple rectangular nylon tarp (not one of those PVC things from Walmart; these work OK but make a rattling noise in the wind, and they have zero class) like a pup tent draped over the mizzen boom and lashed to the stern railings and lifelines. The tarp works just as well as the elaborate cover did, it gives us much more headroom, it can be rigged in a fraction of the time, it stows nicely in a cockpit locker, and it cost a tiny fraction (less than 10 percent) of the old cover. But the best thing is the top of the deckhouse is now free of the flapping bundle of aggravation that got in the way or snagged my harness every time I had to work my way forward in a seaway.

We have found the bloody-thing test essential for everything that comes aboard *Vicarious*. The stupid-thing test works well, too, but I do get a little nervous when Susan looks at me with that analytical eye of hers every time *I* do something stupid.

HOLD ON FOR DEAR LIFE

Handholds are standard equipment on just about any boat you will find, and this is good news for retired cruisers. As we get older, our motor skills—hand-eye coordination, balance, spatial orientation, peripheral vision, hearing, and bladder control—all deteriorate proportionally. We may not like it, but tough luck; the Supreme Navigator has seen fit to gradually diminish our abilities to move about until we have been reduced to the capabilities of infants, at which point we are ready to return to her arms, accompanied, no doubt, by flights of angels blowing trumpets and singing songs of welcome. Most of us have no problem with this, as it is part of the deal we agreed on when we signed on for the voyage of life. There is no way to renege even if we wanted to.

The bad news is, few older boats and even fewer of the newer ones are equipped with handholds adequate for an Olympic gymnast, much less for a tottering old guy who is starting to have trouble tying his own shoes (one reason I stopped wearing the foolish things). Being flung across the cabin by the motion of a boat in heavy seas or the wake of a passing powerboat is among the most common causes of injuries afloat. I don't have the statistics here and am loath to make them up (as I may admit to doing elsewhere in this book), but I am sure head injuries and broken bones caused by falling or being hurled against some unyielding object are in the top 10 of catastrophic disasters to befall cruisers of any age. Older cruisers are just that much more vulnerable.

I fashioned this handhold for Vicarious's *cockpit from a big piece of teak given to me by my brother-in-law (thanks, Bill). It provides a secure holdfast from anywhere in the cockpit as well as a handy way to keep the mizzen halyard and topping lift under control. Normally, I don't tie anything to handholds, but I made this one a double loop just for this purpose.*

Falling accidents are particularly dangerous while offshore, of course, but many cruisers don't realize that they are more likely to happen while inshore or coastal cruising. Offshore cruisers are most often aware of the hazards, and they have more experience with big waves and swells than cruisers who stay in more sheltered waters. They expect to be flung about a bit, so they are ready for it. Inshore cruisers, however, are often caught off guard when some inconsiderate clown in an enormous powerboat comes roaring by from astern throwing a wake that would destabilize an icebreaker.

Handholds and grab-bars are the easiest way to guard against an unscheduled flight across your salon or deckhouse. They are readily available in several materials and in many configurations, and they are ridiculously inexpensive when compared with the costs of a stay in a hospital. Cruisers who enjoy working with wood will find that basic handholds are easy to make and are usually easy to install. (I say usually, because adding them to boats with hull liners can be a challenge, especially if you are reluctant to punch a lot of extra holes in your interior.)

So, how do you determine where you should be putting these additional grabbers? First, get in the habit of always holding on to something as you move around your

One Hip for the Ship

In truth (and we are passionate about honesty here, even when it conflicts with conventional wisdom), it is not possible to always have a grip on a secure boat part. We must carry things fore and aft now and then, and we often need both hands free to do it. We just can't get around it. With our hands full of whatever is being carried, the old cliché, one hand for you and one hand for the ship, doesn't work. If Susan stops to grab a handhold while delivering breakfast to the pilothouse, there goes the soufflé down the cabinhouse steps; if we let go of the leech cringle and grab the granny bar, there goes the reef we were working on as the mainsail tries to flog itself to pieces in the building gale. The answer is the age-old hip-lock.

Developed out of necessity by ancient mariners, the mariner's hip-lock involves jamming some body part, often but not always a hip (thus its official name), into any handy crevice that is close enough and sturdy enough to do the job. A knee stuck into a deck ventilator or a foot jammed under a cleat work well and can keep us just as secure as a handhold.

"One hand for the ship" sounds just right in books, but, once on deck, it often isn't possible. In those times, the careful cruiser will ensure he or she is securely jammed into anything that offers the highest probability of keeping out of the drink and on the boat.

boat. Experienced rock climbers (especially older ones) always keep a three-point grip on the rocks they are climbing. With two hands and a foot or two feet and a hand always locked in place, a careful climber is always secure. Cruisers can do the same, but we usually rely on two feet on the deck and one hand on a grab-bar or other safe attachment.

As soon as you take possession and get comfortable in your new home, start moving about in the manner of the orangutans we enjoyed so much on the *National Geographic* TV specials back before we donated the flatscreen to the Salvation Army. As the friendly orange apes swing through the thickets hand over hand, you do the same moving through your boat. Don't let go with one hand until the other has a firm grip on the next handhold. Do this consistently and at all times (not just when it is rough or you see a sportfisherman approaching), and you will be amazed at how quickly it becomes second nature. You will soon know right where to grab for the next handhold without looking and without thinking about it. You will also quickly discover that there are places on your boat where you reach for a handhold that isn't there, and you end up grabbing the dinette table, the towel rack, or another less-than-sturdy support.

Now you know exactly where you need to add supports, but, before you do that, investigate the possibility of strengthening the things you are grabbing instinctively. That dinette table, for example, should be sturdy enough to support your weight if you grab it on purpose or are flung against it by accident. Test it by giving it the old familiar grab-it-and-yank-it test. If it fails, you can usually make it stronger by adding a heavy backing plate under the floor and through-bolting the base of the table to it.

If the item you are grabbing can't be strengthened—on *Vicarious*, my favorite unauthorized grab-bar was the oven-door handle; Susan's was the paper-towel holder in the galley—you will need to add a proper handhold. As mentioned earlier, the easiest way to do this is with a prefabricated model from the marine store. The ones we use on *Vicarious* are made by Sea Teak, and we have added more than a dozen of them. They are easy to install with simple tools, and they look good when finished to match the rest of our woodwork. If you want a more modern look, handholds can be easily fabricated from stainless-steel tubing by any fabrication shop, or they can be bought pre-made, usually from the same chandlery that sells the teak ones.

So far we have discussed adding handholds to the interior of the boat where the majority of falls happen, but secure grabbers outside on the deck are even more important. The reason I am hypothesizing that more accidents happen inside the boat than outside on deck is the same one we used to argue that inshore waters are more dangerous for falling accidents than offshore. While we are outside

This tiny 18-inch handhold, factory-installed on a 44-foot-long, $300,000+ production boat, is the only one on the exterior of the boat. It is probably better than nothing, but I would be a lot happier with one that ran the full length of the cabintop. It also appears to be held in place by two number-eight self-tapping screws, which may be a worse safety concern than its diminutive size. Whenever possible, handholds should be through-bolted to backing plates.

when under way, we are aware that we are in a dangerous environment, and we are on our guard to stay on our feet and attached to the boat. But down below we tend to be more relaxed, because we are in an environment we perceive as safe and secure. We drop our guard just as an aggressive wake catches the boat on the beam, and away we go.

Most boats are built with grab-rails and handholds on deck and in cockpits that are closer to being adequate than are the ones down below, but most are still lacking. Find out on your boat by going through the same orangutan procedure that you performed inside, and install sturdy grabbers everywhere you think you might need them. But be careful: I have seen many handholds installed on decks where they are a tripping hazard or interfere with winches, block side decks, or otherwise get in the way, sometimes to the extent that they are more dangerous than going without them would be. On *Vicarious*, I usually secure a handhold in position with strong duct tape for a few hours or days before making it permanent. This gives both of us time to get used to having it there and to make sure that it isn't going to be more trouble than it is worth.

One last consideration when deciding where to install extra handholds. It is just as important that any newly added items look good as well as perform a function. When we were installing an extra five-loop handrail in the pilothouse ceiling, Susan pointed out that the three handrails (the two originals and the one addition) might be easier to use if they were installed athwartships rather than in the more conventional fore-and-aft configuration. She was right, as she tends to be, but when we taped them into position for review, it was painfully obvious that they looked weird. We decided to stay with the traditional look, rather than mess with the excellent feng shui that makes our pilothouse such a friendly place.

JACKLINES, TETHERS, AND HARNESSES

Jacklines are well-known to offshore sailors. They are the fore-and-aft lines to which anyone leaving the cockpit of a boat traveling offshore clips his or her harness. Usually a tether, about six feet long with strong carabiner clips at each end, is used to make the connection between harness and jackline. The carabiner slides freely along the jackline, allowing the user to travel the length of the deck while staying attached to the boat.

Most inshore cruisers don't use jacklines. They argue that the boat is usually in sight of land, and a good lifejacket will suffice. Inshore waters are also more populated with boats, so a prompt rescue is likely were anyone to fall overboard. This attitude may be fine for 20-year-old semi-Olympians who are strong swimmers, but anyone over 50 is going to be more susceptible to the shock of cold water and may not have the stamina for a long swim in a life jacket. Also, I am told (by whom I can't remember) that older people are progressively more prone to befuddlement and may not be able to deal with a dunk in the drink with the alacrity of a younger person.

The older we get, the more important security on board becomes. One of the things we can easily do to increase that security is to stay attached to the boat any time we venture on deck while under way. But just staying attached isn't enough, and an inadequate jackline can be more dangerous than just falling overboard.

A proper jackline system has the following essential qualities:

1. All components—the harness, tether, and jackline—must be strong enough to support the weight of the heaviest person aboard times five. There probably isn't any practical way to test this, so just make sure that all parts of the jackline system are super strong.

2. In the old days, tethers had a carabiner at each end, but you often need two hands to open a carabiner to detach it from your harness. The new tethers have a carabiner on the end that attaches to the jackline and a strong snapshackle on the end that attaches to your harness. Snapshackles can be opened with a quick yank on a lanyard, so they are easier to detach in| an emergency. If you have tethers with carabiners on both ends, just replace one of them with a snapshackle, and you will be up to date and ready to go.

3. The carabiner must run freely for the length of the boat. When this is impossible, two tethers should be used so one can be clipped forward of the obstruction before the other is unclipped.

4. The tether should be long enough to allow freedom of movement but short enough to keep the wearer on the boat in the case of a mishap. If the tether allows the wearer to fall overboard and be dragged along beside the boat, he or she might be better off just going for a swim with a life jacket. A boat moving at only two knots or so will create enough force on a body that is being dragged to make recovery difficult, if not impossible.

If you want to experience just how powerful moving water is, throw a bucket attached to a line overboard. But be careful; the first time you do this you will be astonished at how violently the rope can be yanked from your hands with the boat just creeping along at idle speed.

LIFE JACKETS

I won't say a lot about life jackets here because you have already heard it: wear your life jacket . . . wear your life jacket . . . wear your life jacket. You see it and hear it everywhere. It reminds me of my mom nagging me to wear my galoshes to school on a rainy day. She didn't understand that cool guys would rather die of exposure in a snowbank than be seen wearing galoshes. The humiliation would have been unendurable.

Older people need to wear a lifejacket any time there is any chance of ending up in the water. This is especially true while riding in a dinghy. So go out and buy yourself and every member of your crew an inflatable vest-type life jacket. These are comfortable to wear all day, they have a built-in harness to use with your jack lines, and they don't get in the way of most activities on deck. They even look cool, so there is never any reason to not be wearing one.

This lovely Spanish mackerel came aboard in the Gulf Stream about 200 miles from the entrance to the Chesapeake Bay (Spanish mackerel baked in foil with onions, celery, and butter with lots of salt and pepper is delicious). The modern style of self-inflating life jacket with built-in harness is comfortable enough to be worn anytime anyone is outside the pilot house, and the watch person wears his or hers continuously. Note the snapshackle attaching the tether to the harness. The other end terminates with a carabiner that clips onto a 30,000-pound U-bolt.

Inflatable life jackets come in an auto-inflate version (sometimes called the terrorist model because it blows itself up) with an inflation device activated by contact with the water, and a manual version with an inflation device you must activate with a lanyard. Susan has the auto-inflate version because she has a hard time making up her mind, and I have the manual version because I like being in control of my own destiny. The best argument for the automatic-inflating vest is that you will be safe if you are knocked unconscious as you go overboard.

The U.S. Coast Guard has extensive regulations on the number and type of what they like to call personal flotation devices, or PFDs, you must have on your boat. Once you comply with these rules you will be in good shape, so I will add only one more thing here about life jackets: wear your life jacket . . . wear your lifejacket . . . wear your lifejacket . . . .

CODGER-PROOFING THE GALLEY

There will be a full chapter on the retired cruiser's galley later on in this book, but first we should make sure the galley you have is safe, and fix it if it isn't.

The galley is my favorite part of the boat: it's where the food lives and where we keep the beer cold. But the galley can also be a dangerous place. There are often hot liquids that can spill and cause burns, an open flame is a potential disaster in any environment, and anywhere there is electricity in proximity to water is cause for concern. Your galley most likely has sharp things like knives and bottle openers lying around, and, despite your best efforts to eliminate glass, there are probably glass jars and vessels that can break and cause injury. I mean, who would even think of trying to keep the gin supply in a plastic bottle? Some of the noxious liquids that have ended up in *Vicarious*'s liquor locker would melt anything that wasn't made of glass or double-wall Hypalon.

Let's go through these items one at a time to see how we can make the galley the safest place on the boat, as well as the most fun.

Knives

Susan says I am a knife freak, and she may be right. The galley on *Vicarious* has far more sharp things than are required by normal demand. We have a bread knife, a 10-inch chef's knife, a long thin ham slicer, an 8-inch butcher's knife, and three or four paring knives of various sizes. I got rid of the big (and super cool) meat cleaver after nearly chopping off a thumb while splitting a chicken for the grill but remain dedicated to the remains of my collection.

Susan can do all her cooking with a single paring knife, but I function best when I can select just the right knife for the job. Susan is a better cook than I will ever be, so that might tell you something.

No matter how many knives you have, or how few, they should all be kept sharp at all times. Dull knives lying around lead to complacency: if you expect a knife to be dull, you will not be handling it with the same care and respect as you would if

Each knife in the Vicarious *galley is held securely in place by this custom rack that could retain the blades even in a complete rollover (the knives hit the bottom of a cabinet [not visible in the photo]when lifted straight up and must be twisted to be removed). The blades themselves are protected from chance encounters with human flesh by a quarter-inch-thick sheet of tough acrylic plastic, yet the knives remain handy to the cook and are easily removed and replaced.*

you know the knife is sharp. But more important, sharp knives work a whole lot better than dull ones. Unless you are using the knife to spread peanut butter on a cracker, there will be few instances where you will really need a dull one.

Knives must be secured in a dedicated knife rack or drawer so they are kept from shifting about and out of contact with each other. The rack must be convenient enough for the cook to have easy access but be secure enough to prevent the knives from knocking about while under way. The blades of the knives should be protected and covered while they are not in use, both to protect the cook from accidental contact with the knife and to protect the knife from contact with anything that would damage or dull the blade—like the cook.

The Galley Stove

We will talk more about stoves later on, but for now we want to make sure the one you have is as safe as we can make it. Stoves are inherently dangerous, no matter where they are, and the one on your boat has all the potential hazards of the one you had at home with a few extras thrown in. Most cruising boats today have LPG (liquified natural gas) or propane stoves. While this gas is the most popular, it is also among the most dangerous if not stored and used properly. There are other galley-stove fuels you may encounter (we will cover them in Chapter Nine), but we will confine this discussion to LPG.

Of course you will make sure that the flame on your stovetop is a safe distance from any combustibles, you will have a Coast Guard-certified fire extinguisher within grabbing distance, and you will have a proper propane safety shutoff switch within reach of the burner control. But there are a few other things we need to consider.

DON'T GET A GAS OUT OF COOKING

Most boats with LPG systems you buy today will have a propane shutoff solenoid installed near the tanks, in compliance with American Boat and Yacht Council (ABYC) recommendations, but many will not have a shutoff switch convenient to the cooking area, and even more will lack a bilge sniffer to detect escaping gas fumes.

Safe propane management is critically important on any boat but doubly so on boats with older folks aboard. It isn't that we are more forgetful and prone to leaving the oven on after we finish baking the popovers (that's just an ugly rumor started by younger people who are jealous of our accumulated wisdom), but some of us,

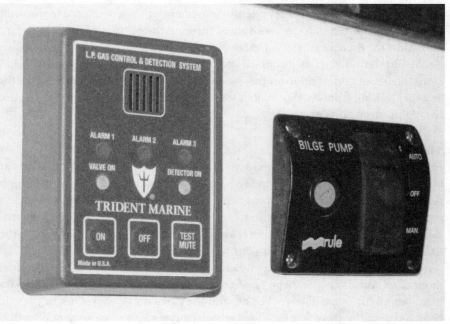

The propane control system on Vicarious *is made by Trident Marine. It was a snap to install, and so far has proven itself reliable. These devices, regardless of the manufacturer, are expensive, and building one would make an interesting project for anyone with moderate electronics skills. Doing it yourself would save at least 80 percent of the end cost. The bilge-pump switch on the right controls the under-sink sump pump.*

like your deaf-as-a-haddock author, can't hear the high-pitched wail of propane (and other) alarms.

This calls for a bright-red light, somewhere adjacent to the stove, that glows anytime the propane shutoff solenoid is activated. And, of course, you will need a switch somewhere close to the light to control the solenoid. While you are at it, make sure you have at least two propane sniffers that activate an alarm and a warning light: one in the bilge and another immediately under the stove.

There are several commercial propane-control panels available (*Vicarious* uses one made by Trident Marine, but there are others) that incorporate a warning light, a loud buzzer, control switches, vapor sniffers, and an automatic shutdown feature that activates anytime a problem is detected.

If you are a do-it-yourself sort who is handy with electrical materials, fabricating a fancy propane control panel makes quite an easy project. All the parts needed are readily available from any online electrical supply, and the money saved can be quite significant.

Buy it or make it; either way, make sure your boat has an effective propane control system with both visual and audible warnings when things go awry.

The next thing to check is the storage area where you keep your propane tanks. ABYC rules dictate that LPG cylinders be stored upright in a dedicated top-opening locker vented to the outside atmosphere through the bottom of the locker. Each tank must have a manual shutoff valve (nearly always a part of the tank itself) and a solenoid shutoff valve as discussed above. We often see cruising boats with LPG cylinders stored on deck or on rail mounts. This works fine; just make sure that any fuel leaking from an externally mounted tank can't find its way into the boat through nearby ports or vents.

STOVETOP GIMBALS

Most marine stoves built today are mounted on gimbals. When the gimbals are unlocked the stove will swing to level when the boat rocks. This feature can be good and it can be bad: good because gimbals can keep the stove level on a rocking boat, allowing the cook to concentrate on things other than keeping the pans from dumping their contents, and bad because, if not used properly and cautiously, they can dump a pot of hot soup onto your feet.

The use of gimbals also depends on your boat and how you have the stove mounted. Gimbals only work on one axis, which would be fine if you had a one-way boat, but all my boats have rocked around the clock on all axes. On our previous boat, *Sultana*, the stove was mounted athwartships, so it swung back and forth on the lateral axis as the bow plunged and rose with the waves. On our present boat, *Vicarious*, the stove is mounted fore-and-aft on the longitudinal axis, so it swings as the boat rolls.

Both these boats are heavy, supremely seaworthy craft, but the difference in stove mountings is profound. On *Sultana* we used the gimbals only seldom as the porpoising of the bow was either insignificant (no gimbals needed) or so severe as to preclude use of the stove at all. On *Vicarious*, however, we use the gimbals most of the time when under way because we are often heeled and, unless motoring in dead calm seas, never on an even keel.

It is rare to have the chance to compare such things as stove mountings in detail, but after using both fore-and-aft and athwartships mountings, Susan and I both prefer the athwartships configuration. Gimbals are tricky and often dangerous to use, so not having to use them often is a big advantage.

When you do use the gimbals, be careful to keep the weight on the stovetop as light as possible and in the center of the stovetop. The more the bottom of the stove outweighs the top of the stove and the closer the pot is to the centerline of the stovetop, the more stable the stove will be.

Sympathetic oscillation is another little-known danger to consider when using the gimbals on your stove. Most musicians know all about sympathetic oscillation (it's what makes guitar strings twang), but if you don't, don't worry about it. Just understand that it can cause your stove to swing on its gimbals much more severely than the rocking of the boat would dictate. And the best way to guard against it is to always have your left hand (for a right-handed person) encased in an oven mitten so that you can dampen and control the swinging any time it becomes excessive.

POT HOLDERS

Those square woven things that your kids made for you back in first grade are wonderful to have in your galley, but that's not what we are talking abut here. We are talking about the funny looking metal arms that reach out from the sides of your stovetop to embrace your pots in an intimate hug and keep them from sliding around and tipping their usually hot contents onto your most sensitive parts.

Akin to gimbals, the pot holders on your marine stove deserve more than passing mention. Pot holders are essential parts of any cruising galley and should be used any time the stove is used while the boat is under way. But, as with the gimbals, there are some problems with the pot holders on most stoves. They usually aren't high enough, for one thing, and there are two sets of them, for another. The higher the pot holders are above the stovetop, the better they work, but the higher they are the more they are in the way. Years ago I saw a set of potholders that were adjustable in height. They were brilliant, but I haven't seen one since.

I raised the height of the pot holders on *Vicarious* by using washers as shims under the supports, but I would be a lot happier if they were a half an inch higher. Someday I will get around to installing metal blocks to get them up to a satisfactory height. Until then, I will just have to limit the height and weight of the pot with which I use them.

Having two sets of pot holders is only a problem if you try to use them together. I am a firm believer in having only one pot going on the stovetop any time we are under way. Cooking on a moving boat is dangerous under the best of conditions;

trying to keep track of two pots at once just makes it worse. Any time the boat is under way and the stovetop is in use, the pot holders should be in use, and the cook, with that off hand encased in a heavy oven mitten, should be there watching the pot. Don't worry about all that "watched-pot-never-boils" nonsense; just don't turn your back on anything being heated on the stove. This is particularly important when the gimbals are unlocked and the stove is allowed to swing.

SAFETY RAIL

Safety rails in front of galley stoves are rarely seen on production boats, and that is a shame. I believe they should be required equipment on any boat equipped with a galley. If your boat doesn't have one, you would do well to get one installed right away.

The safety rail is positioned across the front of the stove, an inch or so above burner level and far enough back from the controls to not interfere with the operation

Every marine galley should have a safety rail in front of the stove to prevent the cook from being thrown onto the stove in a seaway. It also provides him or her with a convenient grab-bar to prevent being thrown backward away from the stove. Note the abbreviated handles on the pots. Cutting a few inches off the handle can make storage a lot easier without compromising the utility of the pot.

of the stove. The safety rail is there to prevent the cook from being thrown against the stove in heavy seas or when the boat is hit by an aggressive wake. It also provides the cook with a handy grab-bar when he or she is thrown backwards away from the stove and isn't wearing the cook-safety strap (see next section).

Safety rails must be as sturdy as any other grab-rail on the boat and able to support the weight of the heaviest crew member without compromise. On *Vicarious*, the safety rail is made from 1-inch, heavy-wall stainless tubing lag-bolted into the cabinet work and has passed the most vigorous grab-it-and-yank-it test we could give it.

COOK-SAFETY STRAP

The cook-safety strap (for want of anything else to call it) is a strap (or, in our case, a rope) that secures the cook within reaching distance of the stove. With it, the cook "straps in" by clipping the strap in back of the waist and leaning back so the strap supports the cook's weight. The strap should be near enough to the stove to allow the cook to lean back against it and work hands-free at a safe distance in anything up to a moderate sea. I'm not a big fan of doing any cooking at all in a heavy sea, but I have to admit we do it occasionally, and, when we do, a sturdy cook strap is invaluable.

Cook-safety straps I have installed are made from double-braid nylon rope with one end spliced to an eyebolt and the other end secured to a snapshackle with a sliding splice to make it adjustable (see photos in sidebar). A cook-safety strap fashioned from a scrap of heavy double-braid looks like a fancy piece of marlinspike seamanship, but it is easy enough for anyone to do. You will need a short piece of heavy double-braid or any other type of braided Dacron—three-strand nylon also works well but is harder on the back and doesn't look as nice—two sturdy padeyes, a snapshackle, and splicing tools. Locate the place you want to attach the cook strap and measure the span or the distance the strap will run. This could be very short, as in the case of *Vicarious* with her compact U-shaped galley, or it could be up to six feet long or so if you have a straight fore-and-aft galley. This type of strap will secure the cook within reach of the stove and keep him or her from being thrown backward, yet it is easy to unsnap so the cook can get away from the stove in an emergency.

I have seen other safety straps that encircle the cook with a belt that then attaches directly to the stove or to the furniture, somewhat like the safety belt used by Glen Campbell when he was a lineman for the county. This might sound like a good idea but there are several arguments against it:

1. Any kind of belt will be cumbersome to put on quickly, which might discourage a cook from using it.
2. A belt might be slow to doff in the case of an emergency. The cook needs to be able to unclip quickly in case of a flare-up or spill and for convenience. Once again, if getting out of the safety strap is cumbersome, it will discourage the cook from using it.

3. The purpose of the cook-safety strap is to prevent the cook from being thrown backward away from the stove, so there is little advantage to supporting the cook being thrown forward. The safety rail (discussed above) should take care of that.
4. It isn't necessary. The safety strap discussed here is strong and dead-simple to make. Why make things more complicated than they have to be?

Find or buy a piece of heavy, double-braid Dacron rope that is triple the length you want your tether to be and at least one-half inch in diameter—the thicker the better. I am as big a fan of recycling as anyone, but I don't recommend using an old bedraggled piece of cast-off rope here. It will look like hell, for one thing, and old double braid is stiff and hard to work with.

Check the sidebar to see how to make your cook strap.

Making an Adjustable Cook-Safety Strap

Determine the minimum length of your cook strap. This would be the length that secures the cook at the minimum distance from the stove. Eighteen inches from the burner is about as close as most cooks would be comfortable, but you want an extra margin of safety so the cook can safely back away from a flare-up or grease fire. This minimum distance will be different for different cooks; that is where the adjustable part comes in:

➤ Measure this minimum distance from the padeye and mark it on the rope.
➤ Make the eye in the eyesplice as small and tidy as you can without restricting the movement of the rope. Be particularly careful not to forget to place the padeye on the rope before you complete the splice. A guy I know did that once. (OK, so he did it three or four times. Who's counting?)
➤ Temporarily securing both padeyes in their predetermined locations before making the final splice will help ensure the proper length.
➤ The open end of the cook strap, the one with the snapshackle, should be on the same side as the cook's dominant hand (on the right side for a right-handed cook, etc.), but don't be pedantic about it.

The cook-safety strap that we use on Vicarious *looks like a fancy bit of complicated rope work, but it is surprisingly easy to make for anyone with basic splicing skills. If you don't have these skills, this is a good time to start learning them. There are dozens of tutorials on YouTube and on the Internet that give clear, step-by-step instructions. The actual techniques vary with the types and brands of rope, so there would be little use in repeating them here anyway. One of the best web sites for splicing instructions is in the Jamestown Distributors how-to section (http://www.jamestowndistributors. com/userportal/how_tos.do), which has detailed instructions for splicing just about any type of rope you are likely to encounter. Jamestown Distributors is also an excellent source of the rope itself if you are in the United States. (Please note: this is a personal endorsement of a company with which I have had many good experiences. I receive no payment or benefit from this endorsement whatsoever. [However, if this fine company were to think it appropriate to make a large cash contribution to the Keep-Vicarious- on-the-Water Sailing Fund . . . . Oh well, probably not.])*

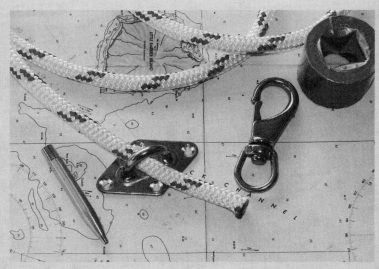

All you need to make a cook-safety strap is a length of Dacron double-braid rope as thick as you can find, two padeyes (one shown), a snapshackle, and splicing tools. (The barrel of a ballpoint pen was pressed into service here when the author forgot to bring his splicing tools to the photo shoot.)

Once you cut the rope to length (see sidebar page 110), remove about half of the strands from the core. The number of core strands will vary with the brand of rope you are using. The rope here is 12-millimeter Yachtmaster XS Braid from New Zealand and has eight core strands, so I removed four of them. The removed strands make handy small stuff, so save them for later. Or, if you are an environmentally insensitive sort, you can just toss them out.

First, splice the rope to one of the padeyes with a tight eyesplice. It is often a good idea to do this first splice before determining the exact length of the safety strap, because splicing techniques can differ, with some using more rope than others. Once you complete the splice, hold the rope in place and mark the minimum length you want your safety strap to be. The ballpoint pen worked OK here because of the missing core strands, but I wouldn't get away with it on unmodified rope.

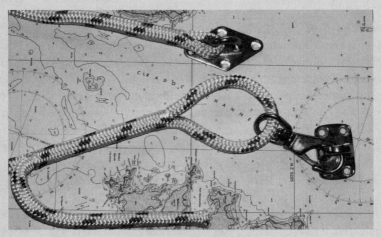

Using a running splice, splice the snap-shackle to the rope at the mark you just made. A running splice is just a regular eyesplice with the tail running out of the rope at about six inches instead of being buried. Sliding this tail in and out of the splice allows the length of the cook strap to be adjusted, yet it will not slip under load.

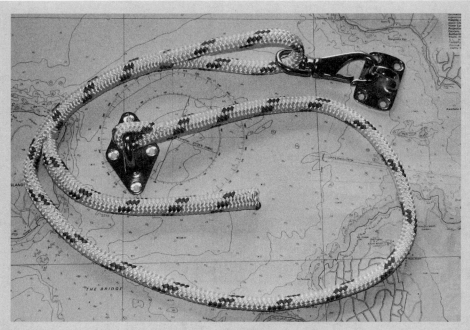

When you are finished, the safety strap should look like this with one end captured in a sturdy padeye and the other secured to a snapshackle with a running splice that lets the rope slide in and out to adjust the length. Bolting the strap in place will finish the job.

The Shocking Story of Electricity on Board

A 120- or 240-volt outlet in the galley comes in handy on many modern boats. And for some of us who use lots of house-style gadgets in our cooking, it is essential to have household current readily available. This is not nearly as difficult or as dangerous as it was in the recent past. The current brands of efficient electronic inverters can deliver usable house current in true sine-wave configuration (the older inverters produced square or modified sine waves that could damage sensitive electronics) without sucking the life out of your batteries. The more sophisticated inverters have cutout circuits that switch to a standby mode any time the inverter is not in use. This means we no longer have to worry about our inverter using valuable battery capacity when it is left on while not being used.

But house current on a boat can still be dangerous, especially in the galley where electrical current and water are in ready proximity. Any moisture will exacerbate the risk of electrical shock, but salt water is about ten times worse than fresh because it conducts electricity that much better. The answer is, of course, a ground-fault circuit interrupter (GFCI), sometimes called a residual current device (RCD). These automatic circuit breakers are required by the American Boat and

Yacht Council (and common sense) to be installed on every high-voltage circuit on your boat, but the one in the galley is the most important.

GFCIs work by breaking the hot (black wire) side of the circuit when any current is detected in the ground (green wire). As you no doubt recall from your basic electricity classes, the ground (green) wire in a household circuit is static and carries no current unless there is a break on the neutral (white) side of the circuit. A GFCI monitors the ground (green) wire, and if even a tiny bit of current is detected, it will instantly open the hot circuit (black wire) and shut down whatever device you have plugged into the outlet.

Without a GFCI on a circuit, many devices (such as an electric eggbeater) will work fine with an internal short until you grab it with a wet hand. Then, if the current sees an easier path to ground through your body it will take it, with shocking results. (Sorry, that's twice for the same clichéd pun.)

There are marine quality GFCIs on the market, but, because they are five to seven times as expensive as the household versions and bear little visual differences, I don't know of anyone who uses them. The only danger to using household GFCIs is rust that can block the spring that opens the circuit when the GFCI trips, in which case the circuit is still hot even after the GFCI has tried to shut it down.

This doesn't happen very often, but you only need it to happen once. Fortunately shocking experiences (help me please, I can't stop) are easy to prevent by frequently using the internal test function of the GFCI, preferably every time you plug anything into the circuit.

Household GFCIs are quite inexpensive, so there is no reason not to have a few spares handy. Then when one fails to test properly, you can quickly replace it with a new one. (Naturally, if you aren't familiar with electrical circuits, you will call in a professional electrician rather than trying to do any house-current wiring yourself.)

A common misconception that boaters have about GFCIs is that they protect against reversed polarity. They don't. Electrical devices that have on/off switches are wired so the electrical current passes through the switch before it gets to the load (the thing that you just plugged in, say that eggbeater again), so when the switch is off, no electricity reaches the device.

Reversed polarity happens when the hot (black) wire and the neutral (white) wire are reversed. Usually wires are crossed at the outlet, but it can also happen at the circuit-breaker panel, or even at your generator or on a shore-power connection. With the hot and neutral wires reversed, your eggbeater will work just fine, but now, with the switch off, the current is going through the eggbeater to get to the switch, making the eggbeater hot any time it is plugged in, not just when the switch is on. This increases the danger of a shock, and it bypasses the protection of the GFCI, so reversed polarity must be guarded against any time household current is aboard your boat.

Your best protection against reversed polarity on a boat is to check the circuit with a polarity tester. These are available from most hardware stores for about $10.

Just plug one of these devices into each outlet on your boat and the array of lights will identify any problems right away. Many newer boats or boats with upgraded electrical systems have a built-in polarity checker on the main panel that will turn off the power to the boat if the wiring is backward. The one on *Vicarious* shows a green indicator light when everything is OK. It is the first thing we check when we are plugged in at a marina and lose power. But these lights only work up to the panel, so reversed polarity at the outlet remains a hazard. To be safe, you still need the separate circuit tester.

Fire! Fire!

Safety regulations and a natural instinct for self-preservation dictate a selection of up-to-date and regularly inspected fire extinguishers on board any vessel used for cruising of any kind. The U.S. Coast Guard, and the coast guard of every other country that has one (a surprising number don't), has specific regulations on fire extinguishers, but this is one area where the statutory requirements fall short. In the United States, any boat longer than 16 feet and shorter than 40 feet is required to have only two fire extinguishers (a 60-footer only needs three). This may be fine on a 16-foot launch, but it is silly on a 40-foot cruising boat. Fire is one of the most horrifying accidents that can happen to a cruiser, and if you have ever seen a fiberglass boat burn, you will know just what I mean. A 40-footer can burn to the waterline in a half an hour.

The retired cruisers need a fire extinguisher within reach anywhere in the boat plus a heat activated automatic extinguisher in the engine compartment. That means a fire extinguisher in the forepeak, one or two in the salon, one in the immediate area of the stove, and one in the cockpit. That is a total of five as a minimum, to my way of thinking. On *Vicarious*, we have seven, and there is no way I feel that is too many.

The Coast Guard designations on fire extinguishers can be confusing to a Phi Beta Kappa member of Mensa International, much less than to normal people like you and me. But don't worry about it. Just make sure yours are Type B, Size I or Size II, and they are current. Size I extinguishers are quite small but are the most popular size for cruising boats. Type II would be a better choice, but they are bulky and difficult to stow where they are handy but not in the way. Type B designates the extinguisher is certified for extinguishing burning fuel or grease and is the only type certified for boats. Type B extinguishers work fine on electrical fires and burning solids so are just right for our use. U.S. fire extinguishers will have an expiration date when they must be replaced. Most can't be refilled so you must toss them and buy new ones.

The majority of boat fires start in the galley, where they are quickly spotted and extinguished, but many others start in the engine compartment, where they can burn long enough to become uncontrollable before anyone realizes there is a fire. Although there is no regulation requiring an extinguisher in the engine compartment, there are reliable automatic ones that you should consider essential gear. *Vicarious* has an automatic Size II extinguisher aimed right at the alternator, where many engine fires start.

Naturally, it does little good to have a fire extinguisher aboard if no one knows how to use it, so all members of the crew should have specific instruction on what to do in case of a fire. Type B, Size I extinguishers are cheap enough that you can buy a few just so each crew member has a chance to operate one. On a calm day on a beach below the tide line with no one around, light up some newspaper and have each crew member extinguish it. This won't mimic an actual emergency in any way, but at least everyone will know how to operate the extinguisher. Repeat the exercise every time an extinguisher reaches its expiration date, just to stay current. The Size I extinguishers you have on your boat are large enough to give two or three crew a go with them before they are empty.

Be sure to dispose of empty or outdated extinguishers in an environmentally considerate and safe manner, of course, and clean up the beach after your test run. In many distant countries with no disposal facilitates, take along a small shovel and bury your trash; just make sure you aren't on a turtle nesting beach before you start digging holes.

Glass on Board

Many experienced cruisers claim that they never allow glass on their boats, no matter what. This sounds like a good idea, but it is practically impossible to achieve, and it really isn't necessary. Glass on board is fine as long as it isn't broken. So rather than expend a lot of effort (and hot air) trying to achieve a glass-free boat, it is easier and makes more sense to make sure the glass you do have on board never breaks.

Broken glass on any boat is a major problem any time it happens. Shards and slivers find their way into every crack and nook on your boat, and it will take forever to track them all down. If glass breaks during a storm or during a knockdown when everything, including the crew, is bouncing around the cabin like a teddy bear caught in a cement mixer, the danger multiplies many times over. When dealing with extreme weather, you are going to have plenty to worry about without having to dodge flying glass, and if a big sliver of beer glass lodges in your toe, you are out of commission right when you need to be at your sharpest.

On *Vicarious* we limit our breakable glass to two heavy wineglasses (we have both tried to tolerate good wine from a plastic glass, but it just can't be done), one two-liter bottle of Sapphire gin, two 750ml bottles of Havana Club dark rum (the real one from Cuba, not the knockoff made in the Bahamas), a bottle of olive oil, and a one-quart Pyrex measuring cup. There are also a few glass jars of condiments (olives and jam and such) that aren't always available in plastic when you are sailing in the wopwops. All these items are secured at all times, and, when we are under way, they are packed so that even if they were to break, the pieces would be contained and not present a danger. The wine glasses are the stemmed type made from the heaviest glass we can find and encased in old socks when we are on the go. The Pyrex measuring cup is practically indestructible, but it gets the same treatment regardless, and the liquor bottles are wrapped in plastic cling wrap and stored in a special heavy fabric bag. In all our years of sailing we have only broken a few glasses, and it was always in the sink while they were being washed and always at anchor.

Mirrors present another danger that should be obvious but, judging by the number we see on boats, isn't. *Vicarious* came with a lovely full-length mirror by the entrance to the forepeak. It was securely mounted with no danger of coming loose, but it was vulnerable to anything flying about the cabin. Experience tells me that when these things break, they don't just crack; they shatter into thousands of needle-like shards. If this happened at sea in a storm, the results would be catastrophic, so, having failed the stupid-thing test, out it went.

EVERYTHING ELSE

A comprehensive safety check is one of the first things you should do after you take possession of your new/old boat. Older folks are prone to falls from slipping and tripping, concussions from bangs on the head, and broken bones from being thrown across a cabin. So be extra diligent in searching out and fixing any condition that looks like it might cause problems. This chapter points out some of the most obvious items and conditions to check, but it is not a comprehensive list. As you become more familiar with your new boat, be alert for any condition that could cause an accident, and fix it before that accident happens. That sounds preachy, I know, but your first responsibility as a captain is to your crew, and an incapacitated captain isn't any use to anyone.

The safer we can make our boats, the longer we will be able to enjoy them. The Supreme Navigator is a patient lady and doesn't mind waiting. And the angels know full well that they will be singing their songs of welcome soon enough. That day will come for all of us, but let's not rush it. The safer we are, the more we can delay the inevitable. In the meantime, I would like to find out if there is any way I can make that trip without those bloody trumpets.

A FEW LABOR-SAVING UPGRADES

. . . as retired cruisers, we should keep our deteriorating motor functions in mind and plan for them lest they sneak up behind us when we least expect it and smack us on the head with the war club of reality.

In this exciting chapter we will investigate some of the ways you can make your new/old boat easier to manage as the years pile up and the vision dims. Your health at the start of your retirement cruise will be fine, and you should be able to manage your boat just as she is. But, as we have pointed out before, the physical abilities of retired persons are destined to change. When you first move aboard, your strength and stamina are likely to show a remarkable increase. We won't be able to wrestle gorillas like we used to, but increased vitality comes naturally when you live aboard a boat. Cruising is a healthful and vigorous way to live, and just getting around the deck, biking or walking to the shopping center, or launching the dinghy can be the equivalent of a moderate workout at the gym. Even the best of us will benefit from the additional exercise and good diet that comes with the cruising package.

But, as wise and forward-thinking retirees, we should provide now for the gradual reduction of our physical capabilities so, when that grim day comes, we are ready for it. With such anticipation in mind, let's look at a few labor-saving devices and techniques that can, by definition, make our retirement cruise less work, less stressful, and correspondingly more enjoyable.

The Outboard-Motor Hoist

One device developed by the rapacious marine industry, in its unremitting search for products we must buy if we are ever to be successful cruisers, is the dinghy outboard-motor hoist: a simple affair consisting of a boom or derrick fitted with pulleys that can help launch or retrieve an outboard motor that is stored on deck or on a bracket fixed to the cockpit railing. Outboard-motor hoists work quite well for their stated purpose (hoisting outboard motors), but they are also useful for hauling aboard all sorts of heavy stuff that our aging muscles would rather not deal with.

Everything that comes aboard *Vicarious*, from cases of beer to groceries to Susan's dog, Nelson, usually makes the trip via the outboard hoist. This cuts down on the physical exertion required for us to load stuff onto the boat, for sure, but even

This simple hoist is designed to help get the outboard motor off the dinghy and onto the mother ship, and it does this very well indeed. But we also use it to load groceries and supplies and nearly anything else that comes aboard when we are at anchor. While preparing for his twice-daily jaunt to the beach, Nelson (Nelson is Susan's hyper-spoiled King Charles spaniel) much prefers the security of the dinghy-motor hoist over the distinct possibility that he will be accidentally dropped overboard when the captain tries to load him into the dinghy by hand.

more important, it reduces the danger of giving a bag of groceries (or Nelson) an unscheduled swimming lesson when it is least appreciated. Transferring anything with even moderate weight from a bouncing dinghy to the deck of a rolling yacht can be tricky even in calm conditions. When the seas are kicking up a bit, it often becomes a feat akin to playing Whac-A-Mole in an earthquake.

The hoist we use on *Vicarious* is made by Forespar (the Nova Lift model) and is rated for lifting 220 pounds dead weight, more than enough to get our little outboard motor aboard without stress or strain.

But a good outboard lifter is not just for hauling aboard outboard motors. *Vicarious's* hoist is essential kit for getting heavy bags of groceries aboard without strain, it is a fast and easy way to free a jammed sheet winch (you know, when the tensioned end of the jib sheet over-wraps the slack end and locks up the whole thing), and it comes in handy when we want to swing the boat perpendicular to the anchor chain, as we do occasionally when we need to get the bow into the wind against a contrary current. (We run a line forward to the anchor chain, let out an extra boat length of chain, then haul it in with the hoist until the bow comes around to where we want it.) It is also Nelson's preferred method of getting into the dinghy for his twice-daily trip to the beach. He developed a paranoid mistrust of being lifted in by hand when I accidentally dropped him overboard—twice.

Another advertised use of an outboard-motor hoist is to get a stricken crew member who has fallen overboard back aboard the mother ship. We haven't tried this, and I am a bit skeptical of how well it would work in an emergency. Perhaps someday when we are someplace where the water is warm and we don't have something more pressing to do, we will give this rather complicated technique a trial run. Until then, we will continue to take every step necessary to ensure that nobody ever falls overboard.

Now for the truth the folks in the boat-show booths don't want you to hear: on many boats an outboard-motor hoist isn't necessary at all. Often a block and tackle at the end of a boom (discussed below) or a halyard used with a gin pole (whisker pole) works as well or even better than a dedicated hoist. Many powerboats, like the venerable Grand Banks, come rigged out with a mast and boom for a steady sail that is a perfect answer to getting heavy items from the dinghy to the deck with little effort.

These hoists are also easy to fabricate, so a clever artisan can often rig one from common materials that is much cheaper, stronger, and more utilitarian than anything you can buy. So before you run out and spend several hundred dollars on a ready-made hoist, think it over and try to come up with a do-it-yourself solution.

Little Dinghies Make Little Work

Selecting the proper dinghy is covered in excruciating detail in Chapter 11 of *The Cruising Life,* Second Edition, so I will gloss over the subject, just to avoid repetition. But there are a few details specific to retired cruisers we need to cover here.

BIG DINGHY VERSUS SMALL DINGHY

A dinghy that is small enough to handle easily but large enough to get the job done is a major challenge for the new retirement cruiser. The utility of a dinghy increases in proportion to its size. Big inflatable dinghies make wonderful diving and swimming platforms; they are comfortable (although usually wet) for long trips of exploration; and in a single mission ashore, they will accommodate enough groceries to provision the boat for a trip lasting for months.

But large, heavy dinghies are cumbersome to handle; they are difficult to get aboard a sailboat and usually need external power to get aboard a cruising powerboat; they are quite expensive; they need a heavy, powerful, and expensive outboard motor to operate efficiently; and if you are planning to visit the Caribbean, they are the number-one target of resourceful and determined thieves.

Small dinghies, on the other hand, are easy to handle, easy to get aboard and stow on deck, still expensive but only a fraction of the cost of a big one, and of little interest (but never immune) to dinghy thieves.

Bigger Isn't Always Better—Not with Dinghies Anyway

When *Sultana* first left Marblehead for our never-completed circumnavigation, we needed a big dinghy with a big outboard engine to make it go. We were a family of four: two adults and two children growing like sunflowers over the septic tank. After weeks of careful research, we chose a 12-foot Zodiac inflatable powered by a 25-horsepower Mercury outboard. That was quite a large dinghy, and rolled up it weighed more than I did.

I selected the big outboard based on my ability to lift the thing off the transom of the dinghy and get it aboard *Sultana* without help from the crew. The motor weighed about 100 pounds, and I could lift it off the ground and over my head with only a few grunts and groans.

Ten years later, when we replaced the now worn-out outboard, I found that I could still manage to lift the thing, but it was no longer easy, and there was no way I could get it over my head. We replaced the 25-horse motor with a 15-horse, because, at 60 pounds, it was the largest outboard I could handle without feeling that important parts of my abdominal zone were going to bust their tethers and head south. We never installed an outboard-motor hoist on *Sultana* because I never felt the need for one.

Now, on *Vicarious*, a boat on which we hope to sail until we can't do it any longer, our dinghy is driven by a propane-powered, 2½-horsepower outboard made by LEHR. This little jewel weighs just 30 pounds, but, even at that weight, I use the outboard hoist most of the time. I only launch it singlehanded when conditions are perfect, which they most often aren't. All other times, Susan and I work together on the hoist to get the little outboard mounted on our little dinghy (see the next section).

DIFFERENT DINGHIES FOR DIFFERENT CRUISING

Your dinghy selection will depend a lot on the type of cruising you plan to do. Cruisers sticking to sheltered waters often tow the dinghy behind the mother ship and can accommodate a larger craft than a coastal or offshore cruiser. In many inland waterways it is common to see a regular skiff, one that is far too large to fit aboard the primary yacht, trailing behind on a long tether. Dinghy dragging is particularly popular in the southeastern United States and in Australia, where aluminum skiffs, called tinnies, are seen being towed behind the popular houseboats on all inland waterways. We spent an eventful week anchored in the lee of Frazier Island (a stunning 184,000-hectare World Heritage site in southern Queensland, Australia) and nearly every private boat we saw was towing the ubiquitous tinny.

Coastal cruisers frequently tow their dinghies also and haul them aboard only when making the occasional offshore passage. This need to get the dinghy aboard limits the size considerably, especially for older cruisers.

You will occasionally see coastal cruisers towing a dinghy far from land, but this is a dangerous practice. A towed dinghy can lower the performance of any boat (in the same way towing a trailer with a car can reduce the gas mileage), and you are in serious danger of losing the dinghy if it ships enough water to create enough drag to endanger the mother ship. The self-bailing feature of most inflatables is nowhere near efficient enough to keep up with the intake of water when the waves start breaking aboard. A swamped dinghy can act just like a sea anchor and stop the mother ship cold.

A flooded dinghy can also lead to unreasonable and unsafe heroics on the part of the skipper and crew when attempting to save the thing. Dinghies are expensive, and most of us are reluctant to cut one free, even when the safety of the mother ship is threatened.

Dinghies used by offshore cruisers tend to be smaller and easier to handle than those used by inshore cruisers. An inflatable, 8- to 10-feet long, powered by a 10- to 15-horsepower motor, is the norm, although larger boats will invariably have larger dinghies. Most offshore cruisers carry the dinghy on deck, so the smaller it is, the less room it takes up, and the less of a nuisance it is when it is time to work the sails or make some emergency trip to the foredeck. Overlarge dinghies lashed to the deck can be a real hazard, and there are many stories of them breaking loose at sea.

THE *VICARIOUS* DINGHY SOLUTION

The solution to the dinghy dilemma is unusual on *Vicarious*. I have long been a fan of two dinghies. The first is a hard dinghy for rowing the dog ashore or exploring within a mile or so of the anchored boat. Rowing is one of the best exercises an older person can get. It provides the upper body equivalent of walking, so alternately rowing and walking two or three times a week offers a full-body fitness program that is fun and easy to follow with no strain or drama.

The solution to the Vicarious *dinghy dilemma is to have two dinghies. The Portland Pudgy (a certified life raft as well as a dinghy, here shown while Susan is giving it a tidy-up) is carried on a reinforced set of davits, where it can be quickly launched. We also carry a small inflatable on the foredeck, where it resides in its storage bag until we need it.*

The hard dinghy we use is called a Portland Pudgy (because it is fat and made in Portland, Maine) and is the only hard dinghy certified as a two-person life raft. We carry our Pudgy on davits, which is normally an offshore no-no. A dinghy on davits is vulnerable to being swamped by a following sea, and, once full of seawater, it will test the strength of the most rugged davits.

I must admit to a bit of apprehension regarding this practice, and, by the time you read this, there is a good chance we have switched to carrying the Pudgy on deck. Our davits are strong, and the dinghy is carried high on the stern, so it would take a monster wave to fill it. But nevertheless, there is a sharp scuba-diver's knife

The second dinghy we carry on Vicarious *is this slick little BoatYak by Saturn Inflatables. It is compact enough for two elderly cruisers and a small dog to handle without expending a lot of muscle power, yet it carries the three of us and a month's worth of groceries without effort. When not in use, it is deflated and strapped to the deck just forward of the deckhouse.*

strapped to the stern rail that I will use to cut the dinghy free if the need ever arises. My anxiety is somewhat mollified by the fact our previous boat, *Sultana*, used this same system and carried her dinghy on davits for 20 years, covering more than 24,000 offshore miles through some of the roughest weather imaginable, and we never had a problem. That, of course, is complacency, and complacency on a cruising boat is just shy of ignorance on the danger scale.

Our second dinghy on *Vicarious* is a small, narrow inflatable, made by Saturn Inflatables, called a BoatYak. At 10 feet long it moves well throughout the water with the little 2½ horsepower propane outboard, yet it will accommodate two elderly cruisers, a small dog, a week's supply of groceries, and a case or two of inspirational liquids. It also rows well for an inflatable.

We have taken the little BoatYak on exploratory trips of up to 10 miles or so without incident, and I wouldn't hesitate to go much farther when the conditions were just right.

OARS! DON'T FORGET YOURS

There is a distressing tendency of cruisers using inflatable dinghies to depend entirely on an outboard for propulsion. This may be because the rowing ability of most inflatables ranges between ridiculous and impossible. The soft-bottom ones are close to impossible to row, and the hard-bottom ones are only difficult. Nevertheless, a functional pair of oars or at least a canoe paddle should always accompany any outboard-powered dinghy.

Selecting a dinghy for your cruising retirement is a personal predicament you must sort out on your own. Just keep in mind this maxim: the bigger the dinghy, the more useful it will be, but the smaller it is, the easier it will be to manage.

Anchors Aweigh

Anchoring in remote places with a few friendly neighbors or even in solitude is one of the joys of the retired cruising life. But to do it safely, you need good ground tackle. The dilemma here is the same as for dinghies but with more profound implications if you get it wrong. The bigger the anchor, the better it works but the more difficult it is to handle, deploy, retrieve, and stow.

Most cruising boats carry at least three anchors: a primary anchor located on a bow roller, a storm anchor often stowed below decks but accessible in an emergency, and a lunch hook for short stops in protected harbors. Many experienced cruisers also carry a kedge anchor to use whenever a third anchor is needed and the storm anchor is too big and heavy to deploy easily. The kedge is used to prevent the boat from drifting into a contrary current or to stabilize a position in a crowded anchorage where swinging room can be tight or nonexistent. Deploying the primary anchor and the lunch hook off the bow and the kedge off the stern is a proven way to immobilize a boat in a specific position.

A favorite trick we use on *Vicarious* is to anchor as close to a beach as is safe using our primary anchor and the lunch hook deployed in a V from the bow, then run the kedge to the beach and use it to haul the stern in until we can easily swim ashore. This same technique is used for careening the boat and for keeping the bow into a swell in a rolly anchorage.

Anchor manufacturers all have charts that dictate which size anchor is appropriate for each size of boat. Sometimes these charts go by boat displacement, but more often they list boats by length. Whichever you choose, your primary anchor should be at least one size larger than recommended, with the correct chain, of course. Your storm anchor should be as large as you can stow without it being in the way. You won't need this super-sized anchor often, but when you do need it you will need it a lot, and you won't need a small one. Your lunch hook can be any size you are comfortable with. You should never use it as an overnight anchor nor should you leave a boat with only the lunch hook out. Since you will be aboard or at least nearby any time your boat is swinging on the lunch hook, it doesn't much matter what size you have, just so it holds in calm conditions and is easy to deploy and retrieve.

The type of anchors you choose is a personal decision. The newer designs, such as the Spade, Manson, and Delta, all seem to offer significant improvements in holding and reliability over the venerable CQR and even the newer Bruce designs. But study the literature, visit the online forums, and talk to experienced cruisers. Then make your selection based on where you are going and what you will be doing when you get there.

A Big Anchor Windlass

The key to handling big anchors for an older person is a big anchor windlass. When *Sultana* crossed the Pacific she carried a lovely old solid-bronze manual windlass on her bow. The crew spent dozens of hours cranking in anchor chain three links at a time and never complained even once. Even so, after the refit we sailed away with a brand-new electric windlass gleaming in the tropical sun just aft of the bowsprit.

Older cruisers, like those over 25, are sure to appreciate the advantages of a powerful electric windlass when it is time to haul several hundred pounds of iron back aboard, but that gob of chrome on the bow does more than make retrieving the ground tackle easier. A big winch allows the use of a larger anchor and chain than you would use when manual retrieval was the norm. And that oversized anchor means that, when the wind rises in the middle of the night, you can just roll over and go back to sleep secure in the knowledge your hook is going to stay hooked no matter what the wind does.

The larger the windlass and the heavier the anchor, the less strain using it will place on the captain's guilty conscience. I used to feel terrible when sending Susan forward during a storm in the middle of the night to add scope to the anchor chain. Now I can sleep on, secure in the knowledge that she has our trusty electric windlass to help her, and she can do it quietly without waking me from my rest. Then, when she is finished her nocturnal re-anchoring, she can shed her wet foulies and get back into her bunk without my having been aware of what she has been about. But, alas, the dream usually ends long before it should, and the reality has me, not she, letting out chain at three in the morning with the drumming rain drowning the sound of the chain rattling through the hawsepipe. The windlass makes short work of a difficult job, and when the breaking dawn reveals the storm abated with *Vicarious* unmoved from her intended position, I can count on a hero's breakfast of pancakes with extra syrup delivered in a grand and timely fashion.

The ground tackle on *Vicarious* consists of a 60-pound Spade primary anchor on 300 feet of ⅜-inch high-tensile chain, a Fortress FX-37 storm anchor on 300 feet of ¾-inch nylon rode and 30 feet of ⅜-inch chain, and a Fortress FX-17 lunch hook on 200 feet of ⁹⁄₁₆-inch rode and 20 feet of ⁵⁄₁₆-inch chain. All this is handled by an oversized windlass with a chain gypsy and a capstan for the rope. We also carry a 35-pound Northill. The Northill has an interesting history (it was developed for Catalina flying boats in World War II) and is popular among fishermen in Maine and in the Pacific Northwest, where anchoring on a rock bottom is the norm. We call the old Northill our extra-backup-spare anchor. We seldom use it, but like the flare gun and the bottle in the bilge with the washed-off label, it is reassuring to know it is there.

Windlasses, no matter what the size, are electrical machines and as such are subject to malfunction. And, while most popular brands are as reliable as such things can get, they can break. When they do, you will need an alternate source of muscle to get all that heavy and expensive hardware back aboard. Most electrical winches made today have a manual override you can use when caught with a dead battery or some other electrical mishap.

I have used *Vicarious*'s windlass to manually retrieve the primary anchor on three occasions. The first involved cranking in all 300 feet of chain, and it took me over an hour to get it all aboard. This compares to about a half hour to do the same job on *Sultana*, so either the old windless was a lot more powerful than the new one or the old anchor cranker (me) is a lot less powerful and needs many more breaks than before.

There is one more alternate method of getting your recalcitrant ground grabber back on deck, which also provides us with a handy lead-in to our next topic, which is:

Big Sheet Winches

Powerboaters across the land can be heard flipping the page to the next section as soon as the term sheet winches pops up. But forbear, kind powerboater, from your frivolous forward-flipping folly, for the subject of *sheet winches* is every bit as germane to you as it is to sailboaters, even though you may be somewhat lacking in sheets (the kind used for trimming sails, not the kind used for sleeping on and [tragically less often] for frolicking about on while at anchor).

Sheet winches, for the uninformed, are the cranky things strategically placed on both sides of the cockpit on most every sailboat built since the 1950s. They are used for adjusting the foresails. There is usually another winch for handling the mainsheet and often halyard winches on the mast for hoisting sails.

But sheet winches can be used for other things, even retrieving an anchor when the main anchor winch decides to take an unannounced vacation day. This is why powerboaters should be paying attention.

Sailboats come ready equipped with at least two winches in the cockpit and sometimes, on more sophisticated sailing boats, four or even more. But winches are expensive, and boatbuilders are as loath as the rest of us to spend money if there is any way they can keep it in their pockets. Thus many winches are not quite as large as they should be, and one of the most elderly-friendly upgrades you can make is to switch your primary winches to a larger size.

On powerboats, the ideal stern winch is a second anchor winch equipped with the same gypsy and capstan you have on your bow winch, but this would be expensive overkill. The number of times you will use this winch does not justify the expense and added strain on your electrical system such an installation entails. A large, manually cranked sailboat winch will do just as well.   *(Continued)*

Upgrading Winches

Susan and I bought *Vicarious* with the understanding she would be modified to accommodate two elderly sailors who had a keen sense of adventure and romance but who didn't want to work too hard to achieve it.

On our first few outings in our new boat we found sail handling could be a bit of a chore when the breeze picked up. The winches that came with the boat were Harken 36 self-tailers, which are excellent winches but a bit small for our purposes. Getting the headsails flat required a lot of effort on my part, and Susan couldn't do it at all without risking a pulled ligament or a painful case of winch-handle elbow.

The answer was to install bigger primary winches and move the old winches to the main mast for oversized halyard winches. This is one of the easiest and most obvious ways to make a sailboat elderly-friendly, so here is a detailed rundown on how we did it.

Good winches are expensive. Come to think of it, so are bad ones. But we were lucky to find a set of used Lewmar 52 two-speed self-tailers that had been removed from a Swan 57 whose wealthy owner was upgrading all his winches to electrics. After making sure these over-large winches would fit on *Vicarious*'s molded winch bases, we bought them for less than half what a new set would have cost.

As you can see from the photo, the new winches were a tight fit, but they would mean a substantial increase in mechanical advantage and a big reduction in the requirement for the application of scarce elderly muscle power. *(Continued)*

The Harken 36 self-tailing winches (on the left) that came with Vicarious *were pathetically small for a 17-ton boat. We replaced them with a set of Lewmar 52s that we bought used from the owner of a Swan 57 who was upgrading to all-electric winches. The Lewmars are much larger than necessary, but the extra power is useful for all sorts of miscellaneous chores from acting as a backup to the anchor winch to kedging off of a mud bank when we venture into areas where we should have known not to go.*

Our new/old boat had gone through three previous owners, each of whom had installed a new set of winches. Each had simply drilled a new set of holes in the winch bases, slathered on some sort of sealant, and bolted them down. Consequently, we had three sets of bolt holes to contend with and three layers of different types of bedding, the last being a thick layer of good old silicone bathtub caulk.

The first step was to get rid of the old bedding compound. A scraper followed by a pad sander with 60-grit paper made short work of it. We had to remove every trace of the old sealant before we could guarantee the new stuff would stick. Silicone is especially hard to remove, and a thorough sanding was the only way to make sure we had it all.

Once the surface of the winch base was clean, backing plates were made from ¼-inch Starboard. These backers fit inside the lockers under the winches. They wouldn't add much strength, but they would keep the new filler from running out the bottom of the old holes and make a tidy base for the nuts and washers when we installed the new bolts.

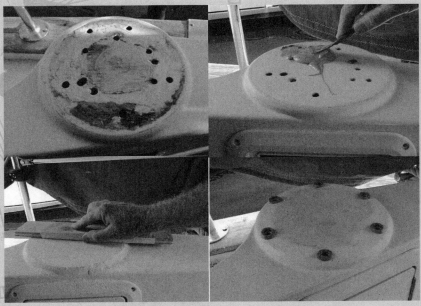

The three previous owners of Vicarious *had each installed a new set of sheet winches. In each case, a new set of bolt holes was drilled and the new winches bolted on and sealed with various types of bedding compound, the last being a thick layer of good old bathtub silicone (top left photo). The old sealant was removed and the base sanded flat (top right photo). Then the old holes were filled and the filler sanded flush (bottom left photo). The holes for the new winches were drilled and sealed with a simple donut of butyl tape.*

The holes were filled with an epoxy and microballoon filler and the base sanded flat. A slight crown (just a fraction of a millimeter) was left in the center of the base to ensure water wouldn't pool under the new winch. Lewmar winches have recessed centers on the bottoms. If your winches are dead flat, make sure the base is dead flat also, and forget about the crown.

When the base was ready, the bolt holes in the backing plate were drilled out. Then the backing plate was used as a template for drilling the holes for the bolts in the base. If you try this procedure, resist the temptation to drill directly through the holes in the base of the winch. There won't be enough room for the drill, the winch gears will get clogged with swarf, and you will risk damaging some very expensive equipment.

There was no reason to use any kind of bedding compound for mounting our new winches, especially not silicone and, even more especially, not 3M 5200 (a diabolical material tragically popular with DIY boat mechanics). Instead, a simple donut of butyl caulking compound was used. This will be plenty to keep water from seeping through the bolt holes. Anyone having to remove the winches for service in the future will thank us profusely for our consideration in using butyl tape instead of bedding compound, especially if that person is us.

Here we are all ready to go with a new, super-powerful winch. Now Susan won't have to interrupt my nap every time she wants to trim the headsails.

Older boats may still have single-action, non-self-tailing winches. And while these worked well enough when we were young and strong, the newer double-action, self-tailing winches are much kinder to elderly folks and should be the only type considered.

Come Along with Me

A come-along (more properly called a handy billy) is any device for lifting, pulling, sliding, or hoisting a heavy object using mechanical advantage provided by gears, pulleys, ratchets, or any similar force-multiplying device. The familiar preventer on a sailboat (the system of lines and pulleys attached to the boom when running downwind, which is used to prevent an accident jibe) is a type of come-along convenient for other jobs where lifting heavy loads is necessary. When the outboard hoist (discussed above) is overloaded, for example, or is at the wrong end of the boat, the come-along/preventer can be used on the end of the boom to get a heavy object, like a dinghy, aboard with minimum muscle strain.

Tie-down straps with a ratchet for tension are another form of come-along useful on a boat. On *Vicarious*, two of these straps doubly secure the hard dinghy on the davits when headed off shore. The ratchets are available in stainless steel, in various sizes, and are just the ticket for securing anything to the deck when you must know it isn't going to move until you want it to move. Two more of these tie-down straps clipped to pad eyes installed just for that purpose secure our small inflatable just forward of the cabin where it is almost out of the way.

The outboard-motor hoist is our first resort for freeing a jammed primary winch (as discussed above), but I know from past experience a tie-down strap will work just as well. All you need is a secure attachment to the boat on the static end of the strap—on *Vicarious*, one of the pulpit stanchions would work—and a line secured to the dynamic end of the strap with a sheet bend, then to the sheet with a rolling hitch. Ratcheting in the strap will haul in the jib sheet enough to clear the jammed winch without the need to head up and lose way.

HALYARD AND SHEET PULLEYS

In days of yore, which for some of us wasn't that long ago, sailors didn't use winches. They used pulleys, block-and-tackles, and brute strength to pull ropes that moved sails and other weighty objects that were happy to stay right where they were. In our elderliness, we may come up a bit short on brute strength, but the old-fashioned block-and-tackle is still a useful labor saver.

We really covered this subject in the above section cleverly titled "Come Along with Me," because a come-along in my somewhat fractured definition can be a system of pulleys. But here we will discuss the use of just a single pulley to assist in handling sails. If your winches happen to be too small, as they usually are, and you don't want to go through the considerable trouble and expense of upgrading them, a simple single-purchase pulley attached to the clew of the jib, through which the jib sheet is rove before being returned and attached to the toe-rail or bulwarks, will do the job. This simple arrangement reduces the force needed to sheet in the genoa by 50 percent. Naturally you will have twice as much jib sheet to retrieve, but that is often a fair tradeoff.

The same system can be used on the mainsail halyard. Just shackle your single-purchase block to the headboard of the sail and secure the bitter end of the halyard to the masthead. Once again we have half the effort required to raise the sail as we did before we installed the block but with twice as much halyard to retrieve. Going aloft in the boson's chair is twice as easy when using a pulley on the halyard, but it will take twice as much rope to get you there.

An easy way to cut in half the effort needed to raise the mainsail is to shackle the halyard to the masthead, then lead it through a single-purchase block attached to the sail before reeving it through the masthead sheave. It will now require half the effort to raise the sail, but you will need a halyard that is one-third longer to do it.

Generators and Water Makers

Somewhere between the Southern Ocean and Niue I picked up the reputation as being opposed to water makers and generators on cruising boats. I did say, in *The Cruising Life*, Second Edition, that they weren't necessary to enjoying a successful cruise.

Generators and water makers are two examples of consumer products that have been successfully promoted by the marine industry to the extent many cruisers are convinced they can't leave the dock for an anchorage without them. But, unless you are cruising on a large powerboat with full air-conditioning and a megawatt entertainment center, neither a generator nor a water maker is necessary, and, once again, may not be worth the time and trouble it takes to own one.

My attitude on this contentious subject has softened a bit as I get older, and *Vicarious* has both a water maker and a generator. Both were expertly installed by the previous owner, so we have kept them against the day we need them. So far, after a bit more than two years of living aboard, we have used the water maker only once, just to see if it worked. Our water needs are met by generous tankage and an efficient rain catcher. This reinforces my feeling that water makers are superfluous frivolities that we can do without.

As I get older, however, and think of those ports to which we are destined where potable water is scarce, of poor quality, and expensive, places such as the Galapagos

At least 75 percent of the fresh water used on Vicarious *comes aboard via this rain catcher that we deploy any time we are at anchor. Rainwater is free, and, because the rain catcher drains straight into the forward water tank, it doesn't take any effort on the part of captain and crew to load the water aboard.*

Islands and many of the smaller atolls of the South Pacific, I have wavered a bit. I have fond memories of filling our tanks on *Sultana* with marginal water from jerry cans schlepped across a crowded harbor in the dinghy. It would take about five trips to get 100 gallons aboard, but we didn't have to do it that often, and I had two teenagers to help out. On several occasions we paid a local boat, usually a cohort of the port captain, to transfer the water for us, but the cans still had to be manually loaded on deck, and the water was still of suspicious quality.

A full jerry can weighs about 40 pounds, and hauling four of them aboard five times is a workout even for a still-full-of-vitality older person like me (I'm still full, for sure, but the container seems to have shrunk a bit). Thus the water maker is standing by for those occasions looming from the murk of the near future where its full utility will be appreciated. By the time we get back to New Zealand, I may have become a full convert to the joys of manufactured water; we'll see.

The generator in *Vicarious* is a Next Generation 3.5-kilowatt model installed in the engine compartment inside a sound shield. It is a brilliant design that runs so quietly we need to look at the gauges to see if it is operating. We use it often to charge the batteries while at anchor and to operate my power-hungry popup toaster in the morning. It is cheaper and quieter to run than the auxiliary motor and not nearly as disruptive. And it is quiet, like many of the new small diesel generators, so running it in a crowded anchorage doesn't bother even the most cantankerous of neighbors.

But generators, even well-designed ones, are a lot of work. They need the same level of care that is lavished on the main engine, with regular oil and filter changes, and they do break down once in a while. In two years I have had to replace the raw-water-pump impeller three times and the condenser once, which isn't that bad, but it is still an effort that adds to the already heavy workload.

The most serious fault was when the thing wouldn't start at all. I had to troubleshoot the entire system only to find the starter and the motor block had both been painted before assembly. The paint acted as an insulator and prevented the flow of electricity through the motor casing to ground. When the thing was still new, the starter current grounded through the ring-gear teeth and pinion drive. After a year or so of moderate use, the ring gear became just a bit worn and rusty, which cut off the flow of electricity to ground, preventing the starter from doing its job. After several days and about 10 hours spent in the hot and cramped engine compartment, I got it going again, and it has run fine ever since. But I can't help but think that those 10 hours might have been better spent doing research in the forepeak (our code for taking a nap), fishing for dinner, or perhaps writing a few clever words for this book.

When the high cost of purchasing and installing a generator is considered along with the amount of work it takes to keep it going, I remain convinced that generators aren't worth the trouble. Running the engine is a pain in the butt, uses more fuel than a generator, and increases the wear and tear on the main engine. Even so, the $7,000 to $10,000 price tag for a full generator installation will buy a lot of diesel fuel. Or better yet, that amount will buy an impressive solar array and a big wind generator, which together can cut your engine-running time by anywhere from 50 to 90 percent.

Climbing the Mast

Powerboaters, who are notoriously deficient in masts, and coastal cruisers in sailboats who are seldom out of range of a competent rigger can safely skip this section, but why not read it anyway? The following paragraphs are full of sound advice that may be irrelevant to your needs, but they are also replete with witticisms, sagacity, and clever verbiage that might put a smile on your face. It may also reaffirm the wisdom of your decision to buy a motorboat that doesn't have a mast to climb instead of a sailboat that does.

Up the Stick

The first time I was faced with the immediate need to get up the mast in a hurry was during a transit of the Cape Cod Canal in my little 21-foot center-boarder, *Aquarius*. My cousin Steve and I were returning from a two-week sojourn from Ipswich, Massachusetts, to Menemsha Pond on Martha's Vineyard. We had departed Menemsha Bight early on the previous morning to ride the flood tide through Quicks Hole, up Buzzards Bay, and through the canal before the current turned against us. Timing was critical for this trip, as the tide through the canal can run at more than four knots making any thought of going against the flow at our top motoring speed of five knots, untenable. The transit went off just as planned, and we stopped for the night at the Sandwich Boat Basin at the east end of the canal.

We weren't in any great hurry to get going the following morning, as the next leg of the trip was a long one for a 21-footer. We were going to try for a straight shot from the mouth of the canal to Gloucester Harbor on Cape Ann, a distance of about 50 nautical miles. With a short waterline, contrary currents, and light winds forecast, we figured on about 12 hours for a trip that would be our first offshore overnight experience. By departing the eastern entrance of the canal in the afternoon, we planned to arrive at Gloucester Light by about dawn the following day.

A late departure would also allow us a generous margin for error should our trip take longer than planned (it ended up taking over 24 hours, but that is a different story), so, after a hearty evening meal of peanut-butter-and-jelly sandwiches (our mainstay for the trip), we motored out of the harbor into the canal. We hoisted the main just in time to catch a broadside from a southwesterly gale with winds of about 40 knots.

The initial gust knocked our little craft sideways like a cat swatting a fresh-caught mouse and sent us barreling toward the granite blocks lining the north rim of the canal. I immediately let go the mainsheet, more by instinct than by any

Climbing the mast is one of the important tasks that an elderly person cruising long distances in a sailboat should be able to perform with relative ease and comfort. Getting to the top of the sticks quickly and efficiently is necessary for lots of reasons, some of which reflect on the safety of the boat and others on the need for routine maintenance. Mast work will be expensive if you can't get up there yourself and must resort to paying a mechanic to do it for you.

When scrambling up the spars is necessary in an emergency, it is unlikely that there will be anyone around to call on anyway, and, besides, we all know that the only way to get it just the way you want it the first time is to do it yourself.

Getting up there isn't easy and will require some practice, mechanical assistance, and a degree of physical agility, so let's take a look at this most important function and see how it fits into our elderly cruising lifestyle.

After we bought our second boat, a sleek and fast Hunter 23, we learned to use

innate sailing ability, but, as the sail flogged violently, we continued drifting sideways toward the rocks at breakneck speed.

In my haste to get under way I had neglected to drop the centerboard, and, without lateral resistance to keep us on track, we were headed full-speed for disaster. As I fought to change course with the tiller, Steve jumped to the mast and let go the halyard, dropping the main just in time to arrest sideways drift enough to give our little Seagull outboard enough authority to keep us off the rocks.

It was a close call, as the boulders on the canal walls bristle with sharp corners that would have made short work of our thin fiberglass hull. It was over in a matter of seconds, and we were both shaking badly as we motored out of the canal entrance.

Once clear of the canal and out of the traffic lanes, we gathered the collapsed main and prepared to continue our journey north. It was then that we noticed that the mainsail halyard had freed itself from the constraint of the masthead sheave and was trailing lackadaisically behind the boat like the overlong tail of a drifting kite. After hauling the errant line aboard and only a brief consultation with Steve, I clamped the bitter end of the halyard in my teeth and went hand-over-hand up the jib halyard to the masthead, where I rove the line back through the sheave, this time with a proper stopper knot to prevent a recurrence of our drama.

So, what's so hard about that? You might well ask, and the answer is: nothing really. But it does serve to illustrate the easier end of the spectrum of mast-climbing techniques. This dramatic tale of heroic derring-do occurred when I was not quite 30 years old and in excellent physical shape, plus the mast was barely 25 feet tall. Then I could knock off 100 chin-ups without breathing hard; now, if I tried to do 10 of them, I would probably never breathe again (OK, make it five then). The difference in time and scale is vast, so we must discover alternative ways of mast ascension if we are to cruise into our sunset years with panache and safety.

a do-it-yourself bosun's chair made from a scrap board and a worn-out dock line. It was crude to the point of being primitive, uncomfortable, and dangerous, but it served us well over the years. After several practice sessions, Susan became adept at cranking me to the masthead with the jib winch every time the anchor light went out or when any other excuse presented itself for going aloft.

The homemade bosun's chair worked just fine for many years but then, some 20 years later, we found ourselves aboard the 40-foot wood ketch, *Sultana,* on an *adventure-of-a-lifetime trip around the world* with our two children, Sarah and Phillip. It was time to upgrade our plank-and-hemp contraption to something more in keeping with my desired world-cruiser image. I found just what I needed at the West Marine store in Danvers, Massachusetts. It was a blue-canvas beauty with padded seat, safety straps everywhere, and heavy stainless-steel hardware that sparkled in the Caribbean sun as Susan cranked me high into the sky. Then one dark-and-stormy night (really) while trying to reef the main amid booming thunder and lightning crackling all around us, the halyard fouled the port lower shroud and was securely jammed. With no way to get up the mast with the new bosun's chair in the middle of the night in rough seas, we were forced to continue the trip to San Pedro under jib and jigger with the half-hoisted mainsail flapping merrily out of control as if it were laughing at us.

This near-disaster precipitated an extended discussion of emergency mast-climbing. After inspecting several boats fitted with permanent means of ascending to the windicator, we decided that either mast steps or ratlines were the way to go. I initially favored the ratlines, as the salty look would be super cool on our traditional old ketch. Ratlines would have also been inexpensive to install. I could make them up out of standard and available materials (wood and rope), and they were an effective way of getting quickly aloft. The downside of ratlines, for all their traditional appeal, was the prodigious amount of work it would have taken to rig them (lots of splicing) and the windage they added to the rigging. *Sultana* was already overstocked with parasitic wind resistance, and I didn't have the spare two weeks that I figured it would take to fabricate and install them.

That left us with mast steps, and, as soon as we got to Guatemala, we ordered a complete set of non-folding steps for both the mainmast and the mizzen.

In the two years that it took us to wend our way down the coast of Central America and across the Pacific to New Zealand, the mast steps worked OK, but there were a few problems. The reputation that the fixed steps have for fouling lines was quickly verified. We actually ended up removing the uppermost steps from the mizzen mast after just a few weeks because of their tendency to constantly tangle the halyard and topping lift. The steps on the main mast worked a little better than the ones on the mizzen, but they, too, would foul regularly.

During the refit, *Sultana*'s mast steps were removed, and we reverted to the blue bosun's chair that had served us so well before our decision to go with a permanent solution to the getting-up-the-sticks dilemma. As it turned out, the emergency

After experimenting with every sort of mast-climbing system conceivable, we settled on the Top Climber from ATN, Inc. This clever device allows one to ascend to the masthead without assistance. Plus, once you are up there, it allows hands-free operation with total security, definitely a recommended item for retired cruisers with sailboats.

situation in the nighttime thunderstorm off the coast of Mexico was the only event of the kind for the entire three-year trip, except, of course, for the many times that we were forced aloft to clear lines that had fouled the mast steps.

Now flash forward 20 years to the other side of the world in New Bern, North Carolina. Susan and I had just purchased the 37-foot ketch *Vicarious*. Our children were grown and gone, I was in my seventies and not much interested in bosun's chairs even if Susan was still willing to man the winches as she had in the past. But we still needed to get to the masthead without killing anyone (specifically me).

Our new boat, a Fisher 37 with a sturdy fiberglass hull and aluminum spars, was a bit smaller than *Sultana* but was otherwise the same boat. It had a roomy pilothouse to keep us out of the weather and wide clear decks with high bulwarks that would make the offshore passages we were looking forward to both safe and comfortable. We still needed a way up the mast, and, once again, mast steps led the competition in spite of our mixed experience with them.

Then I came across a piece on YouTube singing the praise of a new-to-me contrivance called a Top Climber. I had seen ads for this device and had even looked up the price, but at $450 it seemed a bit complicated and pricey, so I didn't pay much attention to it. But the YouTube video changed my mind. The thing worked with two rock-climber's ascenders, and with it I could get to the masthead all by myself. So I bought one, and it has served me well for probably 100 trips aloft. If you are thinking of buying one, keep in mind that it is an aerobic workout to use the thing. If you aren't in good physical condition, you may want to try one out before you buy it.

Whichever way you plan to do it, getting aloft is an important part of cruising in a sailboat, so much so I have promised Susan that once I reach the point where I can't get up the mast by myself, we will start looking at trawlers. (Notice the sneaky use of "start looking." I never said I would buy one, did I? But don't tell Susan that.)

Lighting the Way

As we get older most of our senses tend to get weaker. I have mentioned this before, and to keep bringing it up may sound a bit morbid. But, as retired cruisers, we should keep our deteriorating motor functions in mind and plan for them lest they smack us on the head with the war club of reality when we least expect it. As our knees get wobbly and our hearing becomes unreliable (Warning, Aussie joke: "It's a wizzer day," says one old swagger to his cobbers. "No it ain't, it's Thursday," says the second. "Me too," says the third. "Let's go get a frosty."), our eyes join the rest of the gang on a trip to obscurity. After all, we are retired, so why shouldn't our vision, hearing, balance, and thinking all start to take it easy also?

But it is our eyes that we need to address here. I'm 72 (and a half) as I write this, and my corrected vision is about the same as my uncorrected vision was when I was 14. I can see just fine as long as my glasses are on my nose instead of hiding on top of my head, like they do. But that is in daylight. At night, it is a different story: dark areas of the boat become darker, bright lights become brighter, and the grey areas in between dissolve into murky mysteries.

This decreasing night vision is common as we grow older and as unavoidable as a droopy . . . ah . . . well, you know. Blues and greens become harder to see, while reds and yellows can become brighter; close-up vision and peripheral vision both deteriorate; and bright lights glare and flare enough to temporarily blind us.

There isn't much, besides eating lots of carrots, that we can do about our deteriorating visual acuity, but we can change our environment to accommodate it. One of the best ways is to upgrade the lighting in your new/old boat. And one of the best ways to do *that* is to switch to all-LED lighting.

LED LIGHTS

OK, so changing your old bulbs to LED lights won't help you to see better. They are just another source of illumination, and, because the quality of the light is different from either tungsten or halogen bulbs, some even claim an LED light is inferior to more traditional lights. But you should change all your tungsten, halogen, and even fluorescent bulbs to LED as one of your first elderly-friendly upgrades anyway. The savings in 12-volt electricity alone is reason enough for the change and will pay for the new bulbs quicker than you think. (You're right, it will take a while to break even, but bear with me here.) You can add light fixtures anywhere you need them without worrying about heat buildup, wiring sizes, overloading circuits, or battery drain.

The advantages of LED lighting over traditional onboard lights are discussed in some detail in *The Cruising Life*, Second Edition, so this is another topic we will glaze over, just to avoid unnecessary repetition. But switching to LEDs allows older cruisers the luxury of adding fixtures anywhere they are needed without a penalty of energy consumption. An LED fixture draws only 10 percent of the energy used by a tungsten or halogen fixture of the same brilliance, so, in theory anyway, we can add 10 LED lights for every conventional fixture we have without increasing our use of electricity.

On *Vicarious*, the original fluorescent light in the galley meant cooking after dark sometimes relied on assumption and surmise resulting in mysterious culinary creations. We now have five LED fixtures and plenty of light for creating all sorts of tasty dishes. The original pilothouse had four tungsten fixtures that were barely adequate; there are now eight LED clusters, giving us total flexibility for lighting the chart table during a passage or illuminating the entire cabin when entertaining guests. We have also added small LED lights under the galley sink and in several of the most-used cupboards, those that had always kept their contents a mystery, forcing the use of a flashlight or guesswork.

The color of LEDs is infinitely variable, which is another advantage of using them for us older folks. If your cruising plans include any travel at night, red lighting should be installed anywhere you might need it while under way. *Vicarious* has complete red lighting in the galley, the head, and in the pilothouse, as these are the places most likely to be visited by a wandering watch person. As you know, red lighting will not affect your night vision, which is a marginal advantage to older folks, as our night vision is probably shot anyway. But there is another more subtle reason for using red lights at night: older people can often see things like charts and instruments better when they are illuminated by red light than when they are bathed in white light. White light tends to glare more when viewed with elderly eyes, and red light doesn't. Watch-keeping while offshore is easier and less stressful when everything you need to see is illuminated with red light.

Start upgrading your onboard lighting by buying an assortment of direct-replacement inserts that will fit into existing fixtures just like a replacement bulb. Then use dedicated LED fixtures as you add new lights or change worn-out ones.

There is just one more aspect of LED lighting that we can cover before sailing off to the next atoll, and that is the difference between the hard and soft color choices you may have when buying white LED replacement bulbs and fixtures. Pure white light can be stark and intense, and, while this may work well for work surfaces, it is less desirable for reading lamps and other areas where a more restful light is appreciated. The answer is to install bright white lights in the head and in the galley while using the softer, less intense bulbs with a strong yellow component in your reading lamps and for over the dining areas where the yellow glow is more like candlelight. The brilliant white LEDs emit a large measure of short-wave blue light, which sleep researchers tell us hampers our ability to drop off to slumber-land quickly, so yellow LEDs are doubly important over your bunk. Dimmable LED fixtures are also available that would also work well over the eating and sleeping areas.

DECK LIGHTING

A well-lit deck makes life aboard a boat easier in many ways besides just lighting the way for after-dark chores:

1. Well-thought-out deck lights make the entire boat available no matter what time of day you want to use it.
2. Turning deck lights on when traveling after dark or when other boats enter your danger zone gives approaching traffic instant visual verification of their radar image and eliminates the ambiguity that could be caused by running lights or masthead light.
3. There are many anchorages in the world where local traffic operates after dark in ways that would scare the socks off Evel Knievel. Turning deck lights on as a supplement to the mandatory anchor light is a good way to ensure that the Panamanian panga driver operating his 250-horsepower outboard at full throttle with no running lights can see you.

4. Extra lights will also deter the infamous dinghy thieves that cruise many of these same harbors in hopes of snagging an errant inflatable whose careless owner hasn't secured it properly.

Deck lighting comes in many configurations, and there are many ways to install it. And with LED technology, we no longer have to worry about current draw and battery drain, at least not as much as we did back in the dimly lit good old days.

Sailboats most commonly have spreader lights or a foredeck light and often both. These are intended to facilitate sail-handling after dark, but deck lights serve very well as general-purpose illumination. Powerboats don't have to worry about sail handling, but the same sort of lighting is a useful addition anyway, provided, of course, the boat is equipped with a mast or superstructure on which to mount it. Sportfishing boats with tuna towers have many options for mounting lights. Unfortunately, sportfishers make terrible cruising boats.

Both powerboats and sailboats should have some sort of cockpit illumination; the more the better for elderly retirees. Cockpit lights make entertaining aboard easy and fun while lighting up the barby so we don't char the lamb chops grilling thereon. Most boats, even the older used ones that we are likely to end up owning, are equipped with cockpit lights of some sort, but they are often inadequate and even more often use tungsten or halogen fixtures. Naturally, changing to LEDs is a logical first step in upgrading to elderly friendliness, but adding more and brighter fixtures is also a good idea.

UNDERWATER LIGHTS

Underwater lights are a frivolous sub-theme to the LED story and one I have no experience with other than observing them on the hulls of expensive yachts moored in expensive marinas around the world. There seems to be an active competition among owners of big powerboats to see who can have the most extravagant display of subaquatic illumination. These arrays of blinking, color-changing, and flashing lights remind me of the under-chassis and wheel-well lights of the California low riders of the nineties: cool to the extreme but utterly useless.

Vicarious does not yet sport any undersea lighting, but I can see a practical application for it beyond the coolness factor. These lights are inexpensive, easy to install, and come in myriad colors. Someday I may consider adding a few basic fixtures below the waterline, for practical reasons, of course. Underwater lights are said to be a major boon to night fishing, and that would be an attractive option, especially when needing a few fresh squid to populate one of Susan's sumptuous calamari salads. Swimming at night among the fish attracted to the glow would be great fun, and strong lights might even show the location of coral heads when anchoring after dark.

There may also be security options available here. I can envision a system of blue underwater LEDs triggered by a motion detector that also starts a prerecorded message. As a person of dishonorable intent skulks within striking range of your expensive dinghy, the sea around your boat glows with an eerie blue light, and a baritone voice resonates from above, "forbear ye villain from your nefarious aspiration lest your evil soul be sucked out through your nose and consumed by the light of truth and justice," or some such verbiage designed to make thieves and scoundrels consider a midlife career change. We could also coordinate a burst of air from a scuba tank so that the water around the hull was seen to boil violently as the voice boomed. Who knows, it might work.

LED HEADLAMPS

Headlamps have become standard kit for cruisers in the past decade or so, and elderly cruisers are well advised to have several at hand with strong white and red LED beams.

These headlamps are an excellent emergency illumination if you lose power, and they are useful anytime you are on deck after dark even when you have your deck lighting going at full blast. I wear one at all times while on watch at night just so I don't have to go looking for it when I need to investigate some strange squeaking noise coming from behind the steering gear or faint rattling sound coming from the engine compartment.

LED headlamps have dropped in price over the years, and good ones are now available for less than the cost of a couple of six-packs. You can spend several hundred dollars for a water-resistant, super-powerful model, if you want to, but I find that many of the cheaper ones that put out about 2,000 lumens are about right for general work. Weight is another important consideration. The lights with a separate battery pack mounted on the back of the head tend to be a bit cumbersome for me, but the batteries last longer than in the more compact units.

When I first started using headlamps, many years ago, they would work fine until they encountered a few drops of seawater. I tried using waterproof ones, and this worked OK, but the seal would fail after just a few battery changes. Now, each new head lamp gets a blast of Boshield T-9 waterproof lubrication as soon as it comes aboard, then a refresher blast with each battery change. Lights treated with the Boshield last much longer than the untreated ones, so it is worth the effort. Switching to lithium batteries also helped extend the life of my headlamps. Lithiums last longer than alkaline batteries, which means that the battery compartment isn't opened as often.

There are dozens of headlamps on the market, so take your time and select one you like. If you are going to wear it a lot, like I do, a comfortable strap is paramount, as nothing is as annoying as a light that slips just when you need it not to. If you are going to wear it on deck, a waterproof one is worth a little extra also, and don't forget the Boshield.

Once you find a headlamp the suits your needs and budget, get one for each member of the crew, along with a spare and a pile of batteries.

There are dozens of other ways that you can transform your new/old boat from a complicated nightmare of constant maintenance and repairs into a paragon of easy retirement living, but we can't do justice to all of them here. Just keep in mind that you can simplify your life (and your boat) in ways that most of your contemporaries can't even imagine, and as you simplify it you make living it (and on it) easier and more enjoyable than a more conventional retirement lifestyle can ever be.

 # 7 A FEW COZY UPGRADES

Susan and I may be 40 years downstream from the headwaters of Newlywed Creek, but we still appreciate some queen-sized canoodling once in a while.

Now that we have modified, adjusted, and adapted our new/old boat so that it makes us feel as safe as an egg in a nest, it is time to concentrate on making living aboard so cozy and secure that the thought of moving back into a regular house ashore brings on pangs of dread and despair. Transforming your boat into a warm and welcoming living environment where you relax and escape from all the troubles of the world is nearly as important as making it safe; when the success of your cruising adventures is considered, it can be even more important.

Many of us who could tolerate a marginally unsafe boat, through ignorance perhaps or even misguided contempt for danger, and cruise for years with slippery decks and wobbly lifelines, would bail out after a few short months aboard a damp, poorly ventilated, heat-box of a boat with too-short bunks, too-low headroom, and too-stinky toilet.

Making your boat comfortable will require a bit of study and some rearrangement of interior items along with a few budget-buster luxuries from the marine store. But, even more important, it might also require minor adjustments in personal standards and a fresh look at your conventional shoreside attitudes. Comfort is as much a state of mind as it is physical environment, but before we start on your attitude, let's make sure that your physical surroundings are not going to make the shift in your outlook more difficult than necessary. A wet or even a slightly damp boat is an unlivable boat, so let's address this issue first.

Leaks

Nothing will make life aboard a cruising boat more miserable than a drippy, leaky deck. How can I say this with so much confidence? Because every boat I have ever owned had a problem keeping water where it belonged: outside the boat. Where water doesn't belong is on my bunk, yet keeping a dry sleeping area has been a constant battle through the years, and a personal *bête noire*.

No sooner had I settled into the starboard V-berth aboard *Vicarious* for my first night on our just-that-day-closed-on boat (Susan was still in New Zealand) than it started to rain. It was just a light drizzle, and the gentle sound of the drops falling on the deck served to lull me into a blissful slumber that lasted all of 20 minutes. That's how long it took for a single drop of that drizzle to work its way through a loose bolt on a deck chock to the plumbing for the wash-down hose in the bulwarks to a wire that led to the reading light directly over my head. From there it traveled down to the edge of the light shade, where it ran out of options. After a thoughtful pause, it let go its hold on the light and splashed, with a startling effect, onto my sleeping forehead.

That first drop was only the forward scout for an army of drippy foot soldiers to follow, and, before the night was out, a steady trickle was draining onto a puddle where my mattress should have been. I retreated to the pilothouse dinette berth and spent the rest of the night listening to the steady sound of drops hitting various parts of the interior of our new home and planning my revenge.

That first rainy night aboard *Vicarious* also revealed dozens of other drips and drops splishing and splashing like Bobby Darin in every corner of the boat, all of them in places they didn't belong. Suddenly it was clear why the previous owners

Deck leaks can be one of the most frustrating conditions of boat ownership. My heart goes out to the owner of this sailboat who, perhaps in a fit of enraged desperation, appears to have squirted an entire tube of 3M 5200 sealant onto this leaking sidelight. A more systematic and organized approach to leak fixing would have resulted in a tidier repair, would not have wasted an expensive tube of sealant, and would not have ruined the sidelight, as has been done here. The distressing thing about this sort of amateur repair is that it frequently doesn't work. The next rain could very well find the leak dripping merrily away just as it had done before it was "fixed."

had lavished so much treasure and attention on an elaborate system of canvas covers that, like the cover on a Conestoga wagon, veiled the decks from bow to stern.

That the kind folks who sold us *Vicarious* did not know how to deal with leaks was obvious, and the leaks exalted in their freedom from prosecution. But having owned and rebuilt two large wooden craft from the keel up, and having dealt with every conceivable sort of leak, I was their match. It wasn't easy, but after a year or so of search-and-destroy missions against leaks, I can safely say we are free of them—almost. Susan, it seems, is much more sensitive to the presence of uninvited water droplets than I am. If a drip hits the top of a can of beans in our deep-storage locker in the opposite end of the boat from the V-berth where we are sleeping, she is up like a shot, flashlight in hand, searching for the offending invader. No matter how insignificant the drip, it goes on the to-do list with a priority star next to it.

LEAKS ARE INDIVIDUALS

Leaks are hard to find for a lot of reasons but mostly because each one has a personality all its own. That first deck leak, for example, is one I call Obvious Joe. That's right, I am so intimately involved with deck leaks that I have names for them. Here are a few of my favorites:

Obvious Joe
Average Joe
Sneaky Pete
Windy Wonder
Undependable Bob
Harmless Hanna
Lopsided Louie
Leaky Lena

Obvious Joe sneaks aboard through a simple loose fitting or a fastener that has not been sealed properly, and he is the easiest to deal with. Average Joe leaks in any time it rains, the boat is being scrubbed, or the decks are washed by a wave, and he is easy to track down and fix. Usually tightening a screw or bolt will do the job, but extreme cases might require a fastener or two to be removed and rebedded or resealed.

Sneaky Pete is a lot more difficult to deal with than Average Joe. Sneaky only leaks when you aren't looking. You can be enjoying your traditional sundowner at the dinette, turn around to look out the port at the falling rain, and, when you turn back, there is a puddle of water right in front of you. Sneaky is very difficult to find, so we will give him special attention in the next section.

Some leaks are defined by weather, and Windy Wonder is one of the trickiest. Windy only leaks when the breeze picks up and starts to ruffle the surface of the sea. But he gets more complicated than that. Windy usually only leaks when the wind is from a certain direction. *Vicarious*, for example, had a serious leak over the starboard V-berth that would wet down my feet anytime it rained with the wind over the starboard bow. I eventually located a gap under the cap rail that admitted wind-blown rain, but only under those specific conditions. In another more easily located case, water would come in through the rear flange seal of the forward hatch anytime the wind was blowing from astern at more than 10 knots. The natural slope of the deck would drain the water away from the hatch except when the wind was strong enough to blow it slightly uphill. Fixing this one involved removing and rebedding the entire hatch.

I wouldn't even bother mentioning Undependable Bob (nickname: Undie) if it weren't for Susan. She takes the on-again-off-again appearance of this unreliable leak quite personally with vows to track him down if it takes forever, which it easily can. Undie seems to favor the interior of lockers where we keep stuff that we would rather did not get wet. He may show up once a month or once a year but with no predictable interval in between visits. Susan takes his appearance to heart because he targets the drawer where she keeps her spare knickers (thus, the nickname) with an unpredictable vengeance that almost prompted me to name him Fetish Bob. But Undependable also gets himself into my tool locker on occasion, and everyone knows that you can't have a fetish focusing on tools. (*Now* why is Susan looking at me like that?)

Harmless Hanna is another leak that barely deserves mention. On *Vicarious* she lives under the cap rail where she stays busy dripping away onto the inside of the hull from whence she slides unnoticed into the bilge. Harmless is one of the few remaining leaks we endure in our boat because I have more important things on my mind than fixing broken things that do no immediate damage. But since Susan views all leaks as enemies to be searched out and dealt with, Harmless is doomed. She is destined to join her more troublesome cohorts in obscurity, just as soon as I get around to it.

Like I said: leaks have personalities just like people, and Lopsided Louie (known to his friends and foes alike as Loopy) is one of my favorites. Loopy takes advantage of the athwartship trim of the boat and stays out of sight until the combined weight of water and fuel tanks gets out of kilter enough to tempt him from his lair. When the starboard fuel and water tanks were both empty and the port-side tanks were full, for example, Loopy would find his way into the pilothouse through the bolts at the starboard end of the mainsheet traveler. When the conditions were reversed (starboard tanks full, port tanks empty), he would slip aboard through the head ventilator fan.

Leaky Lena is one of the last leaks we will deal with and one of the most difficult to roun dup and corral. As her eponymous name indicates, Leaky shows up only when we are under way, usually when we are out of sight of land and are taking green water over the bow. She steadfastly refuses to show her face any time we are at anchor or motoring in calm seas, and she laughs at both hoser and spotter (whom we will shortly meet) as we try to double-team her into showing her face in an environment where we can fix her wagon for good. Leaky is one of the most challenging of all the leaks to track down and eliminate.

Leaks are loners by nature, but occasionally they team up and conspire to turn your comfy interior into something resembling the Everglades. Loopy, for example, will sometimes partner with Harmless Hanna for a double, hardly harmless threat. And Average Joe can join forces with Loopy to make your life hell. But, in my experience, all leaks, no matter how devious or insignificant, can be stopped, eventually, so let's look at a few ways to do it.

FIRST YA GOTTA FIND 'EM

One of the first things to learn about leaks is that they are immortal. You can find them, but you can never kill them. They are like zombies in a George A. Romero movie: you think you have destroyed them and all their ilk, but a year or so down the line, while you are basking in the cozy comfort of your bone-dry interior, here they come again. Leaks can be plugged, stoppered, painted over, or slathered with foul-smelling sealants, but, while they may look dead, they are lying dormant waiting for the next conjuncture of high tide, full moon, and a thunderstorm to spring once again to life and drip their nasty drops on your sleeping forehead. The trick isn't to kill them but to keep them dormant, and this takes diligence and an understanding of one basic rule of cruising hydrodynamics: water does not always run downhill.

In order to stop leaks you have to find them, and this is harder than you might think. Leaks happen most often when it is raining, but you can't fix them while the deck is wet. Once it stops raining, it is easy to forget about them; rain stops, leak stops, problem solved—until next time anyway. If you can't fix them while it is raining, you can at least locate them. So stick a few inches of masking tape (the blue or green stuff will be easier to remove than the cheap beige stuff) adjacent to where the leak is appearing. Use a marker to draw an arrow to the exact point where the drip emerges. Two or three arrows might mark the location with more precision, but the point is to mark the spot where the leak is making itself known on the inside of the hull.

Another well-known law of hydrodynamics states that leaks seldom show up anywhere near where they originate, so just going up on deck and finding the spot right over the leak only works with Obvious Joe. Finding any of the others, especially Leaky Lena, is going to take two people and a garden hose. One person, the spotter, remains inside the boat in view of the leaking spot and the other, the hoser, goes up topsides and starts spraying the deck with water.

A gentle flow is better than a spray or a pressure wash, because the hoser needs to concentrate the flow over specific areas of the boat where logic would dictate leaks originate. Deck fittings are immediate suspects, as are the bases of stanchions and the flanges of ports and hatches. When the hoser is hosing over an actual leak, it should be obvious to the spotter, who should then communicate with the hoser by screaming, banging frantically on the hull, or perhaps letting go with a blast from an air horn, whereupon the hoser will mark that location before moving on to the next leak.

This sounds pretty basic and easy because that's what it is, and, after a single session, you should have located all the Obvious Joes, the majority of your Windy Wonders, a few Harmless Hannas, and, if you are lucky, even one or two Leaky Lenas.

If you have never chased leaks using this type of hoser/spotter teamwork before, you may be surprised at how far the spot where the leak appears inside the boat is from the place on deck where it originates, especially if your boat has a molded hull liner.

THEN FIX 'EM

Once you have located all your leaks (or as many as possible—it's always good to save a few for later), you have to fix them, and this can involve a variety of tools, materials, and techniques. Don't succumb to the temptation of slathering some sort of sealant (usually silicone bathtub caulking) over the outside of the leaking seam or fixture. This procedure is popular with amateurs and fools and honest folks who simply don't know any better. Slathered on sealant may work for a while, but it is hopelessly ugly and it is destined to fail, usually sooner rather than later, and almost always at an inconvenient time.

Most leaks are not a condition as much as a symptom, and as such they often point to a problem that can be much worse than just an occasional drip on your sleeping forehead. A leak through a lifeline stanchion, for example, can indicate deteriorated fasteners, saturated fiberglass, or rot in a deck core. Leaking port- and deadlight flanges can indicate deteriorated bedding compound, delaminated fiberglass, corroded fasteners, or a hundred other problems that can occur individually or in combination.

The only way to fix any leak that originates in a fixture, such as a porthole flange or deck cleat, is to remove the entire fixture and re-bed it. Removal allows a careful inspection of the underlying structure of the fixture and an easy evaluation of the condition causing the leak.

Once the leaking forward hatch, mentioned earlier, was removed (no easy task, as the plumber's putty used in the original installation had over 35 years to harden), it was obvious that the bedding compound for the entire aft flange had deteriorated and mostly been washed away. I suspect this leak had persisted for decades and through several owners. Several repairs had been attempted using the slather-on-some-sealant method. This may have stopped the dripping for a month or so with each slathering, but it resulted in an ugly buildup of silicone sealant that took several hours and many sheets of sandpaper to remove. In desperation, someone had given up on fixing the leak itself and had a Sunbrella tarp fabricated that covered the entire bow of the boat. This cover worked very well when at anchor but did nothing to stop the influx of seawater when we were under way.

When the hatch was removed, the problem was revealed to be the badly deteriorated bedding compound. Fortunately, there was no saturation in the exposed balsa-wood deck coring, and the fasteners were all in good shape. I did take the

Simply slathering on some sort of sealant—in this case, silicone bathtub caulking—is not an effective way to fix leaks. It is unsightly, for one thing, and for another, it probably won't work. Sure, the leak might stop or slow for a short time, but it will eventually reappear with a vengeance, prompting some of us to slather on even more ugly gook.

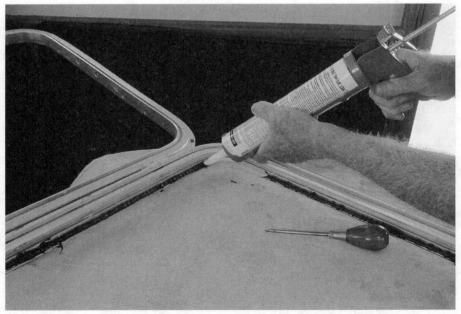

The only surefire way to fix leaks coming from around the base of a fixture, such as this hatch, is to remove the fixture from the boat, give it a thorough cleaning, then reinstall it with the proper bedding compound.

opportunity, while the hatch was off the boat, to re-bed the glazing and to replace the screws with much stronger bolts.

The dripping hatch seal was the worst of the many leaks that we discovered on *Vicarious*, but there were also numerous caprail leaks that we had to deal with before we could claim a dry interior. The caprail on Fisher motor sailers is a teak slab bolted to the top of the bulwarks forming the deck seam. Because of the heavy construction, the fiberglass here is over an inch think in places. To fix these leaks properly would have involved the removal and re-bedding of the entire caprail, a job that would have taken months to complete and cost thousands of dollars. I was able to make suitable repairs simply by removing and re-bedding the individual bolts, which solved about 90 percent of the problems, even though there were a few bolts that were out of reach without major deconstruction on the interior. We are saving these for later.

Whatever you do, don't (repeat: do not) succumb to the temptation to try to fix the leak from inside the boat. Not only will this awful practice brand you as a rank amateur among accomplished leak fixers, it will fail to stop the water, and, worse of all, it can cause serious damage to your boat. When you stop water from dripping by plugging the leak where it is emerging on your boat's interior, you effectively create a small dam. Water trapped behind that dam will eventually find another course, most likely a much worse one, into your boat, and it will become putrid, smell up the interior, and slowly saturate the lining of your boat. If your decks are cored with end-grain balsam, as many of the better-built boats are, you can end up with saturated coring, which is expensive and difficult to repair.

In fact, when water is discovered dripping from saturated coring or from a hidden pool of water behind the interior lining, drilling a number of holes to drain out the backed-up water can save a lot of trouble downstream. Eventually the water dripping through these drain holes should stop, but if it doesn't, track down the leak from outside the boat and fix it there.

Air Circulation

Keeping the air moving on the inside of a cruising boat is one of the most vexing, most often ignored, and most important of problems facing a retired cruiser. Efficient air circulation on a boat is paramount for comfort, of course, but it is also an important way to prevent the mold and mildew that can quickly destroy seat cushions, draperies, your clothing, varnished interior surfaces, and just about anything else that the nasty little microorganisms decide to colonize. If you are going to live aboard a boat, one of the first priorities facing you as a new/old boat owner is making sure that your boat is the virtual center of an air-changing cyclone.

There are two kinds of ventilation you will need to be familiar with if you are to keep your interior dry and cozy: natural (or static) ventilation and dynamic ventilation. Let's take these suckers one at a time.

NATURAL AIR CIRCULATION

Air likes to move, and, left to its own devices, it will happily shift from where it is to another place that it deems to be more attractive. It's like when Susan decides that the anchorage around the corner might have a better beach or the bugs won't be as persistent, so up comes the anchor and off we go to investigate. Like migrating snowbirds in the United States, air likes to move up when it is warm and down when it is cold, and it moves from high ambient pressure to low. Air doesn't like to be restrained, and, given the opportunity, it will move all by itself. The only thing you need to do is provide a course for it to move through and see that nothing gets in its way.

Cowl Vents and Dorade Boxes

Natural ventilation on a boat is encouraged by having adequate open-air cowl vents in dorade boxes. Cowl vents are the attractive metal or plastic funnels you see on fancy boats, and dorade boxes are a baffled box that the cowl vent sits on and through which air flows but water can't (see photo.) Cowl vents allow air to freely pass either into or out of the boat by convection. When air pressure is greater outside the boat than in, fresh air is drawn into the boat. When the pressure inside the boat is greatest, stale air is forced out of the boat.

Cowl vents are directional, so by turning the funnel faces into the wind, the prevailing breeze increases the air pressure, forcing fresh air into the boat. With the funnel facing away from the breeze, a vacuum is created, drawing stale air out of the boat. Thus a system of four cowl vents on dorade boxes, with two facing into the wind and two facing away from the wind, can provide excellent air circulation without any help from electric fans or other energy-eating devices.

Vicarious has only two cowl vents (two more are planned) on dorade boxes, and these are ducted directly onto the bilge to provide a consistent supply of fresh air into this critical area.

Cowl vents are an ideal source of fresh air, but they do have a few drawbacks. They don't work when the wind doesn't blow, for one, and, when cruising offshore, it is easy for a large wave washing the deck to overwhelm the dorade drains and allow a flood of seawater into the boat. Standard procedure on *Vicarious* is to turn both cowl vents so they are facing aft any time we are sailing in fair weather. We do this any time we are offshore, no matter what the sea conditions, because, even in calm seas, small-but-sneaky waves can pile up into one monster and clobber you when you aren't looking. Since most waves come aboard from the forward quarter, aft-facing cowls limit the amount of seawater that finds its way into the cabin.

When the skies darken and the winds start whistling in the wires, we remove the cowls and replace them with sturdy metal deck plates that exclude all water, albeit at the expense of air circulation. Stale air is better than an involuntary saltwater shower any day, even though, after a week or so at sea, any kind of shower might sound inviting.

The two cowl vents on Vicarious *are ducted directly into the bilge and keep the under-floor areas fresh and sweet-smelling. They can be configured to force fresh air into the bilge or to extract stale air just by turning the cowl into or away from the wind.*

Portholes, Hatches, and Windows

First a few definitions: Any opening surface on your boat that is flat and horizontal is usually called a hatch, as is any opening that allows egress from and entry into the interior. Any traditional-looking round, rectangular, oblong, or square fissure with a see-through cover that can be opened and closed is a porthole; if it can't be opened, it is called a portlight. And any large, glazed vertical surface that looks like it doesn't really belong on a boat is a window (whether it opens or not).

Any opening surface on a boat is a good thing when it comes to getting a steady supply of fresh air, so the more the better, or so it would seem. But portholes, hatches, and windows all come with a cost. While all that open area is fine for letting in fresh air, it will also admit water just as easily. And, while this may not be a problem at anchor, where you can just close everything up when it starts to rain and blow, it can present another problem for offshore cruisers. Any opening in a hull represents a structural weakness that must be considered when you first decide what type of cruising you want to do. Thus, classic offshore boats feature small, sturdy portholes and strong hatches with any windows strongly mounted. Coastal cruisers can have larger portholes, big poorly sealed hatches, and huge areas of glass windows without too much worry.

Except for the well-protected center window, which is about four feet wide, the windows in *Vicarious*'s pilothouse are all 18 inches square or less and sturdily mounted in aluminum frames. For my tastes, this is about the upper limit for any windows facing port or starboard. All unprotected glazed surfaces on an offshore boat should be able to withstand the full force of the largest wave the boat is likely to encounter, and that can be a very big wave indeed.

Louvers

Louvers on the interior of your boat are among the most useful of all ventilation devices. They are easy to install, and you can't have too many of them. Most boats have a few louvered doors and vents installed during construction, for both functional ventilation of lockers and cabins and for their nautical good looks. But louvers are expensive, so few boatbuilders provide enough of them. Thus, one of the easiest and most effective upgrades you can make to your new retirement home is to install copious louvered vents.

Louvered vents come in dozens of sizes and shapes made from wood, plastic, and stainless steel, so there are plenty of choices. Any flat surface that hides a cavity behind it, no matter how small or large, is a candidate for this easy-to-install upgrade.

Round plastic louvers are particularly useful for production boats that are built with molded interior hull liners. These liners make the interior look clean and modern, but the cavity they create between the exterior hull and deck is a virtual nursery for mold and fungus. Getting adequate air circulation into this cavity can make a quantum difference in the comfort of the interior. It will smell better once you get rid of the microbes growing in the unseen dark reaches of your boat, and the fresh air is much healthier than the stale, germ-ridden air that it replaces.

Louvered vents installed on the interior liner of production boats also provide access into the cavities where builders like to hide electrical wiring and plumbing. Access to these pipes and wires is only important when you need to make repairs or upgrades, but, with well-positioned vents, getting into the dark spaces is a snap.

DYNAMIC AIR CIRCULATION

Air likes to move around all by itself, as we discovered above, but sometimes it can't. Boats are often sealed from outside air for any number of reasons. Seasonal boaters in the far northern and southern latitudes haul their boats out of the water

The louvered ventilator that we installed on the front of Vicarious's *Engle refrigerator is a simple pre-made panel of teak that came from West Marine. We have installed more than a dozen of these panels throughout the boat, both for their salty good looks and for their efficiency in allowing the free circulation of fresh air into restricted areas.*

every year and encase them in a hermetic plastic cocoon, and we who live on our boats most often seal them in anticipation of bad weather. When it storms, whether at sea or at anchor, windows, hatches, and ports are closed, and air circulation becomes restricted, which can quickly render the interior of any boat stuffy and uncomfortable. The answer here, of course, is powered fans.

Powered Fans

The two basic categories of fans popular on cruising boats are those that blow air into and out of your boat and those that move air around inside your boat. Interior fans are positioned throughout the boat to move air from one section to another.

The theory is that even stale air can feel fresh if it is moving around a bit. Most interior fans are wired into the boat's electrical system and are permanently mounted, although there are battery-operated models that are movable or semi-permanent.

Interior fans are important in hot climates, where they can be a lifesaver, and when sailing offshore in stormy weather. When sailing conditions deteriorate at sea, most cruisers will close up everything that will close. (On *Vicarious*, this includes using duct tape on the forward hatch, on the thimble for the anchor chain were it enters the chain locker, and on the forward portlights in the forepeak. We know from experience that these places will leak when the big waves start coming aboard, so we try to get ready for it before we need to.) When a boat is closed up, the interior soon resembles the inside of a hot-air balloon. A few interior fans going at full blast move the air around just enough to make things bearable, if not exactly comfortable.

Exterior fans vent air into and out of the boat, just like cowl vents, but with an electric assist. The most popular of these fans are solar powered with a rechargeable storage battery designed to keep the fan going overnight and during periods of clouds and rain. These self-contained ventilators usually come with a choice of fans so that they can be configured to draw air out of the boat or to pump it in. Thus, they can be set up with one or two fans drawing in fresh air while others serve as exhaust fans. As with cowl vents, any fan that accesses outside air needs to have a means of closing it down to prevent water coming aboard while at sea. Coastal cruisers don't have to worry about this, but it is still a good idea to be able to shut the fan opening.

Computer Fans

Twelve-volt computer fans have been around since personal computers, of course, but they are just now being discovered by knowledgeable cruisers looking for a way to move air into dark and musty interior spaces of their boats. These little air blasters come in a selection of handy sizes from three inches up to about 20 inches in the 12-volt models. They make little noise, draw only a tiny sip of power, are designed for continuous operation, and can be installed anywhere you need improved air flow.

Best of all, they are cheap. The standard Heller marine fans that we use in all the cabins on *Vicarious* cost about $80 each. Don't get me wrong; we wouldn't be without them in the tropics. But in a cost comparison, the top-quality Heller turbo fans lose horribly, because you can buy about 20 computer fans for the price of one of the dedicated marine ones. At a Florida flea market, I once bought a sack full of four-inch computer fans for $3 each and have been using them ever since.

If you are worried that these cheap computer fans aren't marine quality, don't be. On several occasions I have opened up expensive marine quality ventilation units to find, you guessed it, garden-variety computer fans. In fact, the reason I bought so many at that flea market in Florida was to have spares when the originals burned out. So far, after over two years, that has happened only once, when the fan inside a $120 Vetus ventilator got flushed by a boarding wave.

Blowers

Blowers are powered fans taken to the extreme. They usually draw air from outside the boat and direct it through ducting to an area that needs a steady supply of fresh air, such as into the engine compartment or to a diesel-powered generator. Often they also serve as exhaust fans. They pump hot, stale air out of the boat, creating a vacuum that draws in fresh air.

Although they don't do much to improve the comfort inside the boat, one or two blowers (ideally, one exhaust and one intake) in your engine compartment will make your power plant very happy, especially in the tropics. And, trust me here, if your power plant is happy, you can be happy too, and that can be comforting indeed.

Temperature Control

The easiest way to keep a boat from becoming too warm is with the simple (and cheap) methods of encouraging natural air circulation explored above. And this is the only system we have ever used on all our travels. Even on the equator in the summer we are able to keep the interior of *Vicarious* comfortable by opening ports and hatches, then giving the air a boost with a powered fan. The only exception was while we were living on the boat in Panama while having the decks refinished by a local crew. The sanding dust and flying paint spray made any openings in the hull impossible, so we installed a temporary air conditioner. Without it, we would not have been able to stay aboard.

Heat, of course is another matter, and we will talk soon about various ways to stay warm below.

AIR-CONDITIONING

Air-conditioning is increasing in popularity with cruisers as more efficient and compact marine devices become available, but readers of *The Cruising Life,* Second Edition, know how I stand on the subject: there is no place for air-conditioning on a cruising boat that doesn't spend most of its time tied to a dock with shore power. The reasons are many, but the great expense, the requirement for shore power (or a powerful generator), and the fact that it just ain't cruiserly are the three big ones.

That said, I will begrudgingly admit to the proponents of marine air-conditioning for retired folks living full time aboard their boats that one of the new small, self-contained devices might be appropriate once we reach the point that we are tied to the dock for the remainder of life's voyage. But for now, I sincerely advise against air-conditioning for any boat that is going to be moving from one anchorage to another while avoiding marinas.

The key to staying cool without air-conditioning is to shun marinas in favor of an open-air anchorage. There are many advantages to anchoring out over tying up (it's cheaper, the water is cleaner, it's quieter, the sky is bluer, the birds sing sweeter, and the neighbors are more neighborly—to name just a few), but we shouldn't forget the breeze, which is always fresher and stronger when you are away from the docks, and it always blows from the bow to the stern, which is just the right direction.

HEAT

Anyone reading the paragraphs above, which detail how much I am opposed to air-conditioning on cruising boats, will automatically assume I feel the same way about mechanical heaters. Wrong again! If your cruising plans include areas of the globe north or south of about 40 degrees latitude, you will need some sort of heater. And if you are cruising in the winter, that goes down to 30 degrees latitude or even lower (it can get mighty chilly in Miami in spite of all the gunfire).

Electric space heaters work well when it isn't too cold and you have a place to plug one in. That becomes difficult when you are on anchor, but there are a few portable heaters that can help. Don't even think of using an unvented kerosene (paraffin) heater in a boat. I have seen unvented propane heaters (the type used for camping) used successfully, although I would never use one myself. The additional moisture these things add to the already high humidity, plus the danger of oxygen depletion, make the risk too great for a conservative, eager-to-live-a-little-longer guy like me.

The most popular and safe stand-alone heater for boaters is the little Origo Heat Pal 5100 made by Dometic and available from most marine retailers. Susan and I used one of these alcohol-fired beauties for years while exploring the Canadian Maritimes and downeast Maine on our first three boats.

On *Sultana*, we started with a Newport solid-fuel fireplace from Dickinson Marine and had very good results from it. When we did *Sultana*'s refit, we changed the solid-fuel heater to a similar one powered by propane. Propane wasn't as cozy as firewood, but it did keep the chill off, and it was a lot more convenient and efficient. Gathering firewood on shore was fun and effective exercise, but the wood was difficult to store on board, plus the ashes and soot were a constant bother.

When we moved aboard *Vicarious*, we did without any heater for the first two years, but then installed a compact diesel furnace made by Webasto. This dandy heater supplies hot water to the entire boat, and, while it would be overkill for most cruisers in the mid-latitudes, we are planning to spend the next few years in the North Pacific and the South Island of New Zealand; that alone justified the cost of installing it. Susan has promised to follow me to the ends of the earth as long as I can keep her warm, so hang the expense.

Cushions

Cushions, by definition, are comfortable. So by some extension of logic, most readers would expect the advice here to be "get more cushions," but, of course, most readers would be wrong. (Gee, you guys aren't doing so well in the game of *guess what the author will say next*.) The problem with cushions is that they are cheap, and they are fat and fluffy. Or at least they are cheap for boatbuilders when compared to such things as interior cabinetry, storage space, or larger hanging lockers.

Boatbuilders love cushions for a lot of reasons besides their low cost. Using cushions everywhere they will fit makes the interior of a boat appear to be larger than it really is. And the illusionary spaciousness allows builders to claim, with a straight face, that the 21-foot trailer sailer they are building will sleep five adults. A Catalina 36 (one of the most popular boats built) advertises the ability to sleep six adults, supposedly in some degree of comfort, when four would actually be a crowd, and most other popular production boats exaggerate the sleeping capacity of their products by at least two.

Sleeping capacity is good advertising at the boat shows—"Snookums, Honeybunch, if we buy this boat, there will be plenty of room for the whole family. We can even bring your mother along for weekend trips"—and, like I said earlier, cushions are cheap.

But there is one problem with cushions when it comes time to move onto a boat full time: the fat and fluffy part means they take up an awful lot of room. One of the several previous owners of *Vicarious*, wanting to make her as homey and as comfortable as possible, had a huge custom mattress built for the forepeak (they were newlyweds after all, so who could blame them) that was a full eight inches thick and made from the latest memory foam. It was a lovely mattress, but it took up so much of the already limited space that it made the forepeak claustrophobic and an impossible place to sleep.

As much as it broke my heart to do it—Susan and I may be 40 years downstream from the headwaters of Newlywed Creek, but we still appreciate some queen-sized canoodling once in a while—we ended up taking that beautiful mattress to the recycle center, where it was scooped up by a grateful young man who had enough imagination to project the natural heart shape of the forepeak mattress into his new just-being-decorated bachelor pad.

In total, we took a stack of cushions more than six feet high to the recycle center (all were snagged by the same eagerly expectant Romeo). Much as we hated to do it, especially considering how much the previous owners must have spent on the beautifully done upholstery, it was startling to see how much the absence of all that closed-cell foam opened up the interior of our new home.

In getting rid of about half of the cushions and reverting to standard four-inch mattresses in the forepeak, we made our boat 100 percent more livable. And we still find plenty of opportunity for some elderly canoodling whenever we fancy the urge (OK, so one of us more often than the other, but that isn't what this book is about).

Adjusting Standards and Attitudes

I recently reviewed a book on Goodreads (http://www.goodreads.com/) written by a middle-aged yuppie in California who, fed up with his dead-end job, despondent about not being able to attract an attractive girlfriend, and worn out by his lack of status in a status-oriented society, decided to sell everything he owned, buy a boat, and sail around the world. Our hero got as far as the Sea of Cortez when an encounter with bugs on the vegetables in an open-air market brought reality crashing down on his head like a well-aimed smack from a cricket bat: "I stopped dead. I could not believe my eyes. The produce, all of it, swarmed with insects." (*Breaking Seas*, by Glen Demato: 2011.)

Now, to a lad raised in the country in the fifties, bugs on the veggies are normal. The sterile uniform produce one finds in a local supermarket today is as much an anomaly as "free-range" chickens. All chickens were free range 50 years ago.

Demato's experience in the Cabo San Lucas vegetable market points up the importance of an attitude tuned to the reality of cruising in developing countries. Bugs are a fact of life anywhere you travel outside the areas saturated by various Monsanto products. And the freedom from those Monsanto products is a valid reason to travel.

If you are horrified by cockroaches, terrified of spiders (some as big as your hand), or petrified by slithery things, you will need to make some major adjustments in attitude if you are ever to travel outside of the cruise-ship gift-shop circuit. Once in Panama we were visited by a swarm of five-inch grasshoppers, one of which landed on Susan's back as we enjoyed a moon lit dinner in the cockpit. Her reaction was less than stoic; the ensuing screech probably registered as a magnitude 5.0 on the Richter scale. But, once she realized she was not under attack from a giant killer vampire bat (which she had been told abound in that area), we went back to our taco salad and tolerated their company. Nelson, once he determined they weren't edible (he tried one), just ignored them.

During our stay in Panama, *Vicarious* was also home to an extended family of geckos. There were dozens of them living on our boat, and they would pop up in the oddest places, always when they weren't expected. The paper holder in the head was a favorite haunt of the lissome lizards, as was my book rack in the forepeak. But they were friendly little dudes who were always welcome, especially after Susan learned that they ate bugs. In all our six months in Panama we never saw a cockroach on *Vicarious,* except for the ones that were bigger than the geckos, and I kept a speargun handy to deal with those guys (just kidding).

If you are accustomed to a suburban life in a developed country where all food comes prepackaged, sterilized, and nutritionally enhanced, where chemicals render drinking water safe, where a controlled atmosphere ensures you seldom shiver or sweat, and where "back to nature" means stopping by the park to feed peanuts to the squirrels, you may need a major adjustment in your attitude if you are to appreciate the joys of travel to distant lands.

Bugs are a fact of the cruising life. When this guy flew aboard and landed on Susan's back, the entire anchorage immediately knew about it. Once we determined that it was harmless, and Nelson determined that it wasn't edible, he was invited aboard to enjoy the moonrise.

You may also need to adjust your standards as it applies to creature comforts. On our last trip to New York City, we stayed at the semi-posh New York Hotel across from Penn Station (where the Railroad Restaurant serves the best oysters in the solar system). It was Christmas, and, although we had booked a basic (read cheap) room months in advance, the hotel was full. In desperation, management upgraded us to the only room they had left, a corner suite on the 40th floor with a monstrous king-size-plus bed and expansive views of the Statue of Liberty out one window and the Brooklyn Bridge out the other.

Talk about comfort and luxury. But even so, it couldn't come close to the comfort I experienced many years ago on a lake in backwoods Quebec when I finally crawled into my tent and a goose-down sleeping bag after a long February day of ice fishing for walleye on the Cabonga Reservoir. Comfort is relative, so avoid the temptation to compare the queen-sized bed with the 10-inch bouncy innerspring that you gave away when you moved aboard to the four-inch foam pad on your sea bunk. They are both cozy and comfortable, but the degree to which you can appreciate that depends more on the stuffing in your head than the stuffing in your pillow.

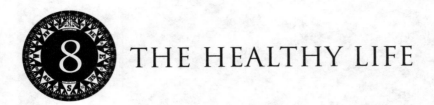

8 THE HEALTHY LIFE

. . . a determined cruiser with a positive attitude can enjoy a life at sea even while disadvantaged by extreme handicaps that would keep most of us locked away in a rest home gobbling mood pills and watching the test pattern on the telly.

Stones off Honduras

Back in the summer of 2014, we were sailing south from Isla Providencia 100 miles or so off the coast of Honduras heading for the hurricane-free ports in Panama. The trade winds had moderated to just above 25 knots off the port beam, pushing us into heavy seas at a heady six knots. The sun was shining for a change; *Vicarious* was steering herself with single-reefed main, full mizzen, and the big yankee; and all was well. We were enjoying the best sailing we had found since leaving Mexico three weeks prior. It was just after noon.

I was in the galley fixing a snack when a sharp pain, strong enough to make me cry out, struck in the left side just under my rib cage. The pain was a familiar one, and, although I hadn't experienced anything like it for nearly six years, I knew I was in for a major episode of kidney stones. I yelled to Susan, who was strapped into the cockpit enjoying the sun, that I was going to take a nap, then stumbled forward and collapsed onto the lee-side V-berth where I lay groaning for an agonizing hour.

I knew from experience that the pain was not going away by itself, no matter how much moaning and twisting and turning I did, so I dug our medical kit out from under the bunk and gobbled 10 milligrams of the oxycodone hydrochloride pain medication that had been prescribed by my New Zealand doctor for just such an emergency. The pills had expired three years earlier, but they retained enough potency to do the job.

With the pain reduced from excruciating to only intense, I was able to get some rest and stand my watch when the time came. I didn't tell Susan about my affliction because I knew that there was nothing she could do about it, and I didn't want her to worry (something she is good at doing when it comes to my health).

After 24 hours the pain had subsided to the point where I didn't need the pills, and we were able to continue to Panama without incident.

Past episodes of this nature had taught me that if the pain didn't recur after two days, the stone had passed, and I was in the clear. So, once safely anchored off Bocas Marina in Bocas del Toro, we went about all the interesting and tedious business that one does when entering a new port, and I forgot all about kidney stones.

Serious problems with the *Vicarious* fuel system meant our planned stay of two weeks was dramatically extended to several months as we struggled to fix the problem in the stifling 90-percent humidity.

Then, two months after our arrival, I had another attack of kidney-stone pain. I struggled through this incident by swallowing pills just as I had the first, and, after a day or so, this one also subsided into an unpleasant memory. But when the third attack came less that a month later, accompanied by high fever and vomiting, I knew I had to get to a doctor without delay. The nearest urologist was in the little town of Changuinola, about three hours away by water taxi and bus.

Dr. Diane O'Brien, a lovely Panamanian lady, whose great grandfather had come from Ireland to work on the canal and stayed after it was completed, immediately checked me into the local hospital for X rays, ultrasound, and an overnight stay for observation.

The X ray showed that, instead of passing, the first stone had lodged in the urethra, blocking it so that subsequent smaller stones had backed up behind, somewhat like ducklings standing behind mother duck while she waits to cross the road. The mother duck had become impacted and infected, and at least six ducklings were in the queue waiting to get through. Dr. O'Brien sent me off to David, a larger city on the Pacific coast located a six-hour bus ride away over the mountains, to deal with the infection. Then it was off to Panama City to the offices of Dr. Enrique Aleman, one of Panama's top urologists. Dr. Aleman checked me into the hospital for a ureteroscopic lithotripsy procedure that stabilized the stones in the urethra enough to allow me to return to New Zealand for their removal.

This longwinded and somewhat graphic dissertation (sorry about that) of a rather common medical condition isn't to solicit pity for the author's pathetic suffering or to stimulate the reader's admiration for his courage in stoically enduring excruciating pain (although such is surely justified) but to illustrate how common health problems that are easily dealt with at home can be serious indeed when they happen on a cruising boat at sea. But it also shows how high-quality medical attention is available just about anywhere in the world a retired cruiser is likely to wander, even in the rainforest and jungles of Central America.

Health Care in the Developing World

One of the oft-heard reasons that people who would dearly love to go off on a retirement sailing adventure give for not going or for staying within sailing distance of their home port is the fear that they will become ill in an area where they can't get health care or where they will be saddled with huge hospital and doctor bills. This fear is generally unfounded, but not completely. I speak from experience when I say that health care in most of the world is every bit as good as it is in the big cities in the developed countries, and it is almost always much cheaper. In our travels, we have needed emergency care or (more often) semi-emergency care in the United States, Mexico, Guatemala, Honduras, Colombia (San Andreas Island), Panama, Ecuador (Galapagos Islands), Australia, and, of course, New Zealand.

A Painful Comparison

An example of how far the cost of medical care has become out of whack in the United States was hammered home recently when we were cruising in coastal Maine. One of the prices I pay for living on a boat is the regular occurrence of *actinic keratosis,* or sunspots, on my face and arms. These nasty blemishes are sometimes painful, and they are potentially dangerous, so I regularly have a medical person freeze or burn them off. (At sea, Susan fries the little buggers with a Dr. Scholls wart-removal kit, but that's another story.)

We were in the Casco Bay area when I noticed that there were several of these spots on my neck and face that looked like they needed attention. We borrowed a car, and I drove to a clinic in Bath, Maine, that advertised seven-day walk-in service. After spending a half an hour filling in forms and another hour sitting patiently in the

Coastal Maine is one of the most beautiful cruising grounds we have visited, bar none, but anywhere you cruise in the United States, if you don't have valid medical coverage, you will find medical care to be the most expensive in the world.

Health Insurance

Another oft-repeated reason aspiring retirement cruisers give for staying home and not realizing their dream is the fear that they will lose their health insurance once they leave their home country. This fear is close to a phobia with many cruisers from the United States, where the delusion persists that U.S. hospitals and doctors are the

waiting room, I was ushered into a separate office where I waited another half an hour for a nurse. She arrived, carrying a fearsome apparatus that resembled a combination of a miniature fire extinguisher and a grenade launcher, and she had the spots zapped to her satisfaction within 10 minutes. When I left the clinic, more than two hours after arriving, I was presented with a bill for U.S. $325.

Now $325 is cheap for any medical attention in the United States, but when we had the same treatment in Mexico, the fee was 100 Mexican pesos, or about U.S. $6. In Panama it was 5 balboas (U.S. $5), and on another occasion it was free. In all three cases, there was no paperwork to speak of, and, if there was any wait at all, it was less than 10 minutes.

If you think that perhaps I was paying for greater expertise and a higher quality of care in the United States, think again. All three of the people who did the work in Central America did a better job than the nurse in the United States (where the spots returned after only a few weeks and had to be removed a second time), and one (the first one in Panama) was a fully qualified surgeon who had worked for many years at the Cook County Hospital in Chicago.

One more example of why you shouldn't worry too much about the cost and quality of health care while enjoying your retirement cruise follows, and then I will climb down from this particular sidebar soapbox and shut up.

In the southern summer of 2000, we found ourselves anchored in the lagoon in back of Surfer's Paradise, Australia, preparing for crossing the Tasman Sea on our way back to New Zealand. A doctor I had visited for a routine pre-departure checkup discovered I had a carcinogenic melanoma that needed to be surgically removed from my arm. It was a simple outpatient treatment that took less than an hour to perform, and the total cost, including a biopsy, came to AU $75 (about U.S. $60 at the time). I have no way of knowing what that treatment would have cost had it been necessary in the United States, but the web site, Health C Hostelper (http://.www.health.costhelper.com), says this about the biopsy:

For patients not covered by health insurance, the cost of a skin biopsy ranges from $150 to $1,000. A needle biopsy performed in a doctor's office would be at the lower end of the range, while a surgical biopsy would be at the higher end of the range.

The point here isn't to denigrate medical care in the United States, which I am sure is excellent even if it is a bit pricey, but to point out that, unless you have U.S. insurance or a lot of excess cash and can tolerate endless paperwork, you may be better off having most medical work done in another country.

best in the world, and comparable health care is not available in other countries. We hear the same thing from cruisers from Canada, Europe, Australia, and New Zealand, all countries that have comprehensive health care that disappears once you cross the border.

But people everywhere need health care, and in every country we have visited they are getting it at a surprisingly high level of quality and affordability. At the risk of repeating myself, health care in most countries Susan and I have experienced on both *Sultana* and *Vicarious* has been excellent and available at such reasonable prices that health insurance isn't that important. Thus, traveling to foreign countries (even those with developing economies (sometimes referred to as third-world countries) without any health insurance at all doesn't carry enough risk to cause concern to anyone in average physical condition. It is certainly not a valid reason to not go cruising.

HEALTH INSURANCE FOR OLDER CRUISERS

If you are still not convinced that the need for health insurance is greatly diminished outside the United States, and you can't face up to cruising without it, there may still be policies available to you. The most popular of these are the individual trip-insurance policies that work well for part-time cruisers who won't be far from home for longer than three months.

There are also more conventional health-care policies available to travelers that offer almost worldwide coverage. Some of these policies have restrictions on where a policy holder can travel and retain coverage. Most of the affordable policies of this type don't cover travel anywhere in the United States and often exclude Canada, and each one I have investigated will drop any policyholder as soon as he or she reaches the age of 65.

The upshot of all this is that if you think that you must have health-insurance coverage to go cruising in foreign waters, it is available, but usually at a high cost and only to cruisers who haven't reached their 65th birthday.

My experience is that if you are looking for international health insurance and you are over 65, you can just about forget about finding it at any affordable level. But once again (and I promise this is the last time I will say it), quality health care in most of the world likely to be visited by cruisers is inexpensive enough so that we don't have to worry about insurance. A few thousand dollars a year salted away in a special contingency corner of the cruising kitty (right next to the engine rebuild one) is more than adequate to cover the vast majority of any medical emergencies that might arise.

Health Insurance in the United States

The United States is the runaway world leader in per-capita costs of health care, spending more than $8,000 a year for each of its citizens. Canada spends about half that much, and New Zealand spends about a third. (These figures come from a Wikipedia article at http://en.wikipedia.org/wiki/List_of_countries_by_to-tal_health_expenditure_%28PPP%29_per_capita.)

Panama, another country where I have experienced excellent care for major problems and another popular destination for expats from North America and Europe, spends only about U.S.$1,200 per person while providing free (or nearly so) health care to anyone who asks for it.

With the United States spending far more than twice as much on health care as the average of all the other 34 countries in the Organization for Economic Co-operation and Development (OECD), it is natural for us to expect care there to be the best in the world, but this doesn't stand close examination either. In the 192 countries recognized by the World Health Origination (WHO), France is ranked as the clear leader in health care for its citizens. Canada comes in at 30th place in front of Finland but ahead of Morocco; the United States is in 37th place behind Costa Rica but ahead of Slovenia; and New Zealand is down at 41st place behind Brunei but ahead of Bahrain. Panama, which isn't a member of the OECD, comes in at 52nd place in the WHO ranking, and yet, even with this low rating, Panama remains a destination for Americans seeking bargains in routine surgeries.

Panama has a two-tier health-care system. On the first tier, basic health care is available to anyone who asks for it for token charges. (My overnight stay in the hospital in Changuinola, mentioned in the sidebar, cost U.S.$7.50 including X rays and ultrasound.) On the second tier, world-class health services are available to those able to pay a fair price for them. (The ensuing lithotripsy in Panama City cost about U.S.$7,000, which is a lot but only a fraction of what the same procedure would have cost in the United States.)

OK that's enough Yank-bashing on the touchy subject of health care. For anyone wanting more information on the comparative equalities of care available in different countries, there is a massive amount of reasonably authoritative information on the Internet; a simple Google search will keep you occupied for days.

Good, or at least acceptable, health care is available at affordable prices just about anywhere a retired cruiser is likely to go, so don't let the fear of not having health insurance keep you from your dream cruise. There are lots of valid reasons for not going cruising, but lack of health care isn't one of them.

THE AFFORDABLE CARE ACT (ACA) AND MEDICARE

Most cruisers from the United States are familiar with both the Affordable Care Act (Obamacare) requirement that all residents buy a health insurance policy or pay a hefty fine and with Medicare, the government insurance plan that pays up to 80 percent of the cost of many common medical treatments and conditions for people over 65. But not everyone realizes that both these health-insurance schemes go away once you leave the country. Here is what the U.S. government website, https://www.healthcare.gov, says about it:

If one of the following situations applies to you, you qualify for a health coverage exemption:

You're a U.S. citizen who either:

➤ Spent at least 330 full days outside of the United States during a 12-month period

OR

➤ Was a bona fide resident of a foreign country (or countries) for a full tax year
➤ You're a resident alien who both:
    Was a citizen or national of a foreign country with which the United States has an income-tax treaty with a nondiscrimination clause AND was a bona fide resident of a foreign country for the tax year
➤ You're not lawfully present in the United States

This exemption from Obamacare payments or penalties can be a blessing because the cost of Medicare, which for me and Susan would be over $2,400 a year were we to apply for it, or your mandatory private health plan, which can be even more expensive, can be saved and placed in an escrow account to cover health-care costs in other countries while traveling.

Here is how the provisions of Medicare play out when we compare the $300 cost of the magnetic resonance imaging (MRI) scan, which my Panamanian doctor ordered to investigate kidney stones, to what it might have cost for the same scan in New York City. According to the Bloomberg Report (www.bloomberg.com) the average 2014 cost of an MRI in the United States was about $4,000 (the cost in New York, for example, was between $474 for the least expensive and $7,332 for the most expensive). Because an MRI for kidney stones is considered elective (regardless of what a doctor might claim), my Medicare compensation for this treatment would have been $441 in New York no matter how much I paid for the MRI scan, leaving me up to $6,891 to pay for myself.

OK, you are right. It is unlikely that I would have opted for the most expensive treatment or the cheapest, but the national average at $4,000 would have still left me with a $3,559 out-of-pocket expense, and even the cheapest would have cost me $141.

It doesn't take a mathematical whiz to figure out that, except for the cheapest option in New York mentioned above, by opting out of Medicare I saved enough to more than pay for the $300 MRI scan in Panama City. The total cost of my kidney-stone adventures in Panama was more than $10,000 including travel and hotel expenses, but that was because it became a highly complex problem that was ultimately solved by returning to New Zealand.

Because of the complexity of my condition, it is impossible to compare what the cost of the same care in the United States would have been, but I am confident that the math would have worked out to roughly the same 10:1 ratio. The savings we have realized over the years from not having to purchase any medical insurance coverage while living in New Zealand more than covered that expense.

THE EXPAT OPTION

One surprising thing we have found while cruising is the number of fellow cruisers from the United States, Canada, and the European Union countries who take up permanent residence in a foreign country. Except for those from the United States, very few of these expats change country of residence because of health care, but all of them certainly keep the quality of health care in mind when considering shifting to foreign shores.

Susan and I are no exceptions. As I mentioned above, we have been residents of New Zealand for more than 20 years and passport-carrying citizens for five. And, while health care wasn't an issue when we made the decision to stay (we became Kiwis because New Zealand is such a lovely place to live, and Nelson has good schools and an affordable and secure harbor), the fact that New Zealand has one of the best public (that means nearly free) health-care systems in the world wasn't a detriment, either.

In many countries (Panama and New Zealand for example) where public health care is available at little or no cost to residents and citizens, there are private insurance companies offering health policies to residents that travel overseas. Qualifying for one of these policies usually requires legal residency in the issuing country, a comprehensive physical examination, and exclusion of all preexisting conditions. This most often means that you must apply for the policy in the issuing country before you start your trip.

Dual citizenship and foreign residency are not ideas to be taken lightly and certainly not without expert professional guidance. The implications of tax laws and the requirement, in many cases, that you renounce your native citizenship can be daunting, and the implications need to be carefully considered.

Be particularly wary of any persons or organizations calling themselves "immigration consultants" who promise quick and easy residency to any particular country for a set fee. You will find lots of these "consultants" listed on the Internet in any country that is a popular destination for immigration, and my experience is that many (perhaps most) are scams. All you need is a legitimate lawyer who is familiar with the immigration regulations of the country in which you want to reside, as well as the emigration policies and regulations of your home country.

DIVERS ALERT NETWORK (DAN)

One form of insurance that cruisers from the United States, Canada, and several other countries should be aware of is offered by the Divers Alert Network (DAN). This nonprofit organization began life in 1980 when a group of SCUBA divers became alarmed by the lack of competent recompression services in exotic areas that were becoming popular with divers. DAN was formed to provide evacuation service to injured divers, particularly those suffering from decompression sickness (also known as divers' disease, the bends, or caisson disease) and to provide training for dive-shop operators and medical personnel in recognizing and treating dive-related accidents and conditions.

Today, DAN has expanded to a worldwide non-government organization (NGO) recognized anywhere divers are likely to congregate. This is good news for cruisers, because divers and cruisers are often attracted to the same places. Also, DAN has expanded its services to include all travelers, not just SCUBA divers.

DAN International has a lengthening list of supporting organizations in other countries that are based on the DAN model, so these critical services are no longer available only to citizens of Canada and the United States.

To see if DAN membership would be of benefit to you and those cruising with you, or to confirm that another DAN-modeled organization is available in your native country, check out their web site (https://www.diversalertnetwork.org), or just ask around in any of the ports and harbors where scuba diving is popular. Everywhere you go you will hear anecdotal stories about some diver, cruiser, or other traveler who was saved from catastrophe when DAN rushed to the rescue. If half of these stories are even half true, DAN is a pretty super outfit and one every cruiser should investigate even if you would never even think of going on a scuba-diving expedition.

One caveat, however: DAN serves as a trip-insurance agency for one or more travel-insurance companies that include medical coverage in their offerings. These plans may be appropriate for cruisers leaving their home waters for short (less than three month) cruises but they don't work for full-time cruisers. In my experience, buying trip insurance through DAN is no different than buying it through any other agency (such as an airline). Buying it directly from the travel-insurance company will make filing claims a lot easier and may even save a few bucks. For recommendations on different trip-insurance plans that include medical and evacuation coverage, check out http://www.insuremytrip.com/.

The Medical Locker

One interesting phenomenon we often observe in other cruising couples as we travel from place to place is the incredible diversity in first-aid gear that they carry. Almost without exception, the longer a couple has been cruising, the smaller and less complicated the kit tends to be.

New cruisers often become obsessive about the stuff in the medical locker and with good reason. When first sailing off on a cruising adventure, novice cruisers don't really know what to expect. If they have read extensively, as most have, they have encountered a wide variety of conflicting advice and opinions, with many cruising authorities insisting on on-board medical facilities worthy of the emergency ward in a big-city hospital. It makes a lot of sense for new cruisers to lean toward the more cautious end of the spectrum and take everything that can be packed aboard. More experienced cruisers know more precisely just want they want and need in their first-aid kit and will eventually get rid of the stuff that they don't feel is important.

On one extreme end of the first-aid-kit scale is the be-prepared-for-anything approach, which, while laudable, can be expensive to the extreme and difficult for a layperson to achieve without extensive training and practice. One online authority, for example, recommends a kit containing several different types of sutures, including ones for sewing up severed blood vessels and another for reattaching nerve ends, ligaments, and tendons. Another authority insists that a dedicated kit for administering intravenous (IV) medications is essential. All this would be fine for trained medical personnel, but the average cruiser is unlikely to have the skills required to stitch severed nerve ends back together. And, although I have watched while a nurse inserted an IV stent into my arm often enough to be familiar with the procedure, and I wouldn't hesitate to try it myself in a truly life-or-death situation, I wouldn't feel comfortable with it.

The big problem is that any comprehensive first-aid kit is going to be a complex affair. The bigger and more complicated it becomes, the more specialized training a person is going to require before he or she can use it effectively and safely. It is one thing to have in your kit the correct sutures to knit nerve ends back together, but it is another thing to develop the skills to do so. My feeling is that some of the advanced kits recommended by cruising experts would require the training of a certified EMT to use properly. And, even if you did possess this level of training, keeping these skills current and maintaining proficiency through practice would be difficult on a boat, to say the least.

On the opposite extreme of the ready-for-everything system we have what I call the Tristan Jones approach. (Tristan, by most accounts, sailed with the least amount of personal gear of anyone since Og on the log, who we met in my last book.) These are the let's-not-worry-about-it-until-it-happens cruisers who have the same first-aid kit they had in the family car before they started cruising. You know, the one you got for free when you signed up for the loyalty card at your local gas station. They haven't looked at it or updated the contents since they moved aboard and often aren't sure exactly where the thing is or even if they still have it.

We recently met a cruiser who used a pair of vise grips from his tool bag to extract an impacted molar, then treated the ensuing infection with an unidentified and probably outdated antibiotic from his much-neglected medical kit. He survived nicely, if uncomfortably, and is now offering his new learned-by-experience dental skills to the entire fleet at no charge. So far, no takers.

Every boat should, of course, have aboard a well-stocked medical kit. It is also important that every member of the crew have the training necessary to use the kit that is on board to its full potential in any emergency. Every member of a cruising crew should seek the best first-aid training available and affordable, then match the kit aboard to these accumulated skills. It makes little sense to have an extensive kit with such niceties as an IV pack and specialty sutures if no one aboard knows how to use them. There is no excuse, however, for not being up to date in CPR. The exact procedure changes with surprising regularity so make sure *(Continued)*

The Case Against Sea-Snake Anti-Venom

One dictate often heard from cruising authorities is that there should be no compromise in your preparation for medical disaster aboard your boat. That certainly sounds like the best approach, but, like the equally oft-heard credo that "everyone who wants to go cruising can go cruising," it is idealistic, unrealistic, and basically not true. Not only can there be compromise in your medical kit, there must be, and a lot of, if you are ever going to sail away from the dock. Here is a poignant example of which I speak (I love poignant examples.):

In Fiji, we met a boat from Australia with a nervous sort of captain, who included sea-snake anti-venom in his regular first-aid kit. Now I happen to know something about sea snakes. While a member of the U.S. Air Force stationed in Okinawa during the early years of the Vietnam War, I enjoyed snorkeling and scuba diving in the pristine waters and coral reefs on the north end of the island. I would make friends with the natives there by collecting any sea snakes I encountered (and there were a lot of them), which they turned into a delicious soup. Yes, I knew sea snakes are horrifically poisonous, and anyone envenomed by one nearly always perishes within hours of being bitten. I also knew that the venom from the several species endemic to Okinawa was particularly deadly—much more so than that from a cobra. But sea snakes are shy, non-aggressive creatures with such small mouths and such tiny teeth that you would have to work pretty hard to be bitten by one. (In one case of attempted suicide by sea snake [unverified urban rumor here], a despondent person jammed his little toe into the mouth of a large sea snake and stomped on its head with his other foot. He apparently survived with no ill effects; tragically, the snake didn't.) There is no way even the biggest can bite through even the thinnest wetsuit. My diving buddy, Paul, would pose for photos with the things draped around his neck, just to prove how brave he was, but in reality he faced no danger beyond making himself look like an idiot.

Sea-snake anti-venom is another matter. It is very expensive, available from only a few places in Australia, is difficult to administer without specific training, has largely undocumented side effects (because it is so seldom used), requires constant refrigeration, and even then has a short shelf life. My call here is that carrying a supply of sea-snake anti-venom in a medical kit on board a cruising sailboat would be extravagant, expensive, and troublesome, especially when considered against the risk of being bitten even while swimming in areas where sea snakes are common.

(Important conscience-absolving disclaimer: If anyone were to expire of sea-snake bite after failing to provide the anti-venom in their first-aid kit because of anything I say here, I would find it difficult to sleep at night. Therefore, please, if you feel the need to include sea-snake anti-venom in your first-aid kit, or any other esoteric medications that your phobias, fears, and apprehensions dictate, please do so. That way we will both be insured restful nights and tranquil days, even though we know that the chances of you ever having to use the stuff are only slightly better than being run over by an Eskimo on a Segway while you are doing one-armed handstands on Bondi Beach.)

you are current on this crucial skill. Skills such as CPR, the Heimlich maneuver, and basic first-aid techniques are taught in an eight-hour Essential First Aid course offered by most national Red Cross organizations. Advanced training, such as the Red Cross Comprehensive First Aid course, is better and recommended to anyone who has the opportunity, time, and money to take it. Most Red Cross organizations offer a periodic refresher course for anyone who has taken their core courses; these should never be neglected either.

THE PREPACKAGED MEDICAL KIT: PROS AND CONS

Despite much advice from established cruising authorities that new cruisers should always develop their own medical kit in consultation with their doctors, I have long been a fan of the prepackaged kits available from numerous sources.

The proponents of building your own kit claim, with many valid arguments, that the build-it-yourself approach is the only way to fine-tune your kit into just the one you want and need. It is true, of course, that anyone taking the time and effort to study emergency medical procedures thoroughly enough to become competent in dealing with every emergency situation that might even remotely be encountered would naturally want to build his or her own kit from scratch.

My feeling is that the best and most efficient approach for those of us without extensive emergency medical training is to purchase as complete a prepackaged

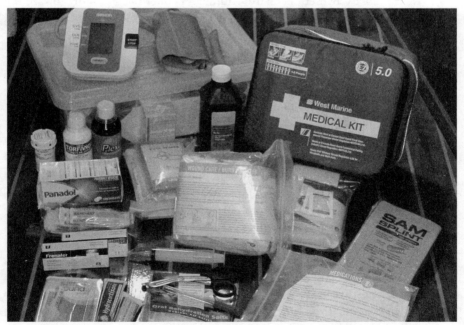

The base for the first-aid kit on Vicarious *was a prepackaged offshore kit from West Marine. To this we have added prescription antibiotics and painkillers, plus a lot of other stuff we hope we never have to use. The kit is a work in progress and always will be.*

first-aid kit as you can find commensurate with your skills to use it. Then supplement the kit with whatever other supplies and medications you think you might need during your cruise.

When Susan and I moved aboard *Vicarious* in the autumn of 2013, we bought the Adventure Series offshore kit from West Marine for about $200, then spent about twice that upgrading and expanding it. We have been refining our kit ever since and now have a reasonable and comprehensive kit that is just right for us. The most important upgrade has been the addition of a supply of general antibiotics (Amoxicillin); prescription painkillers (Tramadol and Paradex); large (one-liter) bottles of disinfectants (alcohol and hydrogen peroxide); and an expanded supply of Band Aids, compresses, and other commonly used remedies for small cuts, contusions, and other minor ailments. We also replaced the scissors and tweezers and added a scalpel and general suture kit.

The alert reader will note that this book has no long list of required items or even recommended items that I feel should be included in your medical locker. This is partly because I am a lazy sod and partly because our individual needs vary with our individual situations, our destinations, and with our training and skills. But it is mostly because these lists exist in their multitudes in just about every other cruising book written, many in precise detail, and most written by writers much more familiar with the subject than I am. For starters, I will point you toward *The Voyagers Handbook*, by Beth Leonard. Although Leonard's list is more toward the EMT end of the sophistication spectrum than my list (had I compiled one) would have been, it is comprehensive, complete, and an excellent reference.

Pre-Existing Conditions

Let's face it. If you have lived long enough to be considered old, even by today's somewhat flexible standards, you are likely to have picked up one or a few medical or physical conditions that you are more or less stuck with. Nearly everyone over the age of 55 has some sort of limiting condition that they need to live with. Some of these conditions are bad, some are worse, and some are truly horrible.

Our oft-mentioned hero, Tristan Jones, successfully singlehanded his tiny sloop for nine years after having his left leg amputated and briefly continued cruising even after becoming a double amputee in 1991. (According to the controversial biography of Tristan Jones by Anthony Dalton, *Wayward Sailor* [International Marine/McGraw-Hill; April 2003], Jones was a bit of a rogue and lot of a liar, but, even so, his books are still fun to read.) This illustrates my point that a determined cruiser with a positive attitude can enjoy a life at sea even while disadvantaged by extreme handicaps that would keep most of us locked away in a rest home gobbling mood pills and watching the test pattern on the telly.

The message we get from cruisers like Tristan Jones and his ilk is that we needn't let mere physical debilitation keep us from our dream of a retirement cruise. But we must be reasonable about it. If you have a medical condition that places limits on your abilities, you can indeed take them cruising with you (probably), but only a fool (like Tristan Jones) would do so without the advice and guidance of a trusted physician. Finding a doctor who understands both your desire to go sailing and your ailments might take a little effort, but it is always worth it. Doctors who aren't sailors are likely to react to your cruising plans with the same incredulity (or even horror) displayed by anyone else who doesn't understand what it's all about.

Medical Concerns on Long Passages

While most retired cruisers don't do long offshore passages, some do, and Susan and I really enjoy them. The feeling of freedom and spiritual renewal that comes from spending weeks at sea with only limited contact with fellow humanity is impossible to explain to those who haven't experienced it.

Actually, the liberating feeling of being in charge of your own destiny that comes from spending long days and weeks aboard a tiny ship on a vast ocean is often hard to explain even to many of those who have experienced extended passages. There are many longtime cruisers who must build their courage and swallow their fears before heading out into dark and unfriendly seas. They often consider offshore trips an ordeal that must be faced and finished as quickly as possible.

But Susan and I have been doing it long enough to have become comfortable with the glorious solitude that comes from being hundreds of miles away from any other human being. We are confident in our abilities and the abilities of our boat, because we have done it before and know we can handle it, whatever *it* turns out to be. Or at least we have been able to handle *it* up until now. As we grow older (and presumably wiser) we have come to realize that if the day comes where we can't handle some unforetold condition that life hands us at sea, then so be it; we are more than ready to place our destiny in the hands of the Supreme Navigator and ride it out to whatever comes next. We have discussed these potential consequences and have agreed between us on quite specific guidelines on when we will and when we will not set off the EPIRB or summon help on the SSB.

These guidelines are personal and apply only to Susan and me, so there is little point in discussing them here. But we are aware that the older we get, the greater the risk of calamity striking when we are too far away to summon timely help. We carefully measure and consider the ramifications of these risks, and we have agreed that when the day inevitably comes that the risk is greater than the reward, we will stop doing it.

There is little argument that cruisers place themselves at risk when they leave on any passage longer than a few days, and that risk necessarily increases, as we grow older. But most passages are not nearly as risky as non-cruisers think they are, and the careful sailor knows just what to do to minimize them.

Once clear of land in a sturdy craft, out where there are no rocks for your boat to hit and not much that will hit your boat, sailors are in one of the most statistically safe environments on earth. Most of the phobias we conjure up regarding sea travel in a small craft are imaginary. Being hit by an errant or angry whale happens but so rarely that it can be discounted as a threat. Striking a floating shipping container—as portrayed in *All is Lost,* a recently popular movie with Robert Redford as the entire cast—is even less likely. (Even though the media seem unable to resist the temptation to mention container striking as probable cause in every disappearance of a yacht at sea for the past decade, I know of no authenticated case of this ever happening.) Rogue waves (another favorite media term) happen infrequently, and the danger they pose to sailors is more likely to be from being flung violently about the interior of a boat than from capsize. Dismasting happens also but is usually survivable if the boat is a strong one. The fear of being eaten by sharks is unfounded (if a person falls overboard in the open ocean, he or she is about 100 times more likely to be devoured by voracious squid than sharks, or so I am told).

The real hazards to health at sea are more prosaic than the sensational dangers we all love to hear about from the popular press. While being flung against an immovable object by a rogue wave is unlikely, abnormally large waves and motorboat wakes are a constant hazard. As discussed earlier, unexpectedly being tossed about in a cabin or cockpit is always a risk but is much more likely to happen close to shore than at sea where sailors know how to prepare for it.

Cardiovascular seizures such as heart attacks and strokes can happen to anyone anywhere, often without warning, and are a legitimate concern of older offshore travelers. The depths of despair that descend when this sort of tragedy happens where help is inaccessible can only be imagined by those who haven't experienced it. The best defenses against life-threatening seizures are a solid background in first aid, a comfortable knowledge of CPR, and a thorough checkup by your doctor before you depart.

Here is a list of the most important items that Susan and I check and recheck before leaving on any passage. The longer the passage, the more carefully we check:

1. **An Unprepared Boat Is an Unhealthy Boat**
   The importance of giving every part of your boat a thorough pre-departure check can't be overemphasized. But, since this is a chapter on health, the things that need checking will vary depending on the individual boat. Numerous checklists exist online and in other books, so there is little need here for a comprehensive list of items to check.

   No boat will ever be 100 percent ready for a long passage, and those who try to make them so seldom go very far, but it is critical that your boat be as ready as you can make it and that you be aware of any shortcomings that exist before you depart on any passage.

2. **Check Yourself and Your Crew**

   Whenever possible, before leaving on a passage of more than a few days, get a basic physical exam from a physician or other health professional for yourself and for anyone accompanying you. If you have any major medical concerns—high blood pressure, diabetes, allergies, arthritis, osteoporosis, or any of those other conditions that make life as an older person so interesting—make sure you have a medical clearance from a doctor who understands the magnitude of your medical liabilities and the impact that they might have on your planned passage.

3. **Your Pets Are Crew; Check Them, Too**

   Don't neglect to have any pets that may be accompanying you checked by a veterinarian, especially if you will be traveling to a new country. You should have already checked that pets are allowed at your destination and what the requirements for entry are. (The country listings at http://www.noonsite.com/ are an excellent source for this information.) Now is the time to make sure all shots and vaccinations are up to date. Many countries now require electronic identity chips and pet passports, so make sure your furry companion's papers are as up-to-date as your own.

4. **Double-Check Prescription Medications**

   Double-check your supply of prescription drugs, allergy-relief medications, and any other supplies and apparatus that are critical for coping with your specific condition(s).

   Making sure you have an adequate supply of prescription medication sounds like a no-brainer, but the voice of experience says that you would be surprised at how often such things are overlooked. A good rule is to have at least enough of any prescription medication on board to last for twice as long as you expect your passage to last (the same rule most of us use for food and water). More is better, of course. Check all the expiration dates of your entire stock of medical supplies, and make sure everything will be still fresh on your arrival date. Keep in mind that the importance of expiration dates varies with types of medications. Your doctor can advise you here.

   Most medications are available in most countries frequented by cruisers, usually at much less cost than you paid at home and often without a prescription. But if something is critical to your health, don't leave home without an adequate supply. It just isn't worth the risk of not being able to find it when you really need it, no matter where you are going or how slight that risk might be. If you require a medication that is difficult to store (one that requires refrigeration, for example) or one that has a short shelf life, you should prearrange a procedure for replenishing your supply. In my case,

Cheap Dope in Guatemala

Once while anchored in the Rio Dulce in Guatemala, we were plagued by native morons playing their music at rock-concert volume. I asked at a local pharmacy for something that might help me sleep. The pills I was given only cost a few cents and worked very well indeed. Not only did they help me drop off to sleep, I didn't seem to mind the racket as much as before. After taking them for a week, I was curious enough to translate the Spanish name of the drug into English and found I had been taking a megadose of diazepam (i.e., Valium).

where the ostomy supplies I require are difficult to find in remote areas, I have a regular replenishment sent to our mail-forwarding service in South Dakota. From there, I can arrange to have them trans-shipped to anywhere in the world.

Medical Problems Endemic to Life on a Boat

Earlier in this groundbreaking book, I made the claim that the cruising life is automatically a healthier way to live than the shoreside life. As with all broad generalizations, this contention is open to dispute and will have a great many contrary arguments ("My Uncle Bob bought a boat and dropped dead the next day. What's so healthy about that?"). But, generally, it is true. For many of us, living on a boat while traveling to interesting and stimulating places, meeting people from different cultures, and making friends with likeminded fellow travelers is one of the most satisfying lifestyles available to a retired person. A satisfying life is what makes us eager to get up early in the morning to catch the sunrise, to move on to the next anchorage just to see what's there, to fully appreciate those blessings the Supreme Navigator has vested on us, and to not worry about those she hasn't.

But as we grow older, our physical condition gradually changes, and we become progressively more feeble in mind and body (but, after reading this book, never in spirit, we hope). Our wrongheaded society has come to treat this gradual lessening of motor function and mental skill as some sort of disease that needs to be treated with pills and tonics and frivolous surgery that we are told will reverse or delay the process, or by locking us away in gated communities and rest homes (which are seldom restful and often not communities). But aging isn't an illness, any more than being born is. It is a natural and healthy process that all of us will go through whether we want to or not and no matter how much we spend on surgery and potions and self-delusional hype to the contrary.

The pleasures of successfully growing old are many and well worth stiff joints, chronic ditziness, and all the other joys of advancing age, but we have dealt with these things in earlier chapters. Being old on a boat is fine, being sick on a boat is not, and being old and sick on a boat is worst of all. You can't avoid the first, so learn to love it, but here are a few things you can do to avoid the second:

1. STAY OUT OF THE SUN

Severe sunburn and sunstroke are largely not a problem with cruisers who have been at it for awhile. One of the things learned early in the cruising adventure is that staying covered up and in the shade pays large dividends in health and comfort. I usually wear a loose long-sleeved shirt and a wide-brimmed hat when in the sun for long periods and always wear a good pair of polarized sunglasses when outdoors. Even so, after a half-century of fun on a boat, I need regular treatments to remove nasty sunspots, which appear out of nowhere, and suspicious blemishes that don't look friendly. Melanoma is an occupational hazard to living on a boat, and it isn't wise to ignore threatening symptoms.

But UV isn't all bad: it is a primary source of Vitamin D, which is especially important to older people. Recent studies have confirmed that Vitamin D is helpful in warding off osteoporosis, several forms of cancer (including colon cancer), and in strengthening the autoimmune system. We also know that most of us don't get enough Vitamin D through our diet and need exposure to the sun to top it up, and the best way to do that is to spend some time outdoors soaking up the rays.

If you are the sort that likes a healthy tan, and lots of us do, don't worry about it. (My skin turns a progressively reddish and motley shade of pink when exposed to the sun, so a healthy tan isn't something that I have ever experienced.) Especially in the tropics, there is enough ultraviolet light bouncing around to insure you are nice and brown without having to waste your time with foolish activities like lying on the decks or otherwise exposing raw skin to direct sun.

A high SPF sunscreen is always a good idea when outdoors, of course, but most cruisers we have met either don't use it or use it rarely. After a few months living on a boat, most people develop a base tan that is enough protection for many of us in all but direct exposure situations. Others who don't tan readily (like your pasty-faced-but-otherwise-healthy author) and, ironically, many people with naturally dark skin, use the big-hat and long-sleeved approach to safety in the sun.

The natural melanin (the pigment that colors skin) in people with genetically dark skin looks great and does afford some protection from sunburn, but it doesn't protect from the harmful effects of ultraviolet radiation. People with dark skin and light-skinned people with dark tans must be extra careful to avoid exposure to UV radiation while at the same time making sure they get enough sun to produce needed levels of Vitamin D. So, it seems that people with dark skin need more sun than light-skinned people to get the needed ration of Vitamin D, while at the same time being extra careful to avoid levels of UV high enough to cause skin damage.

And, you might ask, how do they accomplish that antithetical juggling act? In truth, I don't know. But I strongly suspect that if we all, regardless of skin tone, don't worry about it too much and just go about our business in the sun with due diligence and reasonable care, we will all be fine. The important thing is to be alert for any symptoms of too much or too little sun and take immediate corrective action whenever you spot an anomaly.

2. STOP SMOKING

We will skip right over this one because, if you do smoke, you don't want to hear from me about how you are slowly killing yourself, subconsciously making yourself miserable, supporting one of the most evil corporate empires that ever existed, and insuring your status as a pariah among your fellow cruisers; and it's unlikely anything I say will matter anyway. If you don't smoke, you don't need to hear it at all.

3. DON'T STOP DRINKING

In the early part of the twentieth century, in one of the most ill-advised and disastrous political experiments the world has ever seen, the United States outlawed drinking alcohol. The ensuing social and economic upheaval destroyed the lives of millions of people and shook the very foundations of civilization around the world.

Don't let this happen to you!

A light tipple as you watch the sunset and a glass of vintage red straight from the box at dinnertime are things to look forward to of an evening at anchor in an agreeable spot. It is one of the cruiserly customs that makes elderliness worth waiting for, and it is a hallmark of the contented traveler, so don't mess with tradition.

Naturally, like all things traditional, the sundowner can be overdone. And should the evening sundowner become the morning sun-upper, it is probably time to solicit professional help.

4. BE CAREFUL WHILE SWIMMING

Swimming is one of the most dangerous activities we indulge in, on boats or off. According to the World Health Organization (WHO), drowning is the third most popular way of accidentally leaving this life for the next (among young children, it is in second place in the developed world and a distressing first place in the developing world) and should be of particular concern to cruisers in general and especially to elderly ones.

I don't have any statistics to prove this, but my experience is that, among cruisers, death by drowning is probably near the top of the list. Of the five deaths of fellow cruisers that have occurred in areas where we were visiting at the time, three were drownings, one of which was precipitated by a heart attack. The fourth was a rather messy and tragic suicide, and the fifth was a case of an elderly cruiser crashing headlong into a channel marker while operating the dinghy at full speed at night without lights.

The best defense against drowning is a healthy dose of common sense. Running around in a dinghy without wearing a life jacket isn't sensible at all, but it is common

What could be healthier than two exuberant children (in this case, my youngest son, Phillip, and daughter, Sarah, in a photo taken in 1992) swimming off the boat in the crystalline (but frigid) waters of Grand Manan Island in the Bay of Fundy? Not much really. But, without letting the thought ruin the fun, we need to keep in mind that swimming is among the most dangerous of all the things we do for amusement, on a boat or off.

nonetheless. And what could be worse than driving a powerful dinghy after dark without running lights *and* without wearing a life jacket? How about doing all three while mildly (or not so mildly) intoxicated. These things defy all manner of reason, yet they remain a common sight in many anchorages.

Another less-heralded danger is swimmer's ear (external otitis) which, although seldom fatal, can be debilitating and require hospitalization if not treated promptly.

I learned all about this common affliction the last time I dove to clean the prop in a marina. The next day I noticed a tickling in my left ear. I didn't think much of it, and when my ear started to hurt a day or so later, I simply took a few aspirin. Three days after that, I was in the emergency room getting treatment for an acute infection of the inner ear that had spread into my sinuses and throat. The two lessons I learned from that little episode are (1) don't swim in marinas no matter how clear the water looks, and (2) don't ignore any tickling sensation in your ear; seek medical attention immediately.

Swimmer's ear is a bacterial infection of the canal that leads from the eardrum to the outer ear. Most often, cruisers contract it by swimming in water polluted by *Escherichia coli* (*E. coli*) bacteria from human waste dumped from cruising boats and from shoreside sewage runoff. Marinas, even marinas in the U.S. with adequate pump-out facilities (because people cheat), sport higher-than-safe populations of this potentially deadly bacteria. Most anchorages with more than a few boats can also be sources of swimmer's ear, so the best defense is to avoid swimming around any concentration of boats or in waters directly offshore from any village or town. Observing native people swimming in waters near their homes is not evidence the water is clean, nor is the clarity of the water a reliable indicator that the water is free from pollution.

E. coli bacteria is the evil behind a lot of health problems besides swimmers ear, of course. It can be responsible for a host of ailments from stroke to urinary infections, so it is definitely worth the trouble it takes to avoid it.

Since my first encounter with a serious ear infection, I have worked hard to insure it is my last. My best defense is to avoid going into any water that might be polluted. Then, when I do go swimming or diving, I have Susan slosh a half-and-half mixture of white vinegar and denatured alcohol into each ear. (I do the same for her, of course.) After that, just to make sure I have destroyed all the nasty little microbial beasties, I lightly gargle with a measure of Don Julio tequila that has been recently exposed to a collection of ice cubes placed in the bottom of a rocks glass. After much experimentation, the correct amount seems to be exactly two ounces, and, so far, there has been no repeat of the dreaded swimmer's ear.

9

THE KITCHEN SINK
AND EVERYTHING
THAT GOES WITH IT

*. . . there are multitudes of retirees clogging the gated communities of
Florida and Arizona for each one of us swatting no-see-ums in some
lonesome anchorage in some faraway lagoon most civilized people
can't even pronounce, much less desire to visit.*

Readers of *The Cruising Life,* Second Edition, know well my feelings about the galley
in a cruising boat: without the galley, any boat is merely an oddly shaped depression in the water lined with some non-aquatic, often environmentally obnoxious,
material designed to keep it from sinking. And what the hel—any boat without a
galley might as well sink, for all it's worth.

When Susan and I first started our cruising adventures aboard our little 21-foot
sloop, our galley consisted of a small Coleman ice chest, a five-gallon jerry can of
water, a minuscule sink with a hand pump, and an anemic alcohol stove that took
most of a weekend to heat enough water for a cup off instant coffee. Subsequent
boats didn't have much more than that, and we cruised for many years far and wide
(well, far was the southern Canadian Maritimes and wide was Block Island, Rhode
Island) subsisting on tuna fish sandwiches and peanut-butter crackers.

When our children, Sarah and Phillip, came along, and we were cruising as a
family, some sort of parental instincts kicked in, and we became more aware of the
importance of proper diet while living on a boat. When we bought *Duchess*, our
antique powerboat, and started a long series of family cruises, we were outfitted with
a proper propane range with four burners and a large oven, a Dometic refrigerator
that worked on 12-volt electricity or on propane, an engine-driven hot-water heater,
a large freshwater tank, and a strong desire to advance our competency in the galley
past the toasted-cheese-sandwich-and-Campbell's-tomato-soup stage.

From that early beginning, we have both strived to improve our culinary
virtuosity and can now claim, while keeping a straight face, that we are finally
getting good at it. Both of us have always enjoyed the challenge of cooking without
the limitations imposed by rigid rules or formal training. I have always been (and
remain) the gastronomic daredevil, always trying something new or expedient,
while Susan has always advocated following recipes and convention. Thus many
of my dishes are . . . well . . . interesting, where Susan's are reliable and invariably
delicious. Because of this contrasting cooking philosophy it isn't unusual for my

To say that the crew of Vicarious *eats well is an understatement. No, we don't have homemade Belgian waffles, lean farm-cured bacon, and pure Vermont maple syrup every morning, but this sort of breakfast is far from unusual, especially when it is Susan's turn to man (woman?) the galley. The secret behind producing dishes like this on a boat is repetition; once a dish is discovered that meets with the approval of the entire crew, cook it often enough to get good at it but not so often that it gets tedious, boring, or, as in the case with bacon, unhealthy.*

culinary creations to end up as food for the colony of fish that congregates under our hull in anticipation of my all-too-frequent catastrophes, while Susan fills in with one of her impromptu salads.

A Galley for Retired Cruisers

Chapter 13 in the second edition of *The Cruising Life* has an extensive dissertation on my views about just what the perfect cruising galley should contain, so I won't repeat any of that here. But as we grow older and enter the rarefied atmosphere of the actively retired person, there will be a few differences in the ideal galley that are worthy of mention.

The most important consideration in a galley suitable for older people is (here he goes again, murmurs the crowd) to keep it simple. It is always a mistake to try to make your cruising galley into a copy of what your kitchen was back on shore, but it is deadly for older people. Let's discount the expense of a complex galley for now (while pointing out that the cost of a Force 10 four-burner marine stove with an oven and broiler is almost $1,600 at West Marine, and an equivalent four-burner household stove from Sears costs just under $400—but we will get back to that) and concentrate on operation and function.

When Susan and I downsized from the 40-foot *Sultana* to the 37-foot *Vicarious,* we left behind our dream galley. *Sultana* had a three-burner Force 10 propane stove with a large oven and a functional broiler that was a joy to use. The galley itself was a U-shaped affair (the cook faced aft), with a large sink and counter to the cook's right; the stove with a cover, which could convert to counter space, in front; and a large counter space with refrigerated icebox under it to the cook's left. There was plenty of storage under the sink and under the stove for all of our pots and pans, with room left over for a rubbish bin. Cabinets above provided easy access to commonly used food items. In the 20 years we owned and sailed on *Sultana,* that galley became the ideal by which we measured all others.

The galley on *Vicarious,* by comparison, is small and confining. The tiny two-burner stove swings athwartship on gimbals, the sink and countertop are on the cook's left, and a few cabinets provided limited storage above. On the cook's right there is nothing to do with cooking, just the cushion back of the dinette. That's all there is to it, and of all the trauma involved in moving from a larger boat to a smaller one, learning to cook in the smaller space was the most difficult. But we have lived full time on *Vicarious* for three years now, and in that time we have gradually come to appreciate some of the advantages of the smaller sized galley:

1. One advantage of a small galley is that a bigger one would require a bigger boat, and that would mean a lot more work and expense than we are willing to accept (again discounting the cost, for now).

2. Since the kids have jumped ship to follow their own dreams, we are now cooking for two instead of four, and, while I truly enjoyed cooking for the four of us, the smaller galley is more than adequate for our reduced crew, now that we are used to it.

3. The compact galley on *Vicarious* forces us to be conservative in what we buy and bring aboard. On *Sultana,* if we (and it wasn't always me, in spite of what you might hear to the contrary) bought some foolish gadget, like the large hand-crank meat grinder I bought in Fiji while fantasizing about sausages and meat pies, it would disappear into a remote locker and stay there until it was rediscovered, sometimes years later, so covered in corrosion as to be unrecognizable. ("What's that?" Susan would ask. "Dunno. Must be an old bilge pump, or sumpthin' from the previous owner," I would answer while sending it into watery oblivion.)

4. Our food supplies (called "provisions" by most cruisers, as if we were on a camping trip or a Himalayan expedition) are likewise subject to more careful consideration because of the limited space we have in which to keep them. Our oft-stated practice on *Sultana* was to have enough provisions to last twice as long as our longest passage. This worked in theory, but, because we had lots of storage space for food, we generally just filled it up. Once, on a long Pacific passage, Susan fell victim to a rare panic attack, thinking we didn't have enough food to make it to our destination. When Sarah

and I, in an attempt to assuage her fears, emptied the food lockers and took an inventory, we discovered we had enough food for a mission to a distant galaxy and back, provided we didn't mind Spam, canned tomatoes, canned tuna fish, canned beans, pasta, rice, and Heinz 57 varieties of soups (I think we had them all).

5. The smaller space on *Vicarious* helps to maintain a healthy kitty because we no longer waste the quantity of food we did on *Sultana*, and, of course, with just the two of us, we don't need as much to begin with. With all the space on our larger boat, we often found we were keeping certain items past their use-by dates or until the cans rusted past reasonable margins of safety. This meant we threw a lot of expensive food away. For example, we bought the soups, mentioned above, because having them aboard sounded like a good idea "for emergencies," but we seldom eat canned soups. Why would we when Susan could whip up a batch of tomato-and-lentil wonderfulness in the time it takes to think about it? Now, on *Vicarious*, we are getting much better at keeping our supplies of food at useable levels without the wastage that was such a strain on *Sultana's* beleaguered kitty, and one reason for this newfound economy is the reduced storage space we have for excess food.

A SMALLER GALLEY STOVE

While a smaller galley range is often adequate for the two-person crews on most of the boats cruised by retired persons, there should never be any compromise in quality and safety. Stove safety was covered in detail in Chapter Five, and quality goes hand and hand with safety. Both *Sultana* and *Vicarious* used Force 10 stoves, and I have been pleased with the performance of both of them. The one on *Vicarious* is the smaller two-burner model with a smaller oven than we enjoyed on *Sultana*, and, while it has taken some time to become used to the more erratic heat characteristics, the smaller oven has proven itself over time. We have few requirements to roast a turkey these days, and the baked stuffed fish that I am so fond of fits in the oven just fine when kept to a size appropriate for two people and cooked with the head and tail removed. The most noticeable difference between the smaller and larger versions of the Force 10 is the lower heat of the smaller oven. Because of the reduced interior volume, it is difficult to get the oven to a high even heat, even though the heat controls on the two stoves are identical. This takes some adjustment in cooking times, but it is largely a matter of getting used to. And, no, this isn't a particular endorsement of Force 10 stoves. It is just that all my recent experience has been with these two similar models, and I haven't used any other brand enough to comment on it. I assume other brands are also excellent and that the heat problems caused by the smaller ovens in the smaller stoves are the same.

The lower oven temperature on *Vicarious* means that Susan had to adjust the size and cooking time of her amazing popovers. They are just as savory and delicious

(I've been known to eat the entire bloody pan at one go), but they are smaller, and she can't make as many at one time as before.

The lower maximum heat was not adequate for my pizza either. Pizza requires a hot oven, and even the hotter temperatures on the larger oven on *Sultana* were barely adequate to produce a crispy crust. The development of my widely acclaimed stovetop pizza, driven by the necessity of coping with the cooler oven, is adequately explained in *The Cruising Life*, Second Edition, but there has been even further progress. I have started using a modified flour tortilla dough for the base in place

The problem with the two-burner stove on Vicarious, *versus the three-burner version of the same model we had on* Sultana, *isn't the number of burners—we seldom use more than one at a time anyway—but the size of the oven. The smaller volume of the two-burner's oven doesn't get as hot as the larger one, and the heat is more erratic and uneven. Nonetheless, we have come to love our little stove, mostly because changing it would be an enormous hassle, and, over time, we have been able to adapt to the smaller size just fine.*

of the basic bread base and modified the sauce to suit the thinner crust. This new pizza is entirely different than the old one, so don't throw away the old recipe; it still makes a delectable, if a bit different, pizza.

DON'T BUY YOUR GALLEY RANGE FROM SEARS

Galley stoves on boats aren't the same thing as the kitchen range you used back when you lived on shore. And, in spite of the significant cost penalty you will pay for a proper marine stove, don't be tempted to put a household range in a boat. Marine ranges need certain features that you won't find on household stoves: they are necessarily smaller than household stoves; they must be made of corrosion-resistant materials, usually stainless steel, and, while you can get household stoves in stainless, the controls and other important parts are most likely made of rust-prone mild steel; they should swing on gimbals to keep them level in a seaway; they need integral potholders and high fiddles on the sides to keep the pots stationary as the boat rocks, as boats do; and they must have a sturdy door latch on the oven to keep it from opening accidentally when the pot roast shifts due to the wake of a passing powerboat.

The exception to the rule of never putting a household range (or any other household appliance) on a cruising boat is in the case of large powerboats. Many powerboats are fitted with powerful diesel generators, which are run any time the main engines are shut down (as any of us who has shared an anchorage with one well knows), and the galley is often fitted with a standard electric range and refrigerator. Big power cruisers get away with this because (fortunately for the rest of us) these boats don't anchor out that often. They spend most of their lives tied to a dock and hooked up to 50- or 100-amp electrical power. These behemoth powerboats, most of which were built in the sixties and seventies to accommodate 50¢-a-gallon diesel fuel (and thus tend to be a American phenomenon), don't make good cruising boats anyway, so we won't waste any more ink on them. Big old power cruisers can be turned into fine and economical stationary retirement homes though, so they will be revisited in my next book, which will explore the popular concept of retirement on a stationary (non-cruising) boat.

FUEL TYPES FOR GALLEY STOVES

The galley stoves found in most cruising boats today are fired by LPG, often called propane (by far the most popular galley fuel for boats). There are several other types of fuels available (notably, alcohol, diesel, and kerosene [called paraffin in most of the world], but so much has already been written about them that anything I say here will be repetitive. Just keep in mind that the overwhelming galley-stove fuel of choice it LPG, and there are good reasons for that popularity.

GALLEY LAYOUT

The layout and physical configuration of your galley in relation to the rest of your boat is worthy of consideration on one hand yet not that important on the other. It is important because it will largely determine how much time you spend cooking five-star meals, and unimportant because you are pretty much stuck with the layout that came with the boat when you bought it.

Galley layout is an integral and important part of the design process that the original architect agonized over when he or she first drafted the plan for your boat. Placement of the cooking area is the single most-changed feature of many models of production boats that enjoy long production runs, which serves to underscore the importance of the galley layout and the difficulty of getting it right. The Fisher 37 (of which *Vicarious* is an early example) has been in production since 1974 and has had three major layout configurations, with several more minor variations of each. The first was the L-shaped port-side galley that was used for the first two years and is the one found in *Vicarious*. Then the galley was moved to the starboard side, where it occupied the area formerly used as the head, which was relocated forward. The current standard layout has the galley on the starboard side of the salon, where it runs fore and aft and replaces the only good sea berth the boat ever had. Of the three, the first, in my opinion, is the most useful. The second configuration placed the galley in a tiny enclosed area with poor ventilation, which generated claustrophobia. The third, the starboard side fore-and-aft configuration, is open and spacious but would be a miserable place to work while on a passage.

The center of buoyancy on any boat is also something to consider when looking at galley layout. The closer the stove is to this critical point (it is the point around which the boat moves on all axes when at sea) the more stable it will be, and the more stable the stove is, the easier and safer it will be to use. Of the three configurations of the Fisher 37, the new layout would be the most stable of the three, but I still prefer the L-shaped layout for convenience and usability.

A proper (and safe, as discussed in Chapter Three) LPG locker is gas-tight from the top down, has a top-opening lid, incorporates a solenoid shut-off valve on the feed line to the stove (or any other appliance), has a conspicuous pressure gauge for leak testing, and is vented to the outside atmosphere through the bottom. The squirt bottle lurking in the background contains soapy water and is a permanent resident of the locker, where it is always ready and handy to check for leaks.

The sad fact is that you are stuck with the galley layout that came with your boat, which makes it an important consideration when looking for a liveaboard cruiser.

OUTFITTING THE GALLEY

Once again I am going to try to avoid boring my readers with a long list of equipment that I believe you should have aboard in your galley. There are too many variables in cruising lifestyles, destinations, and personal cooking and dining habits to make any such list even partly valid. I will, however, (at the risk of sounding like a water-front barroom parrot) admonish you to keep the equipment list as short as feasible without detracting from the function of the galley at the level you plan to use it. If you don't like to cook (a surprising number of cruisers don't) and plan to subsist on eating cold sandwiches, canned soup, and in restaurants (as Susan and I did for many years), then you won't need much cooking gear in your galley at all. On the other hand, if you are the aquatic equivalent of Rick Stein and love to spend most of your time in the galley creating imaginative and tasty dishes for your fortunate crew, then you are going to need more than the basic gear.

For the best overview of how to develop a sensible inventory of galley gear, I will refer you to *The Boat Galley Cookbook*, by Carolyn Shearlock and Jan Irons, which is the most comprehensive cruising cookbook you will find. The authors of this fine book are not celebrity chefs but cruisers with a passion for cooking. Together, they have developed a vast storehouse of knowledge regarding how to go about preparing tasty, healthy, and practical meals on a small boat. Carolyn and her husband are full-time cruisers who have lived and cooked on their boat for more than eight years, while Jan and her husband divide their time between the boat and a house on a small lake in the Midwest, with occasional trips in their travel trailer. Each of the coauthors has an entertaining and informative web site: check out theboatgalley.com for Carolyn's blog and commutercruiser.com for Jan's.

Salads

Among the best, easiest, quickest, tastiest, and most nutritious meals we eat on *Vicarious* are the wonderful salads Susan can come up with on a moment's notice. A sumptuous salad can make for a satisfying meal, a tasty side dish, or a quick snack. They can be made up on the spot or a day or so in advance, and they travel well.

The advantages of producing a meal in the tropics without using the stove are fairly obvious, but prepared anywhere a salad saves time and aggravation. Making one doesn't involve a lot of cookware, so the cleanup is easy. Salads come together quickly from commonly available materials, and they are so laden with fiber and minerals that you should try to eat a big one every day.

Susan is a genius at coming up with tasty and nutritious salads on a moment's notice. On the rare occasions when neither of us feels much like cooking or those even more rare moments when we are in a hurry to go somewhere or to do something, a salad can come to the rescue. This simple garden salad was made from romaine lettuce, red onion, cherry tomatoes, and cucumbers, all topped with some canned tuna fish and a dollop of mayonnaise. It served as a satisfying lunch on a hot spring day in Mexico.

The Grill: Unnecessary Nuisance or Essential Kit?

A barbecue grill on a cruising boat is a bit of a luxury and not one that all of us should consider. The decision depends on your personal cooking habits, diet, and tolerance for expensive and aggravating appliances. And, while many boat crews, *Vicarious*'s among them, wouldn't do without a barby hanging off the stern pulpit, an equal number of cruisers do very well without one. Many cruisers in the last category have grills that are seldom used and sometimes never used at all. It seems that grills are on the list of items cruisers buy because the concept sounds good enough to make them mandatory, much like scuba gear, kayaks, windsurfers, sewing machines, and other useful-sounding-but-unnecessary items. But the reality is that the work involved in using a grill (or a windsurfer, sewing machine, scuba gear, etc.) often means they languish in the lazarette taking up more than their share of room, or they hang precariously overboard, where they become an eyesore and gradually rust themselves into oblivion.

Grilled shrimp and vegetables fresh off the grill and served with rice and a garden salad: what could be tastier, healthier, and easier to prepare than that? Often cooking on a grill in the cockpit is quicker than cooking the same meal in the galley, and the cleanup is always lots easier.

All these things are wonderful to have aboard if you use them often, but many of us don't. So think it over before running out and buying a grill based solely on the following arguments, and consider how having one aboard will affect your cooking and eating routine. If you are the sort of cruiser who likes to minimize the time spent at mundane cooking chores, prefers one-pot meals and salads, seldom uses a frying pan, and isn't even sure if your onboard broiler works or even if you have one, you probably aren't going to need a gas grill. If you buy one, you most likely won't use it. But if you are a culinary adventurer who relishes a fresh batch of fish and chips right out of the fryer, salivates over the thought of a medium-rare burger cooked to perfection on a grill (there is really no other way to do them), or invites half the anchorage aboard to share dogs, beer, and lies in a sunset-drenched cockpit, then a gas grill is no longer an option but is essential kit.

When Susan and I moved aboard *Vicarious* from *Sultana*, we had a somewhat traumatic transition into a smaller boat with less storage space for all our essential stuff, so we went the first year without a grill. We reasoned that with only the two of us and our determination to eat healthy foods, we could manage nicely with the tiny two-burner stove that came with the boat. And we did, at first. When we sailed north up the Gulf Stream to Maine, the soups and stews that Susan cooked up in the galley were welcome evening meals, while the heat from cooking them lent a homey warmth to the cabin below. Evenings on the water in Maine can be chilly even in the summer, and heat from the oven and a few kerosene lamps was always welcome.

But when we found ourselves on the west coast of Florida preparing to head even farther south to Mexico and Panama, things changed quickly. It was no longer a pleasure to have the galley oven warming the boat, and Susan's stews and soups, which bubble away on the stovetop for hours at a time, became an ordeal in heat tolerance rather than a pleasant reprieve from the chill. While we were tied to the dock at the Fort Myers Yacht Basin, we found that the multitude of nearby restaurants became an easy alternative to cooking in a hot and stuffy galley. This worked for a while, but restaurant food can become tedious, repetitive, and expensive. The answer to all our eating problems was to revert to a gas grill, and it quickly became the source of over half of our meals.

SELECTING A GRILL

Your first step in selecting a grill appropriate to your specific needs is to decide whether to get one or to spend your money on more useful equipment. Here I will assume that you do indeed believe that a grill will be a valued addition to your collection of culinary gear. So if you decide that a grill is not for you, please feel free to skip over this section. The next decision, for the rest of us, is the type of fuel you will use: wood, charcoal briquettes, or LPG (propane).

Fuel Types

Our first grill used on a boat was a $20 cast-iron hibachi that fit perfectly on top of a board over the stern-mounted fuel tank on *Duchess*, our 40-foot antique powerboat. This location wasn't as hazardous as it might sound, and the grill was held securely even in the most rolly harbors. The fuel of choice was driftwood that we collected on the shore of whatever anchorage we happened to be in, but driftwood has several drawbacks to weigh against several advantages.

WOOD

Wood used as fuel on a barbecue grill has several advantages over any other type of fuel and heaps of disadvantages. Different types of woods impart different flavors to the grilled foods that can be difficult to achieve any other way. And, of course, driftwood fuel is free and often readily available to anyone with energy enough to row the dinghy to the beach and collect a load. The downside of wood is that any type of hardwood suitable for a grill will take a long time to burn down to the coals needed for cooking. If you pick up a bunch of dried pine or other softwood by mistake, it will burn very quickly and turn into soot and ash without leaving any coals at all.

The best fuel for a grill is always a hardwood such as ash, hickory, maple, beech, or oak (depending on the trees native to the area in which you are cruising).

Unfortunately, driftwood weathers to a uniform gray color, and it requires a practiced eye and no little skill to determine which wood is which. The procedure often involves slicing off a sliver with a penknife to expose the inner wood where the species can be identified. This labor-intensive practice can be tedious, and it assumes that you can tell the difference between the different woods once you remove the outer layer. It can also be futile because, especially in the northern cruising areas of Canada and New England, driftwood seems to be nearly all softwood.

On *Duchess* we solved the problem of wood for our hibachi by bringing bundles of split oak from the woodpile at home. This worked very well indeed for weekend trips, but when we went out for a week or more, our wood supplies were quickly exhausted, and we were forced to revert to driftwood. Our most popular cruising ground in those days was eastern Canada, and it is now illegal to transport firewood across the border without a hard-to-get permit. The answer, of course, was to use the ubiquitous charcoal briquettes that are generally available in the smallest and most remote general stores around the world.

CHARCOAL BRIQUETTES

Charcoal briquettes are the runaway favorite barbecue fuel among cruisers who insist on a real fire under their Buffalo wings and burgers. True, the flavors imparted to the food with briquettes aren't as intense or as variable as with hardwood, but the ease of use and general availability can quickly make up for this deficit. Smoky wood flavors are easily achieved by using any of the wood-chip additives that are often sold in the outdoor grill section of many of the larger stores. That rare hardwood driftwood that you pick up on the beach can also be chopped up into chips that are even better than the commercial ones and much cheaper. Just add a handful of either right on top of the coals just before you add your food.

The downside of briquettes is the expense, which isn't that great unless you use your grill every day, like we often do. And charcoal is aquaphilic, which means it will soak up water quicker than a California almond orchard. Wet charcoal can make a horrendous mess in your bilge (voice of experience speaking here), or any storage locker, and render the fuel useless. Most important, wet or damp charcoal has been blamed for spontaneous combustion, which is never a good idea on a boat. Drying wet charcoal takes forever and then it doesn't seem to burn properly. In the humid areas where most of us cruise, charcoal will absorb moisture from the air, so for long-term storage an airtight container, usually a big garbage bag, is required.

In summary, charcoal is an effective fuel if you don't mind the inherent hassles that come with using it. Briquettes are more convenient than hardwood but need supplemental wood chips to impart the smoky flavors that most adherents to cooking on a real fire love, but, even with these drawbacks, a significant number of purest cruisers swear by it. Those that don't nearly all gravitate to the most popular barby fuel of all: good old explosive LPN.

LPG (PROPANE)

LPG has become the dominant fuel for onboard barbecue grills for a lot of reasons. Foremost is the fact that most boats today already have a handy supply in the propane locker. All one needs to do is tap into the feed line with a T-fitting, an independent shutoff valve, and an extra length of hose. This works well indeed, and if you look closely at the photo on page 191 of the propane locker on *Vicarious*, you will notice a notch cut into the lip of the locker at the far right. This notch was cut (rather crudely) by one of *Vicarious*'s previous owners to provide access for a fuel line to a stern-mounted gas grill.

We don't use propane from *Vicarious*'s locker because the small propane-powered outboard motor we have for our inflatable dinghy runs quite well on the two-pound propane bottles available for $3 or $4 at most big-box stores in the United States. These cylinders become horrendously expensive once offshore ($12 to $15 each in Panama and Mexico), so we stocked up on them before leaving Florida. These small cylinders are a bit more expensive option than a tap off the main fuel system, but for us the convenience makes up for it. Once our supply of fuel cylinders is used up, we will revert to the extension hose and a larger tank rather than face the exorbitant prices charged in every country we have visited.

CHOOSING JUST THE RIGHT GRILL FOR YOU

The next important grill-selection decision you make, right after you decide what type of fuel you favor, is the size and type of grill that will do the job for you. Once again, there are so many variables that would go into this decision that all I can do is relate the long trail Susan and I walked to reach our version of barbecue grill nirvana.

Our first little cast-iron hibachi grill on *Duchess* lasted about three seasons of northern cruising.

Each spring, just before launch, I would have to take the thing back to my workshop (that workshop was the only thing I really missed when we moved permanently aboard) and grind away a thick layer of rust. Then, after two thick coats of stove black were applied, it was ready to go again. In spite of these efforts, eventually there was more rust than cast iron, and we contributed it to an artificial reef the locals were building off Monhegan Island.

We replaced the hibachi with a shiny new marine kettle grill from Magma Products, Inc. But, while we moved up to a real marine grill, we stayed with the charcoal-burning model, as we were not yet ready to sacrifice the wonderful smoky taste we could achieve with it by adding a handful of wood chips. It wasn't until we moved aboard *Sultana* full time that we finally gave in to the convenience of hooking our grill up to our propane tanks. The storage needed for a reasonable supply of briquettes was the deciding factor. Trading the new gas grill for the old wood-burning one was as easy as replacing the new one in the old mount and running the new feed hose with the attendant shutoff valves.

GRILL SIZE

The standard size of the Magma kettle grill when we bought our first one and the propane-fired replacement was 15 inches, and that size worked well for the four of us aboard *Sultana*. Admittedly, we could have used a larger cooking surface for preparing many meals, especially grilled vegetables, but, once again, small and simple ruled the day, and we stuck with the smallest size available.

The gas grill we eventually bought for *Vicarious* was also this small size. It is all we really need for the two of us, and, when guests come aboard, we just cook in batches or crowd the grill with food.

Today, there is a much larger selection of good marine grills available than there was many years ago when we bought our first for *Duchess*. Magma (the market leader) has expanded its line with lots of new and enticing products and accessories, while several other manufacturers, notably Kuuma, Dickinson Marine, and Seaward (Whale), have entered the fray with an equally vast array of grills and appendages, more gadgets and contraptions in fact than you will ever need or could fit on your boat.

The most important consideration when choosing a grill size is the storage space available to keep it in while it is not in use. It is common to see boats sailing offshore with a large grill attached firmly to the rail, but this sort of thing brands the sailor as either an unsophisticated beginner or an experienced cruiser who has bought into the cluttered look. Stowing a grill on the rail is fine while at anchor, but both safety and decorum dictate that it be securely stowed out of sight and out of the way while traveling.

Deliberation on the appropriate size of grill would also include the size of your crew, their eating habits, the foods you enjoy the most, and about 100 other considerations that make this a decision that you have to make on your own.

As an interesting and maybe-not-that-important side issue on marine grills, the first two Magma kettle grills we used lasted about 10 years each before any parts needed replacement. The one we bought for *Vicarious* is ready for replacement after less than three years of use, having already gone through multiple burners and control valves. This noticeably shorter lifespan may be because of the way we now use the grill almost every day, or it may be an indication of the new fondness marine manufacturers have for profit-maximizing engineering standards, or it could be a result of the MIC (made in China) syndrome. Who knows? Like I said, it probably isn't that important. These are still good products; they just don't last as long as they used to. But, what the hell, I don't either.

GAS- GRILL COOKING TECHNIQUES

Most everyone old enough to have lived in the American suburbs (that vast wasteland of the go-go years) in the seventies and eighties knows all about cooking on a gas grill. There was one in every backyard of every house in my neighborhood and in every backyard of every house in every neighborhood of all my friends.

They were used on summer weekends to produce great slabs of greasy barbecued beef, each with enough cholesterol to clog a sewer pipe, and to char the American backyard-barbecue standbys, hot dogs and hamburgers, into black cinders, unidentifiable as anything edible.

Today, most retired cruisers have outgrown unhealthy food. Beefsteak is now an occasional treat (or has been dropped from our diets altogether) instead of a staple, and dogs and burgers are likewise irregular delicacies to be looked forward to when something more interesting or exciting doesn't present itself, which it almost always does. The barby has evolved from the backyard meat incinerator of the seventies into a versatile and adaptable onboard cooking tool that is an ideal way for retired cruisers to add variety and interest to their diets. For the roughly 50 percent of us who have the patience and persistence to put up with the troublesome cookers, let's take a look at a few of the more esoteric ways we can use the things.

Deep-Fat Frying

I know, I know . . . frying food in fat is horribly unhealthy, and elderly retired people shouldn't even consider it. But wait! You have to ask yourself if life without fresh-made fish and chips is really worth living. And what about some crusty crispy fried oysters that you shucked yourself within hours of gathering them from the rocks around your anchorage? So, OK, maybe frying food in fat isn't the most healthy way to eat, but it is one of the tastiest ways to prepare food ever invented.

There is a lot of information on the Internet that suggests that cooking in fat has been unfairly vilified in the past (see the article *Health Risks of Fried Foods May Be Overblown*, by Robert J. Davis, *Time* Magazine, Sept. 24, 2013), and, that if we avoid hydrogenated seed oils, like canola and corn oils, and stick with olive oil and maybe peanut oil, we can have an occasional guilt-free fried dinner without worrying about blood pressure or cholesterol. There are other healthy oils, such as avocado oil and palm oil, that can be used in frying, of course, but they can be hard to find and expensive. Olive oil and peanut oil also carry a price penalty over grain oils, but they are generally available, and, for a lot of us, the increased price is worth the healthful benefits.

Olive oil is among the healthiest oils regularly available. With a delicate taste that complements most everything, it is naturally free of both trans-fats and cholesterol, low in the nasty saturated fats and high in the good guys: unsaturated and monounsaturated fats. Peanut oil has many of the same beneficial properties as olive oil but with a stronger, nutty taste that works well with pork and vegetables. Both are sources of vitamin E (an important antioxidant) and phytosterols. I'm not sure just what phytosterols are (or how to pronounce it), but they are supposed to be good for us, and there are lots in both peanut and olive oil.

Here are the *Vicarious* rules for keeping fried food healthy:

1. Limit fried foods to an occasional pig-out. Once every other week is more than enough.

2. Shun hydrogenated or even partially hydrogenated vegetable oils and rely on pure olive or peanut oils.
3. Keep the frying temperature as close to 180°F (82°C) as you can, and don't let the oil smoke. Heating olive and peanut oils to the smoke point can start a breakdown that destroys antioxidants and reduces other health benefits (but it doesn't make them toxic, as you may have read).
4. Balance the fried food with a large fresh salad made with fruit, cukes, tomatoes, peppers, lettuce, and anything else with lots of vitamins.
5. Keep the fried food portions reasonable, and don't serve any other starchy or fatty food with the meal. We can make exceptions for fish and chips, of course, and a drizzle of oil and vinegar for the salad.
6. An hour or so after you eat, go for a brisk walk up a steep hill or do 20 minutes of calisthenics in the cockpit to help settle all that wonderfulness into your system.

DEEP-FAT FRYING ON A GAS GRILL

Deciding that we can do it is one thing, but how to fry foods on a boat without stinking up the interior or depositing a layer of grease over the entire galley is another. Frying food is messy and dangerous, so doing it below decks is inadvisable, so much so that we can add a seventh rule to the above list:

7. Don't even think of deep-fat-frying anything in your galley.

Most cruisers don't consider deep-frying as an option once they move aboard, but it works fine if you are careful and go about it in the right way. Here is a big mess of fresh oysters deep fried on the grill in a kettle of olive oil using the directions above. The olive oil keeps the food healthy, while the grill keeps the mess out of the galley.

Rule number seven is the reason that the majority of cruisers never cook in deep fat on a boat at all. But for those of us who count the days between servings of extra-crispy chicken wings like a kid counts the days until Christmas, there is another way. Deep frying outdoors on a gas grill requires a certain technique that needs to be perfected by practice, and I'm sure it is different with different types of grills. My experience is with the Magma Kettle Grill, so I will herein describe how to go about it using that particular platform:

1. Securely mount the grill outboard of the cockpit so that any spills end up in the water and not on your lap. This first step is crucial to your safety, because the dangers of hot oil are real, and any chance of a spill splashing you or into your boat must be guarded against. Many rectangular grills mount on the pulpit rail so they are half overboard and half inboard; I would not recommend this arrangement for deep-fat frying because the danger of hot oil spilling onto the boat or onto the cook is too great.

2. Only fry on calm days. If your boat is rocking and rolling, save the fried calamari salad (another favorite on *Vicarious*) for another day.

3. On the kettle-type of grill, remove the wire grill itself and the heat-dissipating shield under it. Now reverse the ring that holds the heat shield so that the fingers are pointing down. These fingers form a perfect cradle to hold your cooking pot just above the flame. And your pot is secure even with occasional swells or wakes.

4. Find a pot that fits securely into the fingers of the reversed heat-shield ring. On *Vicarious*, this is a ten-liter kettle that is about a foot in diameter and eight inches deep. The pot should be deep enough so that there are at least four inches of clearance between the surface of the oil and the lip of the pot. This is another safety consideration; the extra height will help keep any spattering oil off your skin.

5. Light the grill and adjust the flame to its lowest setting.

6. Place your pot over the burner and fill it with at least two inches of oil, then wait about 20 minutes for the oil to gradually reach cooking temperature. I never use a thermometer because I cook this way often enough not to need one, but a dedicated frying thermometer would be an excellent investment for anyone who hasn't done it before. The perfect temperature for your oil is 180°F (82°C) for most foods.

7. Watch the pot carefully to make sure that the oil doesn't smoke. The best way to reduce the temperature of oil is to add the food you want to cook. Absent that, add a bit more oil, and reduce the heat a bit. Reducing the heat below its lowest setting is easy: just place a small metal plate directly over the burner. On *Vicarious* we have used the steel lid off a mayonnaise jar (the smell went away after the paint and rubber seal burned off, and it didn't seem to affect the taste of the food at all).

8. Your food (which you have prepared in advance, of course) should be divided into small, finger-food-sized pieces. Small pieces will cook quickly and won't cool the oil excessively when you drop them into the pot.

9. Drop the food into the oil one piece at a time. The oil should bubble enthusiastically when the food hits it but not violently. Violent bubbling or spattering means that your oil is too hot.

Don't crowd the food in the pot. It is always better to fry in small batches rather than trying to get it all done at once.

Turn the food often using a slotted spoon or tongs. Cook until your food reaches a rich golden brown. If it burns or turns dark brown, your oil is too hot. If it doesn't start to brown within about three minutes, your oil is too cold. It is better to cook on a boat by observing the color of the food than by using a timer. Whatever you do, don't leave boiling fat unattended.

THE AMAZING *VICARIOUS* CRISPY FRIED CHICKEN NIBBLES

Of all the fried foods we enjoy on *Vicarious*, chicken has to be the most popular. Chicken is a staple of most areas in Central and South America, and, as long as you are careful that it is fresh, it is safe. In the past we had problems with chicken that had been thawed and refrozen, but, at least in Panama and Mexico, this is no longer a major concern, although you do still have to be careful.

Our favorite form of chicken for frying is the disjointed wings that are popularly called nibbles, but any chicken cut into small pieces will do.

Ingredients

Chicken
Flour
Egg, lightly beaten
Milk
Panko crumbs (or crushed potato chips)
Cajun Spice, made by mixing together:
1 Tablespoon each of:
    Paprika (I like smoked but suit yourself)
    Garlic powder
    Dried parsley flakes
1 Teaspoon each of:
    Onion powder
    Cayenne pepper (more or less to taste—less for wimps, more for macho types)
    Black pepper (fresh ground if possible)
    Oregano
    Thyme (optional)

A generous shake of:
  Red pepper flakes
  Salt (optional)

Technique

1. Cut the chicken into finger-food-sized pieces. If you are cooking wings, discard the tips. Rinse the pieces in water and pat dry with paper towels.
2. Place the panko (or chip crumbs), egg, and flour in separate shallow bowls.
3. Add one tablespoonful of milk for each egg to the egg and lightly scramble.
4. Add a significant amount (to your taste) of the Cajun Spice to both the flour and the egg mix. Mix well.
5. Dip each piece of the chicken into the flour, then into the egg mixture, and back into the flour. Do eight pieces (or one load of your frier pot) at a time, and let them accumulate in the flour.
6. When you are ready to start cooking, dip each piece into the egg mixture one more time, then into the panko (or potato chips) before dropping it lightly into the oil. Wait about one minute between pieces to let the oil recover to its optimum temperature.
7. Turn each piece every few minutes with a slotted spoon, and cook until golden brown and crisp.
8. Drain on paper towels, and serve with a massive garden salad.

This recipe works well with chicken, shrimp, and *langosta* (spiny lobster), but most other foods that lend themselves to frying don't need the cajun spice. For shellfish (mussels, clams, and oysters) drop the spice and add a bit of salt and pepper. For fresh fish, drop the spice, add a dash of salt, dip into the flour only once, and let the mild fish flavors carry the day. Personally, with fish, I prefer the final coating to be in the flour rather than in the panko, but try it both ways to see which suits your taste.

Panko, by the way, is a popular type of bread crumbs from Japan that can be found in many stores catering to yuppy cooks and foodies. If you can't find panko, don't worry about it. The crushed potato chips taste just as good, but the chip crumbs won't make you sound as *au courant* or as exotic as the panko.

STEAMING

Steaming food wrapped in a foil pouch on a grill is one of the easiest and tastiest ways to cook vegetables and fish there is. The method works equally well in your galley oven, but cooking on a gas grill is both more interesting and less troublesome than doing the same down below. And if you are preparing a complicated meal with several different dishes, steaming foods on the grill frees up the galley for more complicated tasks.

Some will argue that the method outlined here isn't really steaming, which usually involves cooking food suspended over boiling water. But when food is wrapped in foil and placed on a fire, the food is cooked in the steam generated from the natural liquids in the food itself and sometimes a small amount of added wine. Whatever it's called, the technique of cooking food wrapped in foil remains basically unchanged no matter what you are cooking, but the ingredients will vary considerably. For our demonstration, let's assume we are going to cook up a fat red snapper, of less than two pounds, that we just caught off the dinghy, accompanied by a mess of fresh vegetables.

Ingredients for the fish

1 fat red snapper (or any other white-fleshed fish of between one and two pounds)
Olive oil
One medium clove of garlic, sliced or chopped (not crushed)
Two or three thin onion slices
⅛ cup of dry white wine (Pinot Grigio and Sauvignon Blanc are good)
A sprig (a quarter of a stalk) of celery with the leaves intact
Half a lemon or lime sliced thin (lemon is best but often unavailable in the tropics)
A tablespoon of dried parsley
Salt
Black pepper (freshly ground, of course)

Technique for the fish

1. Make a tray with a double layer of the aluminum foil large enough to hold the entire fish. Fold up the edges to make a shallow dish.
2. Scale and eviscerate the fish, leaving the head and tail intact. On larger fish, the head and tail may have to go so the package will fit on the grill, but that's OK.
3. Rub the fish inside and out with the olive oil, and place the fish in the aluminum-foil tray.
4. Season the cavity of the fish liberally with salt and pepper, then insert the celery, onion, and some of the garlic and parsley.
5. Drizzle a thin stream of olive oil over the fish, then carefully spoon on the white wine, letting it run into the tray.
6. Season the outside of the fish with salt and pepper and sprinkle with the remaining garlic and parsley. Then garnish with the lemon or lime slices.
7. Cover the fish with a single layer of foil and seal the edges.
8. Set aside until the vegetables have cooked for about 10 minutes, then place the fish on the grill beside the vegetables (as follows).

Ingredients for the vegetables

A collection of just about any kind of veggies you want to serve with your fish will do. Leafy greens like kale and Swiss chard are particularly good cooked this way, and Brussels sprouts, summer squash, carrots, small white onions, bell peppers, broccoli, and cauliflower are all excellent choices. If you are in the tropics, adding a bit of taro and breadfruit will lend a Caribbean flare to the meal. Oh yeah, don't forget the mushrooms.

Heavy-duty aluminum foil
Olive oil
One tablespoon of butter (more or less to taste)
One clove of garlic, sliced or chopped (optional)
Lemon juice
Salt
Black pepper

Technique for the vegetables

1. Cut the vegetables into bite-sized pieces, and place them on a doubled sheet of aluminum foil.

2. Drizzle the olive oil over the vegetables, and mix well with your hands until the vegetables and the foil are completely covered.

3. Add the garlic, sprinkle on the lemon juice, and season well with salt and pepper, then place a pat of butter on top.

4. Close up the foil to form an envelope, and seal the edges. Poke a few small holes in the top to vent the steam.

5. Place the foil packet with the vegetables to the side of a grill preheated to medium-low intensity. (Medium-low is when you can hold your hand a foot over the burner for ten seconds without screaming in agony.) Close the lid of the grill.

6. Cook for 10 or 15 minutes with the lid closed before adding the fish to the grill.

7. Cook the fish and the vegetables together for another 10 minutes (or less depending on the size of the fish).

8. To check for doneness, open a small window in the top of each foil pack and test with a fork or toothpick. The vegetables are done when the thickest root veggie can be easily pierced. The fish is done when the skin peels back and the flesh falls away from the bones. Be diligent and take care not to overcook the fish.

Well, this book is rapidly drawing to a close, and there is neither time nor space for all the wonderful recipes that I planned to share with you here. But don't despair, because spectacular recipes of all sorts are available elsewhere. If the directions to the dish you hunger for aren't available in *The Boat Galley Cookbook*, as referenced earlier, they will certainly be available on the Internet or, better yet, from a fellow cruiser. But, before we end this thrilling dissertation, let's add one more chapter and meet some of the successful retired cruisers whose starboard tack has crossed our bow as we traveled hither and yon (actually, we haven't been to Yon yet but we rather enjoyed Hither).

10 A FEW FAVORITE CRUISING RETIREES

Life is a journey across the ocean of time. When we get to the other side we die. My theory as a cruiser is that if we constantly go places we haven't planned to go, never go anywhere we have planned to go, and never reach anything like a destination, we should live forever.

Susan and I have been cruising on and off for more than 40 years, and in that time we have met hundreds of fellow cruisers we came to admire and respect. The thing about cruisers is that we are all different. We have different boats, go different places, do different things, and cruise for different reasons. We have met several who are cruising to stay ahead of felony warrants, aggressive former spouses, and even the IRS, but this is rare. Most of us cruise for the adventure and freedom that we can only find on the open sea. Still, it is interesting how much the interpretation of these two basic concepts, adventure and freedom, differs among members of our community.

Here are a few profiles of retired cruisers we have met in our travels since this book was first proposed back in 2014. None are wealthy and none are poor; they don't travel the seas on palatial yachts but make do very nicely with basic boats that make up in comfort for what they may lack in beam.

Gregarious cruisers among them gravitate toward the popular destinations like the Bahamas or the Sea of Cortez, where they are never farther than hailing distance from a beach party or a potluck supper. Others prefer the higher latitudes and more remote harbors where sharing an anchorage with another boat is a rare but always welcome opportunity to make a new friend.

The following selection of four profiles was compiled for its diversity and general interest to prospective retirees who are thinking of spending a few years on a cruising boat. None of these couples does the cruising thing the same way as the others, they are all very good at their chosen retirement lifestyle, and they all have a lot to teach the rest of us.

Michael and Gretchen on SV *Syrinx*

I have mentioned in my previous books how cruisers can instinctively spot fellow cruisers the moment they heave into view: a simpatico only partly explained by the traditional cruiser uniform: scraggly beard, tattered cutoffs, sun-ravaged exterior, and casual don't-give-a-damn demeanor that fits the cruiser stereotype so well. The idea that this mutual recognition is more of a spiritual thing than a physical one was driven home recently in Mexico.

As Susan and I were walking north on Avenida Rueda Medina, the main drag in sunny Isla Mujeres, Mexico, looking for the famous Soggy Peso Bar and Grill, where we hoped to sample the acclaimed *alas de pollo rebozado* (barbecued chicken wings), we met a pleasant couple coming the other way. They were the antithesis of the cruiser stereotype, but they were obviously not tourists (who in Mexico manage to wear their tourist appellation like a day-glo armband).

She, with a stylish, silver bob hairdo, was neatly attired in shorts and blouse appropriate to the hot climate. He, a dapper (the only word that works here) gentleman with twinkly blue eyes, had a neatly trimmed Van Dyke beard. Together they bespoke confidence and an outgoing friendliness that invited us to introduce ourselves.

"Hey, you guys must be cruisers," I blurted as they approached. And I was right. They were Michael and Gretchen off the sailing vessel *Syrinx* (named after a nymph follower of Artemis in Greek mythology). Neither of them was at all scruffy, but we learned to forgive them for that betrayal of the cruiser image because they were true cruisers in every meaning of the word.

Gretchen is semi-retired from a long career as managing editor of the popular magazine *Maine Boats, Homes & Harbors* and as a moving force behind the *Maine Boats, Homes & Harbors Show*, which is held annually in Rockland, Maine. Michael had been a carpentry contractor, responsible for much of the fancy woodwork in the interiors of many of the fine homes in midcoast Maine. They met 30-something years ago when Gretchen needed a carpenter to expand the bookcases in her Camden office. Instead of the unkempt, sawdust-covered work-about she expected, Michael walked in neatly attired in a button-down shirt, smiling a beguiling smile. When he tuned his portable radio to the classical music on the local National Public Radio station to inspire his work, Gretchen knew she had met her soulmate.

Michael and Gretchen bought *Syrinx* in 1984, did a major refit, got married, and set out on an extended honeymoon cruise that lasted for the five years between 1986 and 1991. They then returned to work for another 20-plus years, sailing in *Syrinx* when they could and dreaming about it when they couldn't. Finally, in 2013, they were able to once again trade the shackles of the landlubber for the wings of the working-retired cruiser (Gretchen remains editor-at-large for *Maine Boats, Homes & Harbors*, while Michael keeps his chisels sharp and ready for the occasional carpentry job), and they haven't looked back.

Our lead profile introduces Michael and Gretchen on SV Syrinx. This intrepid couple has been cruising on and off on the same boat since 1986 and are the perfect example of commuter cruisers: they are semi-retired and return home to Maine every year to work just long enough to fatten the kitty for another round of winter sailing. They keep it small and simple so they never have to worry about the "Big Boat Blues." (GRETCHEN PISTON OGDEN PHOTO)

So far *Syrinx* has cruised the East Coast of the U.S. and much of the Caribbean, including two years in and out of Venezuela in the late 1980s. Since we met Gretchen and Michael in Mexico, they have covered the length of the south coast of Cuba, explored the wonders of Jamaica and Honduras, and done the Rio Dulce of Guatemala. As this goes to press, *Syrinx* is waiting patiently in Captain John's Marina in the Rio Dulce for the owners to return in the fall to continue the adventure.

Syrinx, *shown here laid up at Oscar's Marina in Isla Mujeres, secured for the 2014 summer while Michael and Gretchen return to Maine to work for a few months. Note the comfortable way the Portland Pudgy dinghy nestles onto the foredeck, where it is secure for storage or for the roughest ocean passage.* (GRETCHEN PISTON OGDEN PHOTO)

I was introduced to *Syrinx* in Oscar's Marina, in Isla Mujeres, where we had stayed for several months on our previous trip to Mexico. She is a green-trimmed beauty of traditional dependability. Her cutter rig and classic lines are built to go places, and she seems impatient while tied to a dock or riding at anchor. *Syrinx*'s design was adapted by Charles Wittholtz as a precursor to his Departure series of sturdy offshore cruisers and was built in 1966 in New Hampshire of welded plate steel. Given Michael's carpentry skills, it isn't surprising she has been extensively refitted by her owners (new deckhouse, mast, engine, interior, electrics), with a heavily insulated icebox and a composting head to replace the old leaky-and-stinky Wilcox Crittenden that came with the original boat.

Michael and Gretchen like the rugged good looks of *Syrinx* ("She's as tough as nails and pretty to look at," says Michael of both his wife and his boat), the characteristic design that sets her apart from the white-plastic norm, and the practical size and layout that provide comfort for two people without costing a lot of money to maintain. The things they like not so much but tolerate are the low freeboard ("makes for a wet ride to windward"), and they are taking a look at the lack of refrigeration:

(Continued)

The retired cruising life isn't an easy life. Boat maintenance is a constant, dealing with corrupt officials and greedy marinas can be unpleasant, sometimes the water and the food aren't to our tastes, and often the pinprick of unexpected expenses threatens to deflate our balloon of optimism. But for retirees like Michael and Gretchen aboard SV Syrinx, retirement cruising offers rewards unachievable in any other lifestyle available. (GRETCHEN PISTON OGDEN PHOTO)

We have a super-insulated icebox, and that has worked well for us for years, but ice is getting harder to find and is of lower quality (cubes with holes in them instead of blocks). We do still have fun trading with fishermen for shaved ice though.

The *Syrinx* crew figures that, between their U.S. Social Security check, Gretchen's much-reduced income as a freelance editor (including doing the copyediting on this book), her summer employment in Maine, and Michael's income from the occasional carpentry job, they can keep cruising for "as long as it remains fun" to do so.

"Fun" in their case requires an income of between $2,000 and $3,000 a month, which allows a reasonable number of meals in restaurants, moderate enjoyment of local cultural attractions, and annual travel to and from the homeland in Maine. The boat is paid for, and they do not carry insurance on it. To me, this is yet one more example of the advantages of a retired couple with limited resources cruising successfully in a smaller-than-average boat (at 35 feet, *Syrinx* isn't small by any means, but she is a compact design built for seaworthiness instead of interior volume) of sturdy construction and comfortable layout.

One of the questions on my cruiser's survey (see appendix) was: "What is your favorite cruising story?" Here is *Syrinx*'s answer, narrated by Gretchen:

We participated in rescuing a boat off a reef in Las Aves, Venezuela. Several boats of various nationalities were at anchor in a spot that required eyeball navigation between some reefs (this was before the days of GPS and chartplotters). It was sundowner time.

We watched in horror as a boat came scooting in toward us with the sun in their eyes and the VHF off—so we had no way to warn them off—and not at all in the deep channel. They were headed straight for disaster, and, sure enough, the inevitable happened.

The boat wasn't taking on water but was hard aground. Luckily it was fairly calm weather. So we all rallied, as cruisers do, and the guys spent the better part of the next day diving and setting kedges and winching and swearing—working really hard in somewhat dangerous conditions on an unfamiliar boat—until finally they got the boat off and safely re-anchored. The crew handed out beers and promised to host a big barbecue in thanks, and we all went to bed early, exhausted.

Imagine our disgust when we got up the next morning to see the boat sailing away. Ticked off doesn't even begin to describe it. Then a month or so later, we were anchored in Bonaire, and in came…the SAME boat! Michael rowed over to give them hell, only to find a completely different crew aboard, a crew that turned out to be the owners of the boat.

Imagine their surprise when he told them that the last time he'd seen their vessel it was up on a reef. Turned out that the owners had chartered the boat to some "friends," and the friends had returned it without ever telling them about hitting the reef. When the owners dove to take a look, sure enough, they could see that the keel was all banged up. They were very grateful, and we wrote a letter for their insurance company.

We heard no more about it, so I can't say how the story ended.

In retrospect, Michael said the crew was oddly clueless about the workings of the boat during the rescue attempt, but he and the other cruisers chalked it up to inexperience. Would we help again in a similar situation? Absolutely, but we might ask more questions first, such as: Is this your boat? ;-)

When we first met Gretchen and Michael, they had a shy but friendly black cat as crew, but, alas, they have discovered the hard way that the commuter cruising life with pets is seriously complicated by the facilities and policies of airlines.

We started out this time with our nine-year-old cat aboard, but left her at home after a summer break. She is long-haired and black, so not a great candidate for the tropics. She also did not adjust to sailing as well as we had hoped. We had a cat aboard during our first stint of cruising, but he came aboard as a kitten. (He was so young that we had him fixed in Venezuela. They let us watch, but that's a story for another time!) We would love to have a cat aboard again, but if we are to continue "commuter cruising," then the costs of flying a pet to and fro have to be figured in, not to mention the stress on the animal. Airlines are not exactly welcoming, airports even less so.

Another reason that the *Syrinx* crew and the *Vicarious* crew hit it off (besides the fact that the cruising community is accepting of nearly everyone, and it is rare to find fellow cruisers who don't get along) is that their cruising philosophy matched so well with ours:

We are advocates of the KISS mode of cruising, (mostly) happy that way, and mostly by choice. Our choices are influenced partially by budget. For example, we are cruising in the boat we already had. If we were to have put it off while we outfitted a "dream" boat, we would have risked not going at all.

It is amazing to us what people consider "essential" now as opposed to 20 to 25 years ago: electric appliances (microwaves, coffeemakers, even, heaven help us, electric stoves), televisions, watermakers, washing machines. . . . Sad to watch how much time and energy (and money) maintaining these things consumes.

Howard and Janelle on SV *Double Trouble*

When I first met Howard and Janelle, they were living aboard their Tayana 42 ketch, *Georgeann,* at a marina slip at Bocas del Toro, in Panama. Both Howard and Janelle are from Australia, and both had recently retired from their jobs as purchasing professionals at large Australian manufacturing plants.

Howard had long dreamed of buying a boat and sailing around the world; in fact, it had been a lifelong ambition ever since he learned to sail racing dinghies in New Zealand. During his working life in Australia, Howard kept his dream alive while raising a family and building a career. He refined his sailing and cruising skills in a succession of boats, from small motor craft to 28-foot sailboats, in the waters of Morton and Bramble Bays, a wonderful cruising area dotted with islands and secure anchorages with lots of rivers and creeks to explore.

Howard and Janelle are sailing their catamaran, Double Trouble, *a 1999 Voyage 37, home to Australia, from where they will continue to explore the many cruising destinations in the South Pacific. Janelle and Howard became friends while they were both still working. Janelle talked Howard into realizing his dream of sailing around the world, then decided, what the hell, she'd go, too. The round-the-world plans were modified when they realized that they had the best cruising grounds right at their doorstep. This same transformation in plans happened to Susan and me in our round-the-world adventure: when we got to New Zealand Susan asked, "How can we improve on this?" and we have been there ever since.* (JANELLE ADAM PHOTO)

Janelle was raised far from the sea, so she is a bit of a sandgroper (from the Urban Dictionary: "Sandgropers are well-known for being taller, healthier and better-looking than other Australians . . . and . . . characterized by high intelligence") who had no dreams of world cruising. But, after Howard and she became friends, she encouraged him to pursue his dream. Then, after she had finally persuaded him to go for it, she decided that there was no way he was going to go for anything without her on board, so she signed on for the duration.

In 2011 Howard and Janelle found the boat of their dreams on the Internet. She was then lying in Panama City, Florida. They put down a generous deposit and flew to the United States to inspect their new home.

Janelle admits that, when they bought *Georgeann*, both she and Howard were naive about ocean sailing, but, after three years of cruising the challenging waters of the Gulf of Mexico and the western Caribbean, they had learned a lot and felt they were ready for the big hop across the Pacific. Unfortunately, they had also learned that *Georgeann*, for all her big-boat strengths and seaworthy construction, probably wasn't the boat they wanted to make the hop in.

Tayanas are large boats for their size: they are heavy at nearly 30,000 pounds; they draw nearly six feet of water; and on *Georgeann*, as with many Asia-built boats of this era, the teak decks had deteriorated to the point that every time it rained (and it does that a lot in Panama) the interior was soaked. A new deck would be an expensive and time-consuming upgrade, and they were more keen on cruising than on spending a year stripping planking and slathering fiberglass with obnoxious chemicals.

Thus, after long deliberation, they decided to sell *Georgeann* and buy a smaller boat, one that would be easier for two retired people to handle and would be more comfortable (i.e., dry) on long passages. While sailing in the Caribbean, Howard and Janelle had come to appreciate the gentle qualities of the smaller catamarans. They liked the spacious interiors that they saw when they visited friends' boats, and the advantages of the fractional sail plan and large deck area also suited their cruising ambitions.

After one look at the convenient layout of the bridge-deck galley on the 1999 Voyage 370 catamaran *Golden Ticket,* which was for sale by a motivated owner, Janelle knew she had found their perfect boat. It took Howard a little longer and a lot of serious inspection time and careful consideration before he agreed that this was the boat for them, and *Golden Ticket* was theirs.

The renaming ceremony, where the old *Golden Ticket* became the new *Double Trouble,* was the event of the season. The entire marina turned out to wish Howard and Janelle best of luck in their new home.

It wasn't long after the renaming ceremony that *Double Trouble* was ready for sea, and they were soon away. Susan and I had hoped to be following them in *Vicarious,* but, alas, more engine problems and my vexing bout with kidney stones meant we were to be stuck in Bocas for many more months.

The Voyage 370 Double Trouble (née Golden Ticket), at 37 feet, is small for a contemporary catamaran (the average cat built today exceeds 40 feet), but her comfortable layout and compact design suit Janelle and Howard just fine. Janelle is particularly fond of the "galley up" layout, which allows her to keep track of what is going on outside while preparing evening tea. Voyage catamarans are built to high standards in South Africa. That radically raked mast gives her a saucy, ready-to-go look, don't you think? (JANELLE ADAM PHOTO)

Every cruiser knows that renaming a boat is fraught with danger. If Davy Jones, Neptune, and Poseidon, not to mention the Supreme Navigator, aren't pleased with the name you pick and the way you go about changing it, you can be in big trouble indeed. I personally know of one poor bloke who changed the name of his boat without the proper ceremony. The very next day his cat ran away, a passing powerboat swamped his dinghy, and the paint he had used to emblazon the new name onto the transom wrinkled and fell off into the harbor. But worry not, for when Howard and Janelle transformed the old Golden Ticket *into the new* Double Trouble, *they followed the ceremony to the letter, and the divinities were pleased. The entire marina turned out to wish them well.* (JANELLE ADAM PHOTO)

On our last contact with Howard and Janelle, *Double Trouble* had successfully transited the Panama Canal, and, after an unscheduled stop in the Galapagos Islands for minor engine repairs and a scheduled stop in the Marquesas Islands and Tahiti, they were on their way to Savusavu in Fiji.

Howard's original dream of sailing around the world was scrapped when he and Janelle realized that Australia and the South Pacific have more spectacular cruising areas than the rest of the world combined. *Double Trouble*, with her shallow draft and easy sailing qualities, is the ideal boat for cruising behind the Great Barrier Reef and for visits to the amazing variety of island nations in the South Pacific.

Howard and Janelle had these answers to our specific questions:

WHAT ADVICE WOULD YOU GIVE TO OTHERS THINKING ABOUT CRUISING AFTER RETIREMENT?

If we had stopped to think about the enormity of what we were about to undertake, we would have had second thoughts and most probably not have attempted it. Luckily we jumped in feet first, or we would have missed the most amazing time of our lives.

Seen here sailing off Raiatea, Tahiti, headed for Bora Bora on a brisk beam reach, Double
Trouble *displays the qualities that endear catamarans to their owners: a straight-up mast and
flat decks with none of that bothersome heeling that the rest of us must contend with. Catamaran
owners are the fastest growing segment of the retired cruising community, and a big part of that
is due to the design's fast-and-flat sailing qualities.* (JANELLE ADAM PHOTO)

HOW DO YOU EXPLAIN YOUR LIFESTYLE TO FAMILY AND FRIENDS AND TO OTHER NON-CRUISERS?

All our family and friends have been very supportive. They are happy that we are doing something for ourselves, as long as we keep in touch and let them know we are okay. We keep in contact with everyone via e-mails, Skype, and of course Facebook. Friends love to see our posts of the places we have been and are envious as we are getting to do what a lot of people only dream about. It is hard sometimes to be away from family on birthdays and family gatherings, but we Skype regularly when we have Internet. I also miss the grandchildren.

WHAT IS YOUR FAVORITE CRUISING STORY?

It was on 26 January 2014, which happened to be Australia Day. This is the day of the year (the equivalent of Canada Day and the 4th of July in North America) when Australian families and friends get together and have a barbecue or picnic and play cricket in the backyard, at the park, or on the beach. We were in Roatan, Honduras, that year, and, to celebrate, an afternoon of games was organized by cruisers berthed and anchored at the Fantasy Island Marina. Of course beach cricket was high on the agenda.

We started the morning aboard Blue Pelican (the only other Aussie boat in the anchorage) with a brunch of Vegemite on toast washed down with large cans of Fosters, Australia's favorite beer. All Australian cruising boats I know of have a jar or two of Vegemite, an acquired taste for anyone unfortunate enough not to be from Australia or New Zealand, and most of them will have an ample supply of Fosters.

In the afternoon we divided into two groups, Aussies against the rest of the world. We had a few English and South African cruisers who were made honorary Aussies for the day. The party games were done, and the outcome was as predicted, the Aussies won; then we were off to the beach for cricket.

Most of the other players were Americans, who had never played cricket before; it was amusing to see them hold the bat like they were playing baseball and watch them try to learn the art of bowling the ball down to the wickets (a strategically placed rubbish bin). The art of holding the bat and touching it on the ground before swinging it as the ball was bowled down was a great source of amusement. As is customary, at the end of the game it was drinks all 'round.

One year later, on Australia Day in 2015, we transited the Panama Canal. Both these pivotal events will be fondly remembered for many years to come.

Chuck and Laura on SV *Lealea*

Of the four cruising couples that I have chosen to profile in this chapter, Chuck and Laura on SV *Lealea* are the only ones that I have yet to meet in person. But that doesn't mean that I don't know them. As a longtime fan of their video series, available for free on their Youtube channel (https://www.youtube.com/user/vega1860), and their detailed and meticulously maintained blog (http://cruisinglealea.com/), as well as their regular podcasts (http://thesailingpodcast.com/sailing-alaska-with-cruising-lealea/), I feel that I know them very well indeed. More important, perhaps, is the fact that I have come to admire them for the lifestyle choices they have made and for the way they have gone about the art of retirement cruising that is the focus of this book.

Readers of *The Cruising Life, Second Edition*, know that I am a strong proponent of keeping sailing, cruising, and life in general as simple as possible. Several informal studies made over the years clearly show that the more complicated a cruising boat becomes, the less likely it is that the owners will enjoy a successful long-term cruise.

The financial advantages enjoyed by some with generous retirement funds, who are able to afford large, complicated boats, don't stand for much when cruising success is measured. In fact, cruisers of modest means who are sailing in basic boats, with only the equipment required to get the job done, often enjoy a greater chance of success than those with fancy and expensive yachts. There are many reasons

Chuck and Laura have been living aboard their Vega 27 sailboat, Lealea, for 16 years. Seven of those have been as full-time long-distance ocean cruisers. They are shown here while wintering in Petersburg, Alaska, in 2013. That Chuck and Laura chose to head for the high latitudes on the second leg of their retirement cruise (the first leg saw them sailing the 1,200 miles from Hawaii to Washington State) instead of heading south for the balmy breezes and piña coladas that most of us seek speaks volumes for their spirit of adventure and individuality. (LAURA WONG-ROSE PHOTO)

for the disproportionate success of basic cruisers, as we have already visited in previous chapters, but the biggest two seem to be common to all large and expensive boats. First is the angst caused by having a large amount of money dedicated to a rapidly depreciating sinkhole for cash. Just the annual insurance premium on a $250,000 cruising boat would finance a year's worth of liveaboard luxury for most of us budget cruisers. Second is the aggravation of trying to keep costly gadgets and expensive equipment operating and updated in a salt-air environment that doesn't much like costly gadgets.

That Chuck and Laura sail successfully in a 27-foot Vega, and have lived aboard for more than 16 years, reinforces my ongoing argument that in the cruising life simple begets success, basic begets serenity, and small begets happiness. They are cruising in the high latitudes away from the throngs who flock to the Caribbean, Bahamas, and the Sea of Cortez, which also speaks volumes about their spirit of adventure and their eagerness to pursue it.

THE CRUISERS

Chuck and Laura met when she applied for a warehouse manager position at the Harley Davidson distributor in Hawaii. Chuck conducted the interview and hired her for the job. They became good friends, started sailing together on Chuck's liveaboard Vega 27, then made the relationship permanent when Laura agreed that Chuck's plans for sailing off to somewhere else after retirement suited her just fine.

Chuck had lived aboard *Lealea* for six years when Laura joined the team in 1996. After sailing around Hawaii for nine years, they both retired from their jobs in the spring of 2007 and sailed away forever. Their first trip was an ambitious one even for experienced cruisers, but from Hawaii you don't have much choice. If you are going to do an ocean passage, it is going to be a long one no matter which direction you sail.

Lealea departed Ala Wai Boat Harbor in Honolulu at 0640 hours on May 26 and arrived at Makah Marina, Neah Bay, Washington, at 2130 hours on July 19 after a rough and eventful passage. The details are documented on Chuck's log at http://americanvega.org/captainslog.html and should be read by anyone who thinks that the cruising life is always an easy one.

But the old saw sings that good sailors aren't made by fair weather and easy passages. Chuck and Laura learned a lot of lessons on their first long-haul ocean challenge, and, fortunately for you and me, they share their experiences with the rest of us in their videos, podcasts, and blogs.

THE BOAT

The Vega 27 is a classic among classics, similar in concept if not in design to the venerable Herreshoff 27 and the Pearson Triton. The Vega 27 was first drafted in 1964 by Swedish designer Per Brohall as a serious offshore cruiser, and, despite her

In addition to being an accomplished sailor, Laura is a talented art photographer who maintains her own web site. "I love having the ability to instantly decide if a shot is good or bad and either save or delete it, but I also see a trend with the digital age to simply 'fix' a shot later. . . . The majority of my photographs posted are not altered in any way." This one, titled Bronze Prop, *is among my favorites. You can view (and purchase at remarkably reasonable prices) more of Laura's work at http://laura-wongrose.artistwebsites.com/index.html* (LAURA WONG-ROSE PHOTO)

modest dimensions, she has fulfilled that mission very well indeed. Those of us who remember John Neal's entertaining book *Log of Mahina*, published in 1994, will recall his adventures in the South Pacific aboard his sturdy and reliable Vega 27.

If that wasn't testimony enough for the seaworthiness of this remarkable design, in 2012, solo sailor Matt Rutherford piloted his Vega 27, *St. Brendan*, through the Northwest Passage and completely around the North and South American continents. He took only 11 months to cover the 27,000 miles, much of the way with an inoperable engine. Many other Vega 27s have circumnavigated, and even more have served their owners well as full-time ocean cruisers.

In the 10 years that Vega 27s were in production (1964 to 1974), nearly 3,500 were built and sold all over the world. This makes the Vega 27 one of the most popular small cruising boats ever, a popularity that continues today, with good Vegas commanding reasonable-but-affordable prices on the used-boat market. There are currently six Vega 27s listed on the Yacht World web site, all for less than $27,000. Alas, only two appear to be good value for ocean cruising, but those two appear to be fine indeed.

Albin Vega 27

In spite of her comparatively short waterline, the Vega 27 is one of the sturdiest and most sea-proven designs to ever materialize from a designer's drafting board. SV Lealea *made the 2,000-plus-mile journey from Hawaii to Port Angeles, Washington, without a radar, generator, refrigeration, SSB, windvane, wind generator, or major problems, proving once again that keeping things small and basic keeps things free and easy. It was Chuck and Laura's first major offshore passage, and it wasn't an easy one. The efficient shape of the hull and the no-nonsense mast-head rig of the Vega 27 are testimony to her sea-kindly voyaging qualities.* (Photo courtesy of http://www. bluewaterboats.org)

Another important advantage to the Vega 27 is the active and enthusiastic owner's associations in the United States (http://americanvega.org/) and Europe (http://www.albinvega.co.uk/) that stand ready to help with parts and maintenance problems.

The features Chuck and Laura like most about *Lealea*, besides the economy inherent in living on a small boat, are the seaworthiness and the self-tending qualities that allow them to sail long distances without a windvane and with only a tiller autopilot (which is seldom needed) as a reserve or backup. High construction standards backed by the fact that no compromises were made in materials when the Vegas were built means that they don't have to worry about deck-to-hull seams opening up in a seaway or about other construction details that can be vexing to owners of lesser boats of this size. The shallow draft (less than four feet) means that anchorages and harbors that bigger boats can only dream about are readily available, and the cutaway keel and hinged rudder means she can take the ground with few concerns.

Lealea is Vega hull number 1,860 and was built in Sweden in 1973. Chuck bought her from his boss in 1990 and immediately moved aboard. Laura moved aboard in 1996, and they haven't looked back. Through the years *Lealea* has had many upgrades, including a new engine, rigging, lifelines, Awlgrip paint job, fuel tanks, and a refinished interior. She is now undergoing a refit in Alaska, which, when complete, will make sure that *Lealea* is good for another 40 years of cruising. If you want to see the step-by-step progress of this refit, just tune in Chuck's entertaining and informative videos on his YouTube channel.

What don't Chuck and Laura like about *Lealea*? Well, not much, really. Laura says she sometimes dreams of a bigger stove with a real oven, and while Chuck hasn't said so, I suspect he would like more room for tools and maybe a bit more room for editing videos. But everything on a boat comes at a cost, and, for Chuck

The clean and efficient lines of the Vega 27 are evident in this shot of Lealea *at the dock with her storm jib ready to deploy. Note the clever way the big Bruce bower anchor is stowed on the split pulpit.* (LAURA WONG-ROSE PHOTO)

and Laura, a bigger boat with a larger stove and working space isn't worth the simplicity they would have to sacrifice to get it.

THE CRUISING PHILOSOPHY

Here are a few gems of Chuck and Laura's cruising wisdom in their own words taken from their blog:

> Our goal is to challenge ourselves and our vessel and by so doing learn and grow, to share our experiences and the lessons learned through our videos and written logs, and to promote small-boat cruising in general and the American Vega Association in particular.
>
> The "stuff" thing for me is fairly simple, there is no extra stuff. I don't have a shoe fetish or a passion for trinkets so it's not a big challenge, but we both still have to occasionally cull our possessions. Books are usually our problem. Secretly I have visions of us leaving a harbor and I am hurling "stuff" overboard. Cell phones, laptops . . . .
>
> There is nothing mysterious or difficult about our lifestyle. We try to keep it as simple as possible with the least amount of anxiety, and whatever it is we are doing it seems to be working. Nearly 15 years of marriage and 18 years of living aboard and we are closer than ever.
>
> The Vega, at 27 feet LOA, is small by today's standards, especially for a full-time liveaboard cruiser. We attribute that to marketing. In our opinion, the Vega, and other boats in her class, are ideal for cruising couples who can get past the idea that they "need" a 40-foot ketch to go cruising. "Go small. Go simple. Go now," and go places that people with bigger boats cannot reach.
>
> We carry six fire extinguishers, two in the forward cabin where we sleep when in port or at anchor, three in the main cabin, and one in the cockpit.
>
> Our first-aid kit is a U.S. Navy item, very complete and well stocked. We have both had extensive first-aid training and have a comprehensive first-aid book for reference. Every crewmember should be able to deal with compound

fractures, burns, severe cuts, poisoning, and any known medical conditions such as heart problems, diabetes, or allergies among the crew.

We both wear a sharp knife on a lanyard at all times while at sea, plus we keep a dive knife in a sheath attached to the base of the mast on deck and another on the aft bracket.

We have three manual bilge pumps, and all hose connections are double-clamped with stainless-steel clamps with tapered softwood plugs handy.

We include ground tackle as safety equipment. We carry two 10-kilogram Bruce anchors, one 25-pound Danforth, and one 10-kilogram Delta. Each has its own rode of 50 feet of chain and 250 feet of ½-inch three-strand nylon rope. Two boat hooks also come in handy.

We carry basic liability and towing insurance through BoatUS (http://www.boatus.com). Electronics: VHF radio with AIS receiver, and depth sounder. That's all folks. When radar systems get smaller and less expensive I may invest in one but for now we'll do without.

Navigation: Best quality compasses possible, two bulkhead-mounted and two hand-bearing. Two pairs of good quality 7X50 binoculars. Complete set of paper charts for the planned cruising area plus plotting tools (I like the Jeppesen plotter because I am a pilot. I also use a U.S. Army Artillery plotting square, a steel ruler, and traditional dividers. I don't like parallel rulers but you should use whatever tools you are comfortable with). I think you need an almanac but doubt the necessity of a sextant and HO249 tables, although we do carry them. We carry four hand-held GPS receivers and plenty of batteries. Also tide and current tables and cruising guides like Charlie's Charts. The more information we can get about our destination the better. We also use a laptop computer with OpenCPN software and electronic charts and Google Earth for planning.

Self-steering: We carry two Raymarine ST2000T Tiller Pilots so we always have a spare. They come in handy while motoring but Lealea has been known to steer herself under sail for up to three days, maintaining her course within 10 degrees with just a piece of shock cord from the tiller to a windward cleat. We are asked frequently why we don't have a wind vane and the short answer is that we are cheap and don't really see the need.

Spares: We carry enough new rope to replace the running rigging two or three times plus several blocks of various types and a handy billy. I used to carry a spare stay but have come to believe that standing rig failure can be dealt with using rope sufficiently well to reach port where more permanent repairs can be made. We carry two water-pump impellers for the engine and spare filter elements for engine and water maker.

While the above may look like just another equipment list, it is actually an expression of our philosophy of self-sufficiency and minimalist cruising *in terms of nuts and bolts. I am talking of actual voyaging as a lifestyle as opposed to life in the marina; exploring remote places and avoiding the crowds. A suitable boat could be bought and fitted out as described above for $15,000 (ca. 2015). As a couple, cruising and anchoring out, we could manage quite well on $600 or $700 a month without sacrificing comfort or safety.*

How much or how little you spend or budget for cruising depends completely on you and your priorities. Don't get caught up in buying a bunch of unnecessary items that other folks think you need to go cruising. Be smart, be safe. Live the Dream!

Jim and Laura on SV *Nilaya*

It is quite remarkable how many retired cruisers we meet who have lived and worked most of their lives far from the oceans and large lakes of the world. These bold souls have little or no sailing experience when they decide to make the big jump from the dreary shoreside existence to the exciting and adventuresome life that only comes from living on a boat. Despite an abundance of valid reasons not to do such a foolish thing, they do it anyway, and here they are sailing to the destinations of their hearts while most of us languish on shore still thinking about it.

A disproportionate number of these erstwhile landlocked cruisers seem to come from Calgary, Alberta, and Denver, Colorado. As usual, I don't have any hard data to support this assumption; it's just that we seem to run into a lot of cruisers from these two places. And a lot from Saskatchewan and Iowa and even faraway places like Gdansk and Uzbekistan (OK, not so many from Uzbekistan). But it seems that a lack of exposure to boats and the water that floats them is not a deterrent to the desire to retire on one. In fact, there may even be an inverse proportion of humanity yearning for the sea simply because they have never been exposed to it.

Jim and Laura on the sailing vessel *Nilaya* are just such formerly landlocked sailors. Laura was born in Denver, and Jim moved there at an early age. Jim retired from a 37-year career in law enforcement (21 as a police officer and 16 as a Colorado state investigator), and Laura retired a month later from her career sewing wedding dresses and making costumes for the local Denver thespian community. They sold the downtown Denver Victorian home that they had remodeled, bought a boat, moved aboard, and haven't looked back. Here's their story.

THE CRUISERS

Jim and Laura first got the idea of a life on the sea at a Denver yard sale. The couple holding the sale were planning to move onto a boat and sail the Caribbean, and they were selling everything they owned. Jim was nearing retirement and facing

When I first met Jim and Laura, they were roasting coffee at the Bocas Marina in Panama, where Jim was picking up a little kitty money by working as a fill-in manager. The marina roasts and markets its own brand of locally grown coffee, which is a favorite with the large cruising community there. Jim and Laura have been cruising in their pristine Bayfield 36 cutter since 2008, when Jim retired from a long career in law enforcement. Their approach to cruising seems to have worked well for them. And, since they got it right the first time around in spite of an acute shortage of experience in sailing or in cruising, they are an inspiration for the rest of us.

the common dilemma of what he and Laura would do with the rest of their lives, and they both came face to face with the idea of retiring on a sailboat.

Jim and Laura had only minimal experience sailing and none cruising, but they didn't let that stop them. Soon the most popular topic in their conversations turned to sailing lessons and charters. All their free time went to research, reading magazines and books to see if the cruising lifestyle might be the life for them. The old Victorian house they were restoring and planned to sell, plus pensions and Social Security became the road to a healthy starting kitty that would finance the adventure.

But they didn't jump in without looking first. They started with a week-long American Sailing Association (ASA) sailing course in Florida, followed up with local Coast Guard courses in Colorado and attendance at one of Bob Bitchin's (Bob is creator and editor of *Latitude 38* magazine [http://www.latitude38.com]) famous sailing seminars in California. Next came a chartered cruise with Jim and

Laura doing all the sailing to the Bahamas and back under the watchful eye of their former ASA instructor as captain. This to-and-fro crossing of the notorious Gulf Stream gave them the confidence and background they needed to start looking for the boat that would see them through the rest of their anticipated adventures. But first they wanted to find a place to keep it.

After a search of the Internet for hurricane-free cruising areas in the Caribbean, Jim discovered the remote archipelago of Bocas del Toro (which means "the mouth of the bull") on the Caribbean side of Panama and decided that it looked like an ideal base for their planned retirement cruise. A quick plane ride south confirmed that, yes, indeed, Bocas was all it claimed to be, so it was back to Florida to look for the perfect boat. When they found *Nilaya* lying in Punta Gorda, Florida, they knew they need look no farther.

After dragging the remains of their possessions (by this time nearly everything material had been sold or given away) to Florida in a small U-Haul trailer, they moved aboard and immediately began preparations to move south ahead of the impending hurricane season.

THE BOAT

The boat Jim and Laura bought in Punta Gorda is a Bayfield 36C cutter with a 44-horsepower Yanmar JHE four-cylinder diesel engine. Her complete name is *Shante Nilaya*, which is Sanskrit for "house of peace," but her documented name is the shortened version because it is easier to say and more understandable on the radio. *Shante Nilaya* was her original name, and the new owners saw no reason to change it.

Although Jim and Laura claim that they knew little about cruising boats when they bought *Nilaya*, they must have had strong instincts (or a bit of luck), because they couldn't have found a more suitable craft for two people sailing the Caribbean. Designed by Ted Gozzard and built by Bayfield Yachts in Bayfield, Ontario, Canada, the Bayfield 36 has earned a firm reputation as a sturdy, seaworthy, dependable, and safe offshore cruising boat. To those of us who appreciate classic lines, she is also a lovely boat to look at. From the sinusoidal curves of the wineglass stern to the tailboards on the clipper-style bow she exudes time-honored charm, and the radical sheer with generous tumblehome does nothing to detract from this traditional appeal. But she isn't a pirate ship either; her efficient cutter rig, cutaway forefoot, perforated toe-rails (which sit atop low traditional bulwarks), inboard shrouds, and a dozen other modern features show that the designer was never blinded by tradition and was quick to incorporate contemporary features where they were most useful.

As this is written, there are only two Bayfield 36s listed for sale on http://www.yachtworld.com/, one in Florida and the other in Ontario. The asking price of each is around $65,000, both appear to be in excellent condition, and both would be worth a closer look from anyone seeking a compact and comfortable offshore cruiser.

THE CRUISE

The first long passage for *Nilaya* was the 1,300-mile trek from Punta Gorda, Florida, to Bocas del Toro, Panama. Although they had gained a world of experience sailing *Nilaya* in the Port Charlotte area and the Peace River, with an occasional foray into the eastern Gulf of Mexico, they didn't feel ready for a long nonstop passage through challenging seas, so they hired a professional skipper to accompany them.

Was that a good decision? Here's what Laura says about it:

> You can probably imagine the excitement we shared that evening, walking to dinner with our captain to go over a few final details, and . . . the next morning, April 22nd, as we motored out of the harbor on the start of our 1,300-nautical-mile adventure. The plan was no stops along the way unless needed for fuel, provisions, or emergency. (No, we didn't sleep much that night.) On the morning of May 2nd, we entered the Bocas del Toro channel and we both agree that we learned more on that nine-day trip than on all our previous lessons and charters combined.

Nilaya's classic lines and efficient good looks are evident in this photo of her lying at anchor in the San Blas Islands complete with all the cruiserly details: a Panamanian courtesy flag (just above the flag of the Guna Yala community) flying in the breeze, a sturdy shade tent to keep the tropical sun off the deckhouse, a wind generator keeping the batteries under control, and laundry drying on the lifelines. (JIM AND LAURA PHOTO)

Jim and Laura have now lived full time on *Nilaya* for eight years and during that time have crisscrossed the Caribbean many times. They have visited their favorite anchorage in the snug harbor at Providencia, Colombia, six times so far. They have also visited San Andreas Island, Colombia; Albuquerque Cay, Colombia; the San Blas Islands, Panama; the Bay Islands, Honduras; Isla Mujeres, Mexico; and Cartagena, Colombia; and they have cruised the south coast of Cuba. Most seasons they return to the sheltered marina at Bocas del Toro, but twice they have summered in the popular hurricane hole in the Rio Dulce of Guatemala.

Jim and Laura's longest passage, perhaps the one that saw them graduate from advanced novices to seasoned veterans, was a trip through the canal and on to Hawaii as crew on a friend's boat. This trip saw stops at the Las Perlas Islands of Panama, then up the west coast of Central America to Maderas, Mexico. From there it was a 30-day nonstop run to Hawaii.

As for future destinations, the crew of *Nilaya* isn't sure: a return to Providencia is in the cards for the upcoming holiday season, given an acceptable weather window (the western Caribbean is notorious for aggressive winter trade winds and steep short-period seas), but, beyond that, who knows. Most likely is a transit of the Panama Canal sometime in 2016 and a journey north along the eastern Pacific coast.

Here are some of Jim and Laura's answers to my survey questions:

WHAT IS IT YOU LIKE MOST ABOUT THIS BOAT?

She's a sturdy, well-made, full keel with skeg rudder, and has a good reputation for ocean voyages. She's simple to operate with very few complicated systems or equipment to maintain. Although she is a smaller boat than we had originally been looking for (we thought we wanted a boat 42 to 44 feet long), her size is a plus when it comes to upkeep and costs for maintenance and docking. We both like her classic lines and "old boat" character.

WHAT WOULD YOU CHANGE OR ADD TO THIS BOAT IF YOU COULD?

Jim is finding the maintenance of the teak not to his liking. A larger fuel tank (we currently have a 45-gallon tank and carry 20 gallons in jerry cans on deck during ocean passages) would be an asset; a stern shower (we have a small tub-type shower below, but it tends to hold cases of beer and other essentials during a passage); more refrigeration or even a freezer; a larger engine room; and more storage! But all this would require a bigger boat, which we really don't want.

ARE THERE ANY ITEMS . . . YOU WOULD CONSIDER ESSENTIAL GEAR FOR A SUCCESSFUL CRUISE?

The most important item of equipment to us has been our Autohelm 6000 auto pilot simply because it takes care of a lot of the work and relieves the stress of long passages. We wouldn't want to go cruising without a chart plotter, solar panels, refrigerator, VHF, radar, AIS (at minimum a receiver), life raft, EPIRB, or SSB radio. Some of these items may not be essential, such as the chart plotter when adequate GPS receivers would do, but since we've always had them, it would be hard to give them up. We've installed a water maker but don't consider this essential to cruising due to the upkeep it takes. There have only been a couple of instances where we couldn't get adequate drinking water before we installed it, but it does take away the hassle of ferrying water with jerry jugs, or collecting rain, etc. We do have a wind generator, but the solar panels do the vast majority of daily charging. Also, a sturdy dinghy and reliable outboard are essential. We also have "chaps" for our dinghy, but many cruisers don't bother with them.

We like to have paper charts of the areas where we intend to travel, and reference books, cruising guides, and maintenance manuals for equipment on the boat are all considered necessary equipment. Adequate ground tackle and sufficient anchors are important, along with a windlass. A wash-down pump for raising anchor may not be essential but is certainly both a time- and back-saver.

Something else we consider necessary is what might be classified as diversions. This includes books (now mostly on Kindles for us), movies, games, hobbies, etc. You spend many hours by yourselves and will have need of entertainment when the ubiquitous Internet isn't always available.

A good set of basic tools is essential along with some spare parts. We carry a spare alternator, a few various spare pumps, GPS, and a handheld VHF. We also have various rebuild kits. We can use either a computer or iPad as a backup for navigation. For docking, decent fenders and dock lines are important. In a marina, sun/rain shades are a must. We carry a small house-window-type air conditioner to use in the marinas, but this is not essential, merely a comfort item.

ARE THERE ANY ITEMS ABOARD THAT YOU BOUGHT BUT HAVEN'T USED?

We didn't use our computer printer much when we had one, although it was handy for both printing and scanning of official documents when checking in and out of harbors, and for copies of photos that we would give to locals or send home to relatives. It was difficult to maintain, and the ink cartridges would usually dry out between uses and were expensive to replace. Laura still wants a printer, but we haven't found the right one, and we are not currently traveling to the areas where it would be of use.

Laura also purchased a Sailrite sewing machine before leaving the States and worked on some canvas items for the boat with the thought that (relying on her long experience with sewing machines) she might pick up some canvas and sail work if our cruising budget wasn't adequate. She has since sold the Sailrite and replaced it with a smaller, lighter home-type machine along with a serger (a machine for binding the edges of fabrics). The realities were that she really didn't enjoy working on canvas and sails. We don't have the space for the supplies it would really require to do an adequate job, and the big, heavy machine didn't work well for clothing repairs and such. There are also difficulties of working for pay in foreign countries without a work permit, along with our desire to give to the local economy rather than just take. We didn't want to take a job from somebody local who might be doing it. With the small machine she has now, Laura can take care of most of our repairs and maintenance, and we can usually find someone to do any larger jobs.

WHAT WILL YOU LOOK FOR IN YOUR NEXT BOAT, IF THERE IS GOING TO BE ONE?

We thought we might eventually trade up to a larger boat, but after seeing and hearing of issues with larger boats (including crewing on a larger boat across the Pacific to Hawaii) we have decided that we like the simple systems of our boat.

WHAT IS YOUR FAVORITE CRUISING STORY YOU TELL TO NON-CRUISERS?

Jim's Story:

One day while anchored off the mainland of Panama in a remote area mainly inhabited by indigenous people, a small Indian boy about 6 or 7 years old paddled to our boat. He was alone in a cayuka, which is a small canoe carved from a large tree trunk. He knocked at the boat and, in rather bashful Spanish, asked for sugar. In questioning him, we found that his mother had sent him for sugar as she needed, it for something she was cooking. Laura asked how much she needed and he thought for a while then said a "sack full," which we took to mean quite a bit. We keep very little, if any, sugar on the boat, so we searched and found three small packets like what you would be given for a takeout cup of coffee back home. When we handed him the sugar, he looked dumbfounded, as if he was thinking how would he explain this to his mother, and we tried to explain to him that was all the sugar we had.

He was a cute little boy with a dirty face. We also gave him some crayons and a few pages from a coloring book, along with a small baseball cap from Colombia. As he paddled away, he would stop, look intently at the items we gave him, then continue on paddling. He did this several times as we watched him return to shore.

A few months later we returned to the area and anchored nearby. One day a young couple with a small child about three years old paddled to the boat hoping to sell us some fruit they harvested. While Laura went below to get payment, I noticed the young boy was wearing the baseball cap we had given the other boy. It was now extremely dirty but was obviously the same hat. I laughed and indicated to them in English that this was a hat that we had given to a boy several months ago. The father, who spoke nothing but Spanish, thought I wanted to buy the hat, took it off the boy's head, and started to hand it to me saying "ten dollars." It took awhile to sort it all out, finding out that the boy we had given the hat to was their older son, but in the end we all got a laugh out of it. The younger son was relieved not to have to give up his hat.

Laura's Story:

Right before we left to find our boat, I started a blog to chronicle our adventures for family and friends (see http://www.jimandlaura.mysite.com), especially as we didn't know how much contact we would have with them once we got to Panama. Right after we arrived in Bocas, I posted an entry on the blog highlighting the trip down and mentioning a few mechanical issues we had along the way. There was a minor issue with a frayed spinnaker halyard. Our shift cable to the transmission broke, and we didn't have a spare, so we tried various fixes during our leisure hours on the trip.

Another day, our high-water bilge alarm sounded, and, after some anxious moments, we discovered a loose fitting that allowed the fresh water tank to empty 80-plus gallons into the bilge. We had extra water on deck and a saltwater hand pump at the galley, so we were OK for the passage, but the fresh water pump located just below the tank didn't survive the drowning. Then we found a connector on the automatic bilge-pump switch had been accidentally knocked off, so that pump wasn't working either.

We weren't able to come up with a workable solution to the broken-cable problem, so, when we arrived at the marina in Bocas to dock, Jim had to lean over the hot engine to shift gears following shouts from the captain at the helm. We made it into the slip without too many close calls, Jim just a little worse for wear, having shredded his arm on cable ties and hardware in the engine compartment.

Anyway, I mentioned in the blog that we would now be spending our time on boat repairs. One of the first comments I got back said something

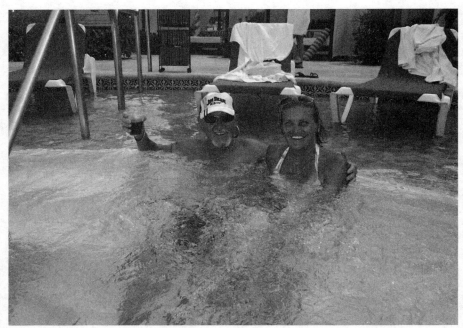

One of the comments that the crew of Nilaya *get from non-cruising friends and family is that they admire Jim and Laura's life of leisure. People who don't live on boats don't seem to realize how much work and aggravation the cruising lifestyle entails. They think "retiring on a sailboat is a life of luxury lying around on white sandy beaches, with bikini-clad women and bronzed young men serving you exotic food and drinks." Now were in the world would they get a crazy idea like that?* (JIM AND LAURA PHOTO)

like, "You spent three months getting the boat ready and were only gone nine days and you're already doing boat repairs?" Eight years later, we know only seasoned cruisers who have been out more than 10 days can understand how normal this is.

The reason this is my favorite story to tell non-cruisers is that some of our relatives and friends (still) think we hang around in hammocks all day sipping umbrella drinks. A few have commented that they are living vicariously through us and enjoy reading our blogs and posts on Facebook and the like. Some have even admitted that they would not be able to let go of what it would take to have a similar lifestyle. If we were retired back in the States, we'd probably need such things as a car, insurance, rent or mortgage, utilities, etc. Then add on the luxuries such as cable TV, dining out, movies, and it wouldn't take much to spend our monthly budget. The whole culture and environment make it difficult to keep from acquiring "stuff." Although I may have gotten a little off topic, my point is, the dream vision of retiring on *a sailboat is a life of luxury lying around on white sandy beaches, with bikini-clad women and bronzed young men serving you exotic food and drinks. The fact is, living on a sailboat, we have many of the same problems as anywhere else. The difference is really where you go, how you got there, the people you meet, and your attitude about it all.*

To me, all four of the cruising couples profiled here exemplify the basic philosophy that has served me and Susan so well over the years. The retired cruising life does not have to be complicated. When we make it such by indulging in larger, ever-more-expensive boats, we risk losing the dream to the reality of excessive overhead, disheartening work load, and paralyzing costs, all in the elusive pursuit of greater comfort and convenience, and, although few will admit it, in the futile quest for prestige and the admiration of our fellows. I have lost count of the friends and acquaintances (some of them very good friends indeed) who have been forced to abandon the cruising life because they attempted to "grow" or "move up" into a larger, more complex boat. We also see many cruisers give it up because they just don't like it, never realizing that a big part of not liking it is dealing with the expense and complexity of an unnecessarily large and elaborate boat. In other cases we see happy cruisers who love the cruising lifestyle and are good at it decide that it is time to move up to their dream boat. After pausing in their cruise to build or outfit their larger and always more complicated cruiser, they never return to full-time cruising, simply because they must go back to work to pay for their folly.

IN SUMMARY

The cruising life isn't for all of us; it isn't even for most of us; but it is for some of us; and, for a few of us, it is essential to life itself.

The best advice I have heard for a successful retirement is "don't do it." Many studies have shown that moving from an active working life to a sedentary one can knock years or even decades off your life expectancy. Inactivity can cause the senses to atrophy and the muscles to deteriorate to the extent that we soon echo the stereotypical caricature of the elderly retired person: a shuffling, hunched-over, drooling shell who can't be trusted with sharp things and makes loud political pronouncements to the rose bushes.

So the answer is clear: if we want to delay the day when the highlight of our existence revolves around pills and a place in front of the TV at the Sunnyvale Senior Habitat, we need to stay employed. Not gainfully employed, perhaps, but busy doing something productive that we can point to as a reason for being here and to justify the oxygen we consume and the space we occupy.

Moving onto a boat and cruising from place to place is a noble way to spend our time after we outgrow the need to live our lives the way others expect us to live them. Visiting faraway lands, be they across the sea or in the next township, broadens our horizons to their limits. Meeting new people who talk funny and wear strange clothes, then making them our friends, expands our understanding of the world and the humanity walking on it. Visiting famous destinations that previously existed only on the Travel Channel or sailing off to obscure places where few have gone before gives us a sense of accomplishment seldom found working for pesos or rupees or dollars. And breathing deep the air of freedom that comes with being what we were meant to be, going where we are meant to go, doing what we are meant to do, and sharing all we have with whomever else we want in our lives refreshes our soul and nourishes our internal self beyond what societal convention, structured religion, or spiritual creed can ever do.

When these very real metaphysical benefits of the cruising life are coupled with the healthful physical demands that living on a boat entails, is it any wonder so many of us are sailing away to our ultimate destination? No, it isn't. The wonder is that so many are not.

INDEX

F

fans
  computer, 158
  powered, 157–158
Fiji, 57–58
fires and fire extinguishers, 116–117
first-aid kits, 172–173, 175–176
fish recipe, 204
flopper stoppers, 19
food and cooking
  cleaning up diet, 31–32
  galley and, 186–192
  salads, 192–193
  variations in, 185–186
  see also galley
Force 10 stoves, 188
foredeck lights, 143
Forespar, 121
Fortress, 127
free-market system, 27–28
freedom, 4
friends, changing, 33–34
fuel
  costs of, 18, 74–75, 78
  for galley stove, 190
  for grills, 195–197
  in shore bag, 63

G

gadget obsession, 82–83
galley
  layout of, 190–192
  outfitting, 192
  safety upgrades for, 103–118
  size of, 186–188
  see also food and cooking
galley stove, 104–114, 188–190
generators, 134–136
Georgeann, 214–215
gimbals, 106–107
gin poles, 121
glass, 117–118
Gozzard, Ted, 228
GPS unit, 64

Great Barrier Reef (GBR), 41, 42
Great Barrier Reef Marine Park, 41
Great Loop, 42–43
GRIB charts, 47
grills
  cooking techniques for, 198–206
  selecting, 195–197
  size of, 198
  types of, 195–197
  usefulness of, 193–195
ground-fault circuit interrupter
    (GFCI), 114–115
Gulf of Mexico, 51–52
guns and ammunition, 65

H

Ha'apai island group, 56
halyards, 121, 132–133
handholds, 96–100
handy billys, 132
Harken, 129
harnesses, 100–101
hatches, 155–156
headlamps, 63, 144–145
health care
  conditions endemic to boat life,
      180–184
  in developing world, 165–166
  expat option for, 171
  kidney stones and, 164–165
  long passages and, 177–180
  medical locker and, 172–173, 175–176
  pre-existing conditions, 176–177
  in United States, 166–167, 168–170
health insurance, 167–172
heat, 160
Heller fans, 158
hip-lock, 98
Honker, 20
hoser, 150
hull-speed-to-waterline-length ratio, 69
hurricanes, 57
Hydrolite emergency rehydration
    tablets, 64